OUTSIDERS TOGETHER

OUTSIDERS TOGETHER

VIRGINIA AND LEONARD WOOLF

Natania Rosenfeld

PRINCETON UNIVERSITY PRESS   PRINCETON, NEW JERSEY

Library of Congress Cataloging-in-Publication Data
Rosenfeld, Natania.
Outsiders together : Virginia and Leonard Woolf / Natania Rosenfeld.
p. cm.
Includes bibliographical references and index.
ISBN 0-691-05884-9 (alk. paper)
1. Woolf, Virginia, 1882–1941—Political and social views.
2. Literature and society—England—History—20th century.
3. Woolf, Leonard, 1880–1969—Political and social views.
4. Women novelists, English—20th century—Biography. 5. Political scientists—
Great Britain—Biography. 6. Married people—Great Britain—Biography.
7. Woolf, Virginia, 1882–1941—Marriage. 8. Woolf, Leonard, 1880–1969—
Marriage. 9. Marginality, Social, in literature. 10. Moderism (Literature)—
England. 11. Authorship—Collaboration.   I. Title
PR6045.O72 Z8672 2000
823'.912—dc21
[B]   99-053742

This book has been composed in Janson

The paper used in this publication meets the minimum requirements
of ANSI/NISO Z39.48-1992 (R1997) (*Permanence of Paper*)

www.pup.princeton.edu

Printed in the United States of America

1   3   5   7   9   10   8   6   4   2

**for Sidney Rosenfeld and
Stella P. Rosenfeld**

I thought how unpleasant it is to be locked out;
and I thought how it is worse perhaps to be
locked in. . . .
(*A Room of One's Own*)

She knew from the effort, the rise in his voice to
surmount a difficult word that it was the first time he
had said "we." "We did this, we did that." They'll
say that all their lives, she thought. . . .
(*To the Lighthouse*)

Contents

Acknowledgments

I WOULD LIKE TO THANK the many friends who helped this work to felicitous completion. Its first incarnation was conceived under the tutelage of Maria DiBattista, a kind and incisive critic and reader, and of Sandra M. Gilbert, whose lively teaching inspired and whose encouragement fed the project. Larry Danson gave tough love from the beginning, reading several chapters in succeeding drafts, catching every instance of sloppiness, but never stinting his praise. Mimi Danson helped me with Anglicisms, and Brenda Silver gave wise and canny suggestions, steering me on the right path.

In the summer of 1989, the Donald and Mary Hyde Fellowship enabled me to visit the University of Sussex, which houses the Monks House Papers and the Leonard Woolf Papers. There, I was assisted by Bet Inglis, and by Helen Bickerstaff, who also arranged and conducted my pilgrimage to Monks House and Charleston. Sadly, I can no longer thank Helen for her kindness, as she died of breast cancer in early 1998; I hope her surviving relatives will be warmed by the knowledge of an American scholar's gratitude.

The final stages of the project received much nurturance. The students in my two undergraduate seminars on Woolf at Duke University, in the fall of 1996 and the spring of 1997, inspired and heartened me. One young woman, who refuses to come out from the bushes, suggested the punning possibilities of "Moor" and "moor" in *Orlando*. Thanks to the Dannenberg Mentorship fund, I had two research assistants at Duke whose labors were invaluable: Kate Hagopian and Laura Podolsky, both of them lovingly diligent and quick on the uptake. And Amira Jarmakani performed a small but important service for which I remain grateful.

Vicki Mahaffey cannot be thanked enough. She read the introduction in an early form and, through caring "resistance," launched me on a maturer intellectual journey. Vicki sustained me in lean professional years by the compliment of her unwavering faith in this book, and in my virtues as a teacher and scholar. The desire to go on deserving this compliment inspires me continually.

My editor, Mary Murrell, was gratifyingly forthcoming from prospectus to final copy; her responsiveness and humor made the process of revision a pleasure rather than a burden. Lauren Lepow was a sensitive and clever copyeditor—she, too, deserves thanks.

The debt I owe Neil Blackadder, my partner and "linchpin," can never be repaid. "I snuggled into the core of my life, which is this complete comfort with [Neil], & there found everything so satisfactory & calm that I revived myself, & got a fresh start; feeling entirely immune." I have teased out so much, writing, and always found this core again.

My parents are the dedicatees of all the book except chapter 3. That part is for my grandmother, Stella Pagales, who came to this country and labored at night, cleaning and sewing; like Rezia, she created with her needle. As for my parents, they have given me everything that matters—and have been colleagues, too. "I sing back to you / my sticklegged words."

A version of chapter 3 appeared as "Links into Fences: The Subtext of Class Division in *Mrs. Dalloway*," in *LIT* (*Literature Interpretation Theory*) 9 (Summer1998): 139–60.

Abbreviations

BA	*Beginning Again*
BTA	*Between the Acts*
CDB	*The Captain's Death Bed and Other Essays*
CE	*Collected Essays*
CSF	*The Complete Shorter Fiction of Virginia Woolf*
D	*The Diary of Virginia Woolf*
DAW	*Downhill All the Way: An Autobiography of the Years 1919 to 1939*
DM	*The Death of the Moth and Other Essays*
G	*Growing: An Autobiography of the Years 1904 to 1911*
GR	*Granite and Rainbow: Essays*
JNAM	*The Journey Not the Arrival Matters: An Autobiography of the Years 1939–1969*
L	*The Letters of Virginia Woolf*
LAWHKI	*Life As We Have Known It*
LLW	*Letters of Leonard Woolf*
LWP	Leonard Woolf Papers, University of Sussex
M	*The Moment and Other Essays*
MB	*Moments of Being*
MD	*Mrs. Dalloway*
ND	*Night and Day*
QQ	*Quack, Quack!*
ROO	*A Room of One's Own*
S	*Sowing: An Autobiography of the Years 1880 to 1904*
TG	*Three Guineas*
TS	*Two Stories*
WV	*The Wise Virgins*
VO	*The Voyage Out*
WFP	*The War for Peace*

OUTSIDERS TOGETHER

Border Cases

THIS STUDY is animated by two contrary, yet intimately related, tropes: marriage and annexation. While Virginia Woolf often represents real marriages as microcosmic forms of colonization, tyranny, or warmongering, marriage as a *metaphor* in the writings of both Virginia and Leonard Woolf always stands for the opposite: a dialogue, in which neither subjectivity drowns out the other and both partners thrive. Their own marriage negotiated the dangers of inbuilt hierarchy through self-awareness on both sides, always leaning toward the metaphor and away from the traditionally conceived actuality.

My focus on the relationship of Virginia and Leonard Woolf for the greater part of the chapters that follow emphasizes the intersubjective principle in Virginia Woolf's prose and links it with larger sociopolitical questions about belonging and exclusion. While this study gives primary attention to analysis of Virginia Woolf's writings, my new readings of her works depend on an understanding of both the irritation and the inspiration provided by Leonard Woolf (with "irritation" understood as creative and intellectual restlessness rather than malaise). Although Virginia's feminist beliefs and her shrewd observations of gender relations under the rule of patriarchy were spawned early in life, her husband's ardent political engagements created fertile ground for their growth and expression. More provocatively, her alliance to an impecunious Jew with the highest connections in British academe and politics multiplied and illuminated the contradictions in her own identity and politics. Leonard Woolf, at the time of their marriage in 1912, was a former colonial administrator turned fervent anti-imperialist, an active socialist engaged particularly with feminist questions within the British Labour movement, and a theorist of international relations whose work contributed directly to the formation of the League of Nations. Most compelling for my particular perspective is his divided sense of ethnic and class identity: an assimilated Jew, he fluctuated between fierce pride in his heritage and a repudiation of it—a repudiation partially expressed in his gravitation toward Virginia Woolf and Bloomsbury. Nothing was simple in this story, however, and fundamental to my examination of the relationship and writings of the Woolfs is the idea that Leonard Woolf brought to the marriage, but also to the wider currents of literary modernism and political theory, the complex and vital perspective of the social outsider.

In opposed yet complementary ways, the Woolfs were outsiders together—she privileged by her background, but excluded from centers by her gender, he privileged by gender and marginalized through background. Such a chiasmic alliance forces social borderlines into relief, making them inevitable objects of scrutiny—all the more so as Leonard Woolf, in his political scholarship, was by vocation a student of borders, between nations but also between groups such as colonizers and colonized, male capitalists and female workers, and different political camps within one governmental structure. In their marriage the Woolfs enacted, and in their work they fantasized, theorized, and attempted, the crossing of borders intently policed in the "real world." As the founders and editors of the Hogarth Press, moreover, Virginia Woolf and Leonard Woolf laid a crossroads in the dissemination of avant-garde literature and ideas; it is difficult to imagine literary modernism without their wide influence, and this study is also, finally, a denotation of that influence.

The violent deaths that embody the opposite of mutual recognition and cooperation in the work of Virginia Woolf, occur in places at once central and obscure: Judith Shakespeare, the invented sister of *A Room of One's Own*, died for the historical and literary sins of patriarchy, and is buried at a crossroads; Septimus Warren Smith, the World War I veteran of *Mrs. Dalloway*, whose impaled figure is the emblem of my middle chapter and irradiates its outskirts as well, expired on the railings that divide two properties. Both were technically suicides; both were victims of larger social forces, just as surely as Andrew Ramsay, killed in the war, Prue Ramsay, whose father "gave" her in marriage only to see her die soon after of "complications resulting from childbirth," and Mrs. Ramsay, overworked by her demanding husband and an ethos requiring the endless self-sacrifice of wives, are such victims.[1] All of them could have lived if the spirit of negotiation had won over the will to annexation.

Woolf gives Septimus Warren Smith a cannily ambiguous label: he is "a border case, neither one thing nor the other" (84), and his absurd name is emblematic of between-ness, being divided in three parts. "Septum" itself is a dividing wall or membrane, frequently osmotic; and Septimus, polysyllabic and Latinate, suggests both grandeur and last ("seventh") things, God's chosen and God's afterthought. His surname is as prosaic and "common" as his given name is high-flown and extraordinary: he is a private person, a son, a dreamer, and a middling citizen of a class-bound state that sends Smiths by the thousands to die *in war*. His middle name, transposing those two words, reminds us of this—reminds us that this would-be poet, this private thinker and possible genius, is and was inevitably co-opted by a force (by parties, by people) to whom he is both marginal and essential. The Smiths of the world are throwaways, but without the Smiths, government cannot operate.

This introduction takes its title from Septimus's designation; but I dilate the word "case," with its suggestions of enclosure and categorical discreteness, to focus on its other implication of the exemplary individual instance. Like Woolf, I am concerned with the energies contained *within* a border figure and with imagining an internal dynamic that works against encasement and toward the connection of disparate objects. Septimus's credo is "Communication is health; communication is happiness"—finally bursting through the window (the "casement") that represents his psychic internment, only to be impaled on the fences he rails against, Septimus nonetheless embodies a hope for communicating territories, plots, and neighbors. Like Judith Shakespeare, he is a Messiah figure, who will rise again when humans embrace the border as a place of possibility, a fecund ground where opposing energies, intersecting, *need* not stiffen into ancient, deathly postures. It is this resurrection that Woolf's prose continually works for, in an evolving effort not so much to reconcile opposites as to imagine the varied configurations formed by difference.

The rejection of simplistic notions of "centrality" that underlies Woolf's concern with borders also informs recent discussions of literary modernism, which question the idea of a "central" current even while continuing to interrogate the work of those figures traditionally denoted as the definers of high modernism.[2] James Joyce, W. B. Yeats, T. S. Eliot, and Ezra Pound have been increasingly examined from the point of view of ideology, and the intersection of their own politics with larger political movements such as fascism and socialism has received particular attention. Virginia Woolf dealt consciously, and often explicitly, with ideological and political questions;[3] through her husband, but also through inclinations developed early on, she was involved in Labour issues and actively engaged with an offshoot of the Labour movement, the Women's Co-operative Guild. Not only was she alert and sensitive to the class divisions of her world; she was also, as the descendant of imperialists and judges and a liberal-humanist child of privilege, both prone to and aware of her class, racial, and ethnic prejudices.

Woolf's marriage played a vital role in the engagement with injustice that informs, I believe, every one of her works; her husband, a Jew of financially straitened circumstances, a skeptic and lifelong socialist, was overtly the friend and secretly often the butt of Woolf's family and social circle—both central and marginalized, a "border case" himself. Certainly, as a man, a Cambridge graduate, and an imperial administrator, he was more centrally located than Virginia Stephen. Yet one might call Leonard the Septimus Warren Smith to Virginia's Clarissa Dalloway—the scapegoat who pointed up her privilege, the dark horse who drew her from the window to the street, from the well-lit room to more obscure and disturbing spaces. (He played the opposite role, too, however; as Thomas Caramagno has shown in *The Flight of the Mind*, Virginia Woolf's bipolar illness imposed regular forays into mental darkness—and I am convinced that Leonard Woolf took it on himself to keep these forays as safe as possible.)[4]

The Woolf marriage, too, was a dynamic border case. Its counterpoint of prejudice and empathy complicated the relationship in the same ways that it does Virginia Woolf's work—and can complicate our own conceptions of modernism. For Woolf herself was both the one really English figure among the "greats" of English high modernism, and not English at all—as she points out so cogently in *Three Guineas*, nation belongs to men and men belong to nation, and women are part of that construct only by virtue of daughterhood or marriage. She calls into question the whole notion of centrality; indeed, her oeuvre rests on a paradox: the central is precisely the marginal, the vital what others (fathers, rulers, men) call trivial. The image of a "trivium" is, in fact, apt here: the space where three roads come together (*OED*), it suggests the vitality that may arise when inconsequential things meet at a junction.

Because Woolf's political critiques lie in subtly drafted narratives in which the grid of middle-class lives and values still firmly overlies the cobweb networks of the powerless, with the spinning of gorgeous prose superimposed on the messages of protest, even now more stringent political critics tend to concur with Leavisites of yore that Woolf's primary impulse, born of luxury, was toward the aesthetic. She openly said so herself, and it is my aim both to explore and to justify this unabashed commitment to politics *through* an aesthetic practice rather than the reverse. Woolf's art was a "project": perpetually in progress, perpetually yearning and straining, both in subject and in form, toward the other side. Whatever that side is— the ethnic Other, working women, men—what the end of her project might have looked like is a moot question; her work embraces and upholds inconclusiveness as strategy, and the process itself is the thing that matters. (By the late 1920s her work was generically uncategorizable, and she wished it this way, calling *The Waves* a "playpoem" in her diary and fliply naming *Orlando* a biography.)

If Woolf left the activist life to her husband and other friends, her works did not deny admission to political and social facts—it is her way of admitting without expressly highlighting these that has earned her the label of effete from some critics (while others *too* readily claim her for Marxism or feminism). As Margot Norris writes of James Joyce's work, "Art's aesthetic discourse tells political lies about itself. Joyce's texts, too, tell such lies— but Joyce provides multiple mechanisms whereby they are repeatedly caught" (*Joyce's Web* 7). In fact, while Woolf's credo—and that of modernism more largely—has seemed clearly antirealist, it is the genius of her work so consummately to envelop hard fact in the tissues of consciousness (the breathing and wishing of her characters and her prose, in one) that the dialectic between real and ideal, or objective and subjective, could scarcely be better illuminated by a professional philosopher or political theorist. If sociopolitical observation, like the charwomen of *To the Lighthouse*, occupies the obscurer spaces of Woolf's texts, it is precisely these spaces to which she draws our attention, illuminating the interdependence of the obscure and the "enlightened," the parenthetical and the supposedly essential.[5]

This study defines an endless traffic between and across lines as Woolf's aesthetic and political principle—political *because* aesthetic, Woolf would have said, since there is no change, in life as in art, without dreaming; and her work is an enacted dreaming, an illumination of possibility. In it, there is no resolution to ambivalence, there is only transition, or transitional space, between two sides. Images for this dialectic abound, both in Woolf's work—"granite and rainbow," "the wing of a butterfly against a cathedral"—and in that of critics. Françoise Defromont calls it a "double rhythm": "on the one hand, there is for instance the sharp rhythm of Big Ben (in *Mrs. Dalloway*) or 'tick, tick, tick' (in *Between the Acts*), and on the other, there are fragments of sentences relentlessly repeated, underneath, as gently as the murmur of ebb and flow" ("Mirrors and Fragments" 76).[6] Rachel Bowlby makes Woolf's frequent trope of vehicular travel the embarkation point for her study, *Virginia Woolf: Feminist Destinations*, focusing especially on trains; inspired in part by Bowlby, the image of a railroad track comes to mind as emblem for Woolf's prose—with the "vertical" lines—the ones that lead forward—functioning as framework for the ties that bind them. Consider the lines as the markings of power—the power of government, of patriarchy, and of social law to carve out property and channel human (e)motion in one direction—and the ties as the weavings, shuttlings, knittings of human subjectivities, individually or in concert. The vital trajectory is from side to side, without end, rather than forward, conclusively: a constant crossing within or even over the borders.

Two kinds of border, in fact, form the locus of these crossings: both are containers of human energies, the one inhibiting and the other, one might say, preserving them. Borders can be neglected edges, margins, repositories for refuse—prisoning yet often fecund spaces, like the East End of London, the unnamed originary locus in Leonard Woolf's short story "Three Jews," to which social force relegates the unacceptable. But borders are also, and more often, boundaries, marks down the center of contested or quiet territory. If the latter, they can be closed, absolute, policed—and permeable only by violence; or, more rarely, they can be porous, open, as good as unnoticeable. Both psychologically and politically, neither of these extremes is desirable: absolute separateness, the "splitting" of parts of the self, of the self from others, of bodies of selves from bodies, or groups, of other selves, frustrates and leads to violative acts; conversely, when lines are dissolved, individuality disappears, which leads either to panic or to that state of mass hypnosis whose danger theorists such as Freud, as well as twentieth-century history, have all too clearly illuminated.

Nonetheless, in literary experimentation as in politics, risks must be taken, and Woolf saw more potential for good in merging than in distinction. As she said once of the "screen" obstructing her perceptions of working-class women, "If we had not this device for shutting people off from our sympathies, we might, perhaps, dissolve utterly. Separateness would be impossible. But the screens are in the excess; not the sympathy" (D 3:104). Yet she knew well, and illustrates in the relationship of Lily Briscoe to Mrs. Ramsay, that the wish to merge can be the mere inverse of the wish to violate, a desire for engulfment as problematic in its way as the desire *to* engulf.[7] The exorcism involved in writing *To the Lighthouse*, the book in which she laid the ghost of her mother, inscribed Woolf's reluctance to substitute a goddess for the God; what she always imagined was *dialogue*, and of this there was hardly enough in the "real" world[8]—so she made it the principle of her fiction.

My ideas about both borders and their crossing derive partially from object relations theory, particularly as that theory is rearticulated in the forms of intersubjectivity Jessica Benjamin envisions in her feminist rethinking of Freud, Winnicott, and Hegel, *The Bonds of Love: Psychoanalysis, Feminism, and the Problem of Domination*. Writing against objectification, Benjamin, like Woolf, imagines a world of subjects. "Domination," she argues, "is a twisting of the bonds of love" whereby self objectifies other; an ideal, desirable politics untwists these bonds, making them channels of communication rather than instruments of subjugation—and such a politics begins and ends at home, in the relations between gendered individuals.

The dialectic I have described, a dialectic that informs all Woolf's works, also inscribes a politics that crosses from the home to the world (of class, ethnic and gender relations, labor relations, and, finally, international relations) and back again with no clear starting or end point. "Granite and rainbow" stands not just for the interweaving of elements but also for a representation of power politics both *as they are* and *as they might be*. Thus, for instance, as I show in chapter 3, the fine threads that link disparate consciousnesses in the famously fluid narrative of *Mrs. Dalloway* also signify the barriers between subjects in a society based on division rather than connection. "Only connect," that principle Woolf shared with Forster, here serves the vision of an end to hierarchy by acting to highlight rather than ignore the ubiquity of class structures. In the realm of gender relations, the "marriage of opposites" that is imagined in the late 1920s in *A Room of One's*

Own and exposed as a sham or double-crossing in the "real-life" Victorian marriage of the Ramsays in *To the Lighthouse* is finally enacted in both the form and content of *Orlando*; the "translation" or successful crossing begins to break down again in *The Waves*, to be tentatively resurrected in Woolf's final novel, *Between the Acts*.

Jessica Benjamin uses the terms "tension and breakdown" to describe just such inevitable and interdependent vicissitudes in her conclusion, which she terms "both modest and utopian"—a phrase Woolf would readily have applied to her life's work, and one I hopefully adopt for the study that follows in these pages. "Tension," Benjamin writes, is the desirable state in which subjectivities as well as parts of subjectivities sustain what she calls "mutual recognition"; but to avoid breakdown is too much for us humans to ask of ourselves:

> After all, breakdown of tension is as much a part of life as recreating it once more. The logic of paradox includes the acknowledgment that breakdown occurs. A sufficient ground for optimism is the contention that if breakdown is "built into" the psychic system, so is the possibility of renewing tension. If the denial of recognition does not become frozen into unmovable relationships, the play of power need not be hardened into domination. As the practice of psychoanalysis reveals, breakdown and renewal are constant possibilities: *the crucial issue is finding the point at which breakdown occurs and the point at which it is possible to recreate tension and restore the condition of recognition.* (Benjamin, *The Bonds of Love* 223; italics mine)

The "point" Benjamin describes is a border in or on which opposites meet and can engage in battle or in dialogue. That this border is both inter- and intrasubjective goes without saying in the psychoanalytic paradigm but is a fact Woolf was constantly at pains to illuminate. In *A Room of One's Own* she refers to the "infantile fixation of the fathers" as an insatiable craving for fixity in the social order; for that fixity to be unsettled, "intercourse" must occur between parts of the brain as well as between brains. When such traffic comes about, "fixation" phases into paradox—two points of view existing simultaneously, both of them valid—and in those two "x" words all the difference lies: one of them embodying an ancient, monistic, and dictatorial worldview, the other filled with the energy of endless renewal. Thus the censoring Professor von X of *Room*, for instance, is occluded by *Orlando*, X becoming O in a ceaseless circulation of energy.

I think of these crossings as the politics of intersubjectivity, and by illuminating them I wish to excite and complicate perceptions of the modernist movement. Far from monolithic, that movement, as many recent critics have shown, derives its ethos from internal conflict rather than overriding coherence; richly riddled by differing points of view, modernism in all its actual plurality is not, in fact, one "movement" so much as a contained period of copious opposings (not unlike a border case overflowing with ambivalent energies).[9] My first principle in this study is to show Woolf in dialogue with other voices, both within and outside her own thinking. The book both begins and ends with marriage—her own marriage to the culturally Other Leonard Woolf, but also, by extension, the difficult intersection of opposing (and sometimes overlapping) principles and ideologies so often metaphorized by Woolf herself as "marriage" or conjugation. A marriage, of course, all too easily becomes a battleground, even a burial ground; thus the "Strange Crossings" of chapter 1 culminate in the "Monstrous Conjugations" of chapter 5—not, however, in the Woolf marriage, which I read as a remarkably successful negotiation of tension and breakdown, but rather in the collective consciousness of fascist Europe.

Chapter 1, "Strange Crossings," chronicles the events and images surrounding the actual engagement of Virginia Stephen and Leonard Woolf—an engagement fraught with ambivalence on both sides: ambivalently ambivalent, so that in effect four points of view argue among themselves. The strange crossings inscribed in the colonial fictions both Woolfs wrote soon after their marriage were not only literal crossings to alien territory but hybrids, crossings of one species with another. Virginia Stephen/Woolf's profound dubiousness about sexuality emerges in *The Voyage Out*, in her association of male sexual desire with a beastly rapaciousness she locates both in the jungles of South America and in the drawing rooms of Edwardian England (here already she deconstructs polarities even as she subscribes to them, launching a critique of colonialism while she relies upon some of its basic tenets). Louise DeSalvo's examinations of the book's genesis, *Virginia Woolf's First Voyage*, inspired me to conjoin certain passages of *The Voyage Out* with Woolf's transcribed memories of her half-brothers' incestuous gropings and to find in them an analogous concern with splitting mind from body in order to deny or refuse the violation of the latter. Thus the novel's heroine, Rachel Vinrace, metaphorized as a mermaid, "goes under," or is dragged that way, dying of a tropical fever soon after her engagement to be married; this is the first of Woolf's equations of marriage with engulfment—the female ego, overwhelmed by the male ethos, which itself splits women into parts, simultaneously excoriating and fixating upon the nether half, finally destroys itself.

Such destruction was not the result of the Stephen-Woolf engagement, but the fears inscribed in *The Voyage Out* translated in life into a repulsion that complicated Virginia's attraction to Leonard, a repulsion directed expressly toward his strange or "foreign" class and ethnic identity. Himself ambivalent, both as a Jew and as a sexual being, Leonard wrote two novels in the late 1910s that illuminate these and other rifts in his subjectivity; his first, *The Village in the Jungle*, stands in contrast to *The Voyage Out* as the chronicle of a successful crossing. The novel inscribes Leonard Woolf's political conversion to anti-imperialism in its sympathetic portrayal of the lives of a group of Sinhalese peasants under colonial rule—a portrayal lauded by Ceylonese readers and critics since the time of publication for its extraordinary freedom from bias and ethnocentrism.[10]

Leonard Woolf's second novel was *The Wise Virgins*, an autobiographical work in which a young Jewish painter *unsuccessfully* courts a thinly disguised Virginia Stephen; the book is a tortured narrative, exposing the author's self-hatred along with his often prideful alienation from the echelons of Bloomsbury. Virginia Woolf's engagement-narrative, *Night and Day*, is a conservative and far more genteel transposition of the story, with the emphasis on class and manners rather than ethnicity. These two works form the point of departure for chapter 2, "Incongruities; or, The Politics of Character," which takes its title from both form and content of the Woolfs' first Hogarth Press production, the jointly authored *Two Stories*. This slight volume encapsulates not only the conflicts already described but also the contradictory notions of character and realism embodied in Woolf's early short fictions and expounded in 1924 in that famous modernist manifesto "Mr. Bennett and Mrs. Brown." *Two Stories* contains a short story by Leonard entitled "Three Jews," followed by Virginia's much more famous "The Mark on the Wall"—stories that, on the surface, could not be more different, but whose common wellspring is resentment toward reigning ideologies. In Leonard's case, the ideology is "Englishness," that social ethos by which English Jews feel enslaved even as they fail to assimilate; in "The Mark on the Wall," patriarchal hierarchies of class and rank are the bogey of both narrator and author, whose move against stultifying convention is a deliberate denial of demarcation that forms both the subject and the method of her narration. And while Leonard's short story is comparatively stiff and realist in its method, the sociological issues it raises, issues of belonging and exclusion, find their way into Virginia Woolf's interrogation of the author's attitude toward character—an attitude that can be authoritarian, as in the case of Mr. Bennett, who effectively ignores "the old lady in the corner opposite," or respectful and empathic, rescuing the old lady from her corner and placing her at the center of a horizontal trajectory between author and audience. Thus Mrs. Brown becomes a "border case" in Woolf's test of the real; truly "real" characters will convey not only sociological truth but also the truth of "human nature," and this truth is determined in the exchange between author and readers. Woolf establishes a chiasmic grid within the architecture of the railway carriage where the Bennett-Brown encounter takes place: as author is toward character, so is character to author. She thus rectifies the Hegelian mirroring of the two "B" 's by adding a third party, the audience, to monitor their relations and keep them just.

Just relations are the ultimate concern of *Mrs. Dalloway*, that novel Woolf wrote to "criticise the social system, to show it at work, at its most intense" (*D* 2:248).[11] Under Leonard's influence, Woolf had become involved with the Women's Co-operative Guild, attending a Guild convention in 1913 and collaborating over a period of years with the Guild general secretary, Margaret Llewellyn Davies, to produce a Hogarth Press volume of short memoirs by working women (1931). Woolf wrote the "Introductory Letter" to this volume; in it, she chronicles her own journey from alienation to greater sympathy for the women whose stories follow, and does her part to "translate" them and their lives to the educated readership that constituted the Hogarth Press audience. Her exposure of the gulf between herself and the women laborers, her frankness about her own ambivalent attitudes, illuminates the limitations of Clarissa Dalloway's egalitarian musings; more important, it sheds light on the extraordinary structure of *Mrs. Dalloway*, a structure whose diaphanous threadings paradoxically embody the iron rails of a society based on a spurious concept of Proportion—a society superficially democratic, but founded in divisive, ultimately fatal notions of property and propriety. *Mrs. Dalloway*, like "Mr. Bennett and Mrs. Brown," complicates the apparently simple rejection of realism that seems to constitute Woolf's modernism; in its illumination of a social system "at work, at its most intense," the novel shows us what is at the same time as it imagines what might be. Casting the borders into relief, it enacts the crossings as yet impossible in the "real world"; in dreaming of such crossings, it draws our attention to the existing barriers.

Chapter 4, "Translations," continues the focus on Woolf's work of the 1920s, considering how that work carries the political deployment of metonymy over from *Mrs. Dalloway* into images of hybridity, traversal, and mutation. In both "The New Biography," the essay that broaches the image of "granite and rainbow" for different styles of narration, ideally combined, and *A Room of One's Own*, with its famous excursus on androgyny, she attempts to imagine virtually indescribable reconfigurations of gender by positing as-yet-unassayed ways of writing. While *A Room of One's Own* is hopeful in its dreams of progress, *To the Lighthouse* records its author's ambivalence: the text is both nostalgic for a marital mode embodied by the Ramsays and absolute in its critique of that mode. Mrs. Ramsay's knitting adumbrates the boat crossing at the end of *To the Lighthouse*, mirroring her efforts to unite people in agreements that prove spurious. The stocking she intends for the lighthouse keeper's son never reaches him; the match she concocts for Lily Briscoe won't materialize; her effort to mediate between her husband and her son James founders on the former's stubbornness and the latter's dream of revenge. That dream, classically oedipal, is reconceived in Woolf's vision of an ultimately nonviolent severing of constrictive bonds at the novel's conclusion, and *Orlando* becomes the embodiment of an altogether different sally against censorious fathers.

Orlando's principle—its central image—is creative engulfment, the incorporation of a dictatorial "I" by a copia of words that spawns innumerable "I"s. Gender becomes a mutable category in this text that incarnates mutability, whose protagonist comes unmoored from his very sex. In the marriage of Orlando with Marmaduke Bonthrop Shelmerdine, acts of simultaneous translation take the place of the husband's traditional desire to dictate, and the bond of relationship, represented by reversals of syntax, becomes a conduit of communication. In Woolf's next novel, *The Waves* (1931), however, conduits are blocked once more; links turn into gulfs or barriers, and the characters batter and frustrate themselves in acts of failed translation. The "escapade" of *Orlando*, whose radicalism lay precisely in its apparent frivolity, gives way to a sobered vision of a world in which power politics determine social relations and even those who love each other rarely if ever commune.

My final chapter records a sad turn back to the world as it was, beset in the 1930s by the monstrous menace of fascism. Here I focus on the metaphors of obscene coupling that inform both Woolfs' antifascist writings—images in contrast to their own vision of marriage as "co-operative labour," where the principles of alliance are democratic rather than dictatorial. To counter the rhetoric of dictators and warmongers, both at first turned to satire, Virginia in *Three Guineas* (1938), Leonard in *Quack, Quack!* (1935). Satire, however, was still an echo of the thing satirized; in the late thirties, therefore, in *Between the Acts* (published in 1941, but begun as well as set in 1939) and *The War for Peace* (1940), they proposed new plots as a radical alternative to the tiresome master narratives of the authoritarians. These two very different books—the former a generic hybrid, the latter, in style at least, a conventional tract—are based on an antiauthoritarianism that translates as anti*authorial*ism. Both Woolfs are concerned with the autonomy of the reading/playgoing public; both books posit an open-endedness, a plot whose outcome is decided, democratically, by others.

Curiously, Woolf turns back here on her own earlier critique of Bennettian social realism, a method that left the reader with a feeling of "incompleteness" and the need to take action; and while *Between the Acts* fully maintains the devotion to character, it relates the individual to her society more integrally than did any preceding novel. Having generally eschewed activism in favor of what I have called "enacted dreaming," at the start of World War II Woolf felt the urgency of doing something more, an urgency that cast her frequently into despair at the same time as it gave rise to ever more determined experiments in her prose. My chapter ends with a scene from Virginia Woolf's diary, a vignette in which the two Woolfs are both united and polarized in their concern for a third party—a destitute Jewish seamstress whose life Woolf imagines and despairs of writing in all its sociological fullness. This "border case" is my final image for the simultaneous comprehension of a productive marriage—the two Woolfs paradoxically brought together by the very polarities of gender and background that divide them—and death at a crossroads: yet another figure victimized by social forces beyond her control, the seamstress seems on the verge of expiration when she collapses on the Woolfs' doorstep.

In the final book of his five-volume autobiography, Leonard Woolf described an excursion he took with Virginia and Vita Sackville-West on June 14, 1940, the day the Germans occupied Paris. They went to Penshurst, the Elizabethan mansion belonging to the Sidney family, and had tea with Lord de L'isle, the last descendant of the Sidneys:

> There was something historically absurd and touching, ironically incongruous and yet, in that particular moment of history, appropriate in the spectacle of Vita and Lord de L'isle and Virginia and me sitting together. . . . [Vita's] ancestor, Thomas Sackville . . . might well have driven over from Knole to visit Lord de L'isle's ancestor, Sir Philip Sidney, at Penshurst four hundred years ago. He would not have taken either Virginia's or my ancestors with him, for Virginia's ancestors were labouring as little better than serfs in Aberdeenshire and mine were living "despised and rejected" in some continental ghetto. . . . In 1940 the descendants of the Scottish serf and the ghetto Jew, on payment of 2s. 6d. each, visited the [Sidney mansion], while Lord de L'isle, the owner, and the descendant of Thomas Sackville, sat in a poky little room drinking tea from rather dreary china. I felt that in that room history had fallen about the ears of the Sidneys and the Leicesters, the Sackvilles and the Dorsets, while outside, across the Channel, in France, history was falling about the ears of us all.

Leonard Woolf's post-World War II reflections on this absurd but poignant scene echo Lily Briscoe's ruminations after the First World War on Mrs. Ramsay's outdated obsession with the primacy of marriage over all other human bonds and enterprises. The Sackvilles and the Sidneys take the place of Mrs. Ramsay: the outdated attitude they represent is not the "mania for marriage" but an ancient and ingrained social snobbery that held certain human beings to be organically superior to others. Leonard and Virginia, the descendants and representatives of those others, are the couple who have not only reauthored the marriage plot but dispensed with chauvinism. My final chapter ends with Virginia's clear-eyed vision of herself and Leonard as social equals. Here, Leonard, in his denotation of himself and Virginia as equally lowborn, dispenses once and for all with his own sense of inferiority, as well as with his wife's occasional claims to superiority. He echoes E. M. Forster, who asks, in his wartime essay "Jew-Consciousness," whether anyone can be certain who his great-grand-parents were. We all are border cases beneath the surface; even Vita Sack-ville-West's mother was the illegitimate daughter of a Spanish dancer.

In her 1937 radio broadcast, "Craftsmanship," Virginia Woolf describes words as border cases too. She thus links literature, inextricably, to the human capacity to empathize, to recognize the other as our equal. More-over, she relates it to our defiance of conventions: conventions that forbid miscegenation, enforce matrimony, exclude the "illegitimate." Words, she says, "are much less bound by ceremony and convention than we are. Royal words mate with commoners. English words marry French words, German words, Indian words, Negro words, if they have a fancy." And she insists that "they are highly democratic, too; they believe that one word is as good as another; uneducated words are as good as educated words, uncultivated words as cultivated words, there are no ranks and titles in their society" (*DM* 205). On the eve of another world war, in the midst of a cataclysm of hatred and cruelty, Virginia Woolf pins the hope of a new era on the literary capacities of human beings. We must all, she says, become the authors of a new, truly intersubjective plot, a plot that excludes no one and accounts for the complexities of the human soul.

My stance in the pages that follow is clearly more celebratory than censori-ous, locating in Woolf's work and politics the recognition of her own impli-cation in an oppressive social system as well as the lifelong desire to revise that system. It is difficult to ask for more than this; I choose, therefore, to illuminate rather than excoriate those moments when Woolf failed to overcome her ingrained ethnocentric, antisemitic, and racist tenden-cies, her class biases, her resistance to activism. Woolf is unique in her centrality and her marginality, as an intellectual aristocrat deeply affected both by the ideological cataclysms of her era and by her private involve-ment with a "penniless Jew." Woolf's modernism reflects those influences in its continual embrace of polyphony, the "mating" of alien voices, even when she could not effect a true crossing to the "old lady in the corner opposite," a lady she construes as fallen from gentility rather than as an aged Jewish seamstress, for example. These failed crossings are as instruc-tive as the successful ones that define Woolf's prose experiments, and can help us in our current interrogation of the often-antagonistic ideological currents that constitute literary modernism. In her conflicted identity, her marriage, and her writing, Woolf exemplifies these very currents.

In "Virginia Woolf and English Culture," his early defense of Woolf studies,[12] Tony Inglis referred to "the intense *transitivity* of [Virginia Woolf's] writing" and situated her at a vital crossroads in literary history:

Woolf is one of the converts to modernism . . . ; and, like Yeats's, her converted style continues to grow and develop instead of hardening, as did, say, Pound's. Moreover the date of her conversion—just after the intensely polemic, promotional period associated especially with Pound, yet before the time when the epigoni Auden and Beckett deploy various stylisations to resolve (and in part to evade) modernist technical and substantive dilemmas—puts her at a distinctive stage in the movement, less frenetically doctrinaire than her predecessors, more fruitfully direct than her immediate successors. In these, and doubtless in other connections, taking Virginia Woolf seriously will illuminate problems of continuity and tradition in modernism—a prerequisite both to clear thinking about our current relation to inter-war modernist art and to the development of a properly aware successor culture to modernism. (Bowlby, *Virginia Woolf* 58–59)

That "successor culture"—whether we dub it postmodern or postcolonial—is, of course, informed by, if not always "properly aware of," the issues I have outlined as central to Woolf's project and encapsulated in the phrase "border cases": issues of gender, class, racial and national identity, and the hybridization of these categories that causes such instructive confusion.[13] In a century of mass migrations, persecutions, and expulsions, when refugee status has constituted the fastest-growing form of national affiliation, few can avoid the designation "border case." Such homelessness can be tragically unsettling; it can also become the ground of fertile productivity.[14] In Woolf's life, dislocation was both choice and imposition: she wrote about wanderers and street-dwellers from the comfortable heights of her middle-class life and an inherited sense of social superiority—yet she was aware as a woman of her exclusion from centers of power, and, as a manic-depressive, of the constant threat of a violent change of mood. Her work celebrates displacement, cherishing the mind's capacity to inhabit two places at once; but in so doing, it always enjoins attention to the tragedy of the forcibly displaced:

> When [nature] set about her chief masterpiece, the making of man, she should have thought of one thing only. Instead, turning her head, looking over her shoulder, into each one of us she let creep instincts and desires which are utterly at variance with his main being, so that we are streaked, variegated, all of a mixture; the colors have run. Is the true self this which stands on the pavement in January, or that which bends over the balcony in June? Am I here, or am I there? Or is the true self neither this nor that, neither here nor there, but something so varied and wandering that it is only when we give the rein to its wishes and let it take its way unimpeded that we are indeed ourselves? Circumstances compel unity; for convenience' sake a man must be whole. The good

citizen when he opens his door in the evening must be banker, golfer, husband, father; not a nomad wandering the desert, a mystic staring at the sky, a debauchee in the slums of San Francisco, a soldier heading a revolution, a pariah howling with scepticism and solitude. (*DM* 28–29)

Woven into the civilized language of Woolf's experiments, the pariah's howl makes itself heard through the end of our century.

CHAPTER I.

Strange Crossings

I am going to found a colony where there shall be no
marrying—unless you happen to fall in love with a
symphony of Beethoven—no human element at all,
except what comes through Art—nothing but ideal peace
and endless meditation. This world of human
beings grows too complicated. . . .
(*Virginia Woolf, letter to Emma Vaughan, April 1901*)

"It's you novelists who're responsible, you know. You've
made a world in which everyone is always falling in love—
but it's not this world."
(*Leonard Woolf, "A Tale Told by Moonlight"*)

Love . . . and sensual pleasure . . . are two different
phases of a single fact. . . . The man of superior mind
as well as the imbecile . . . feels the need of the ideal
and the need of the sensual; all alike go about in
search of this mysterious hermaphrodite, this *rara avis*
which, in a majority of cases, is found to be a work
in two volumes. This search is a form of depravity for
which society is to blame.
(*Balzac*, La Cousine Bette)[1]

AMPHIBIANS

Marriage is a paradox. In legally uniting man and woman, society attempts
to author a hermaphrodite: a single, ambivalent being. Yet flesh is an insuperable barrier, as is subjectivity: bodies cannot meld, nor brains join. And
"falling in love" means embarking on a self-created fiction that has no
simple resolution in marriage but receives there a continuation either fecund or embattled—or both. What began, often, as mutual cathexis is then,
with luck, complicated and enriched through dialogue. For Leonard and
Virginia Woolf, who experienced barriers to physical conjunction, true intercourse was verbal, and largely expressed through the remarkably fertile
literary output of both partners.[2] Marriage, for them, was a cowritten narrative: one work in two volumes.[3] The many actual volumes the couple

wrote were the products not only of intellectual cross-fertilization but, even more important, of the sense of strengthened individuality each gained from the other.

The novels Virginia and Leonard conceived before marriage, and ended by dedicating to each other, inscribe attitudes and fantasies that initially placed them at odds and ultimately brought them together. Both novels are set in colonial venues, invoking problems of gender and sexuality through the ambiance of imperialism—an ambiance shown to shape the hierarchical relations of men and women in the metropole as well as the riddled postures of servitude and domination in the colonies.[4] Virginia's *The Voyage Out* (1915) and Leonard's *The Village in the Jungle* (1913) present that ambiance in different ways, from the perspective of the very different experiences that shaped the young adulthood of each author. Virginia Woolf's first novel chronicles the sea change of a young woman who travels to a former colony in South America and is assailed and, finally, destroyed by a social malaise: the hypocritical ethos that denies sexual subjectivity to women even as it constructs them as consummately sexual creatures. The subtext of Rachel Vinrace's tragedy is Virginia Stephen's own journey to adulthood via loss, illness, and unsavory familial experience—a traumatic crossing that led ultimately to a psychological crossing of sensual creative energies with inhibition in the realm of sexuality. Leonard's novel, and the short stories he published later as *Stories of the East* (1924), expose the moral bankruptcy of British colonial rule by representing tragic losses in translation between colonizer and colonized; their background is Leonard's own crossing from England to Ceylon as naive colonizer-to-be, and his return crossing to England and a new vocation as anti-imperialist writer.

Together, these works illuminate the ambivalent attitudes toward body and intellect, self and other, that, writ so large in the ideologies of imperialism, also informed the two writers' initial conceptions of each other. Their fictional works both inscribe and revise the mental fictions each created about the other—fictions whose elements of truth needed finally to be distinguished from those of masquerade inherent in their respective social identities. In part, the novels functioned to help make that distinction, to enable the couple's embarcation on the further, lively crossings of their marriage: crossings that dispensed with simplistic social paradigms of falling in love and living in wedlock, of the separation between public and private domains, politics and emotion, intellect and sexuality.

In an essay written for the Bloomsbury "Memoir Club" in 1921, Virginia Woolf recalls her brother Thoby's description of Leonard Woolf as a Cambridge undergraduate, and her own fascinated response:

Thoby [told me about an] astonishing fellow—a man who trembled perpetually all over. . . . He was a Jew. When I asked why he trembled, Thoby somehow made me feel that it was part of his nature—he was so violent, so savage. . . . I was of course inspired with the deepest interest in that violent trembling misanthropic Jew who had already shaken his fist at civilisation and was about to disappear into the tropics so that we should none of us ever see him again. (*MB* 166)

Of course Virginia did see Leonard again. After seven years as a colonial civil servant in Ceylon, he returned to England in 1911 with the hope of persuading her to marry him—a hope that had been spawned by epistolary intercourse with his closest male friend and fellow Cambridge graduate, Lytton Strachey. It was only then that she came to know him well. But her initial impression—better labeled a projection authored primarily by Thoby—had been a powerful one. Indeed, her construction of Leonard as "savage" stands in inverse parallel to Strachey's casting of *her* as spiritualized virgin maid, the perfect and pure intellectual who might take his own place as Woolf's platonic companion (without, perhaps, draining from the earlier companionship its few drops of playful verbal eroticism).

Leonard's intensity, his congenital tremor and verbal vehemence were legendary among his friends—legends played up *by* his friends—and invariably associated with his Jewishness. David Garnett, another acquaintance, describes Leonard as "a lean man with the long hooked nose and burnt up features and ascetic lips of the desert dweller rather than the typical Jew. [He] had spent ten years shaken by fever and burnt by the tropical sun as a District Magistrate in Ceylon" (*Flowers of the Forest* 162). Both Garnett's and Virginia Woolf's descriptions of Leonard are absurdly hyperbolic; both lay stress on his Jewishness, and on its combination with the supposed effects of the Orient. Under the guise of absolving him from a stereotype ("the typical Jew"), Garnett merely reemphasizes his foreignness, turning him into the acceptable, though still alien, Oriental and collapsing the considerable cultural and geographical space between Arabian desert and Ceylonese jungle (as well as the psychopolitical space between colonizer and colonized).[5] Inevitably, Leonard is the Other: in Garnett's account a desert nomad, in Virginia's a species of "savage" like those toward whom he migrated, with apparent Darwinian inevitability, in 1904. What Virginia's brief impression also ignores—though elsewhere she emphasizes it to the point of parody—is the fact that Leonard went to Ceylon to impose order rather than to engulf himself in primitive *dis*order. In the course of his seven (not, as Garnett has it, ten) years among people toward whom he felt sympathy for reasons considerably more complex than a visceral attraction to "savagery," his ideas of order underwent a change that may, indeed, have made him seem a very different man from the intellectual undergraduate who had also been a surprising success in the rarefied (and almost exclusively Gentile) circle of the Cambridge Apostles. As he reiterates time and again in his memoirs, he changed from a political naïf into a thoroughly "political animal."

In a chapter of his autobiography entitled "The Voyage Out," Leonard described the start of his career as a colonial civil servant as a second birth, far more "strange, frightening, and exhilarating" than the first (*G* 11). Most striking in this chapter (with its noteworthy title) is Leonard's emphasis on the voyage itself—the embarcation—as the real shock, rather than the debarkation in a "strange" new world. Given the notorious English project of precisely reproducing England's own society in the colonies, the shipboard "microcosm" Woolf encountered on the voyage out was the true and perfect locus of familiarity and estrangement to prepare him for his new position. It reproduced in more blatant forms the metropole's hierarchies of class and gender; cast those hierarchies into relief; and, in some instances, collapsed them through the inevitable intimacies of so small and delimited an environment.

In this setting, Woolf's ambiguous status as fledgling colonizer was brought home to him with considerable intensity through the behavior of others. On the one hand, his low marks in the Cambridge tripos had barred him from more prestigious occupation—Thoby Stephen had gone up to study law; Lytton Strachey stayed at Cambridge to pursue an intellectual career—and cast him into Ceylon, the preferable alternative to a job in the Postal Service. On the other hand, as he quickly learned on board, he was already on the top rungs of the colonial hierarchy, automatically resented as a civil servant by mere merchants and shopkeepers in "the class war and hatred between Europeans which in 1904 were a curious feature of British imperialism in the East" (*G* 16). According to *Growing*, Leonard's Jewishness played no role in this warfare, but—as the memoirs also reiterate—he was clearly "not a gentleman" who nonetheless passed as one, incurring the patronage of superiors, the liking of colleagues, and the resentment of the lower ranks. He adjusted quickly on board ship, as he had adjusted at prep school, by concealing some attributes and emphasizing others—skillfulness at sports and games, love of dogs, and rage for efficiency. All that remained to discover was the gulf between himself as ambivalent colonizer and the natives he was meant to order.

Virginia Stephen, debarred as a woman from the privileges of university and the chance of a public career, made no great voyages during the same period of her life. Her story of Rachel's journey was based on experiences as a tourist in her twenties that left her with little taste for travel. Indeed, she embarked on these journeys in a spirit of rather determined ethnocentrism and returned with her prejudices confirmed. Unlike the Leonard Woolf of Thoby's mythifying description, who slipped easily from the shores of England to join his fellow fist-shaking savages, Virginia resisted the unwashed Other all the way out and all the way back. The same woman who professed "astonishment" at Leonard's misanthropy was capable of rather astonishing remarks about people of different national or ethnic background from her own. The virulence of her reactions suggests a kind of viral paranoia, an intense fear of infection from the "dirt" of foreigners. The natives of the Mediterranean she viewed as barely human; from Italy she wrote in 1904, "There never was a beastlier nation than this . . ." (*L* 1:139). On a trip to Spain the following year she objects to her fellow ship-passengers: "There are a great many Portuguese Jews on board, and other repulsive objects . . ." (*L* 1:184). Her goal on this sea journey, to which she refers in her next letter home as "the voyage out," is to "keep clear of [the repulsive objects]." On the way back, however, she fears she may "have to sleep with a Portuguese Jew" if there is insufficient space on the ship.

Perhaps it was a fear of contamination that made Virginia view travel as a disease from which "the brain recovers in a month or two," and feel that "coming home [is] the best part of being away" (*L* 1:187). Later, she must have been traumatized by the result of a Greek tour in 1906, on which her brother Thoby, her sister Vanessa, and her friend Violet Dickinson all contracted typhoid, which killed Thoby within a month. The fears and devastation that attended and resulted from these travels were all too famil-iar: the mood of Virginia's adolescence had been largely defined by the premature deaths of both her mother and her half-sister Stella, both vic-tims of illnesses Virginia Stephen associated with the predaceous sexual, emotional, and material demands of Victorian husbands. On trips, the de-fenses Virginia Stephen must have developed to cope with what she came to call the "random unheeding flail" of sudden illness and death most likely combined with an inherited and class-based xenophobia to heighten her fears. All these feelings and experiences help explain the disastrous ending of her first novel, *The Voyage Out*, in which the newly engaged heroine dies of an obscure tropical illness—an illness, moreover, falsely diagnosed in its early stages by a South American doctor whose dark face and "hairy hands" almost suggest a collusion with the beastly force that is killing her.

The most frequently invoked explanation for Rachel Vinrace's inexplica-ble disease and senseless-seeming death is the profound ambivalence about sexuality exhibited by Rachel and attributed to Virginia Woolf herself by most, if not all, biographers. Certainly the South American atmosphere seems fresh enough, in Woolf's depiction, not to harbor hordes of danger-ous germs; indeed, the eponymous voyage is hardly a genuine journey "out," as the writer W. H. Hudson complained shortly after the novel's appearance in 1915: "Here are a lot of people . . . —all English people of one class (that of the author) all thinking, talking, and acting exactly like the people one meets every day in every London drawing-room. . . . Somewhere in S. America it is supposed to be and once or twice 'natives' are mentioned. The scene might just as well have been in some hotel on the south coast of England."[6]

Perhaps the author of *Green Mansions: A Romance of the Tropical Forest*, a Tarzan-style best-seller admired by Conrad and Galsworthy, misses the point. Woolf's unexotic ambiance may be the book's most radical move, despite—indeed, because of—its apparent timidity: in imposing the Edwardian drawing room on more liminal territories, she exposes the imperialist dichotomy of civilization versus savagery precisely by reproducing it. Woolf "borrows" her postcolonial setting for her own interests—just as the British "borrowed" their colonies to suit their own profits—and shows, at the same time, that the very doctrines which buttressed the imperial venture underlie the rituals of English social intercourse, and even of "falling in love" and marrying.

There is a biographical explanation for the setting as well: Phyllis Rose suggests that the novel chronicles the most important voyage Virginia took in the years before it was written. "It may seem odd," Rose admits, "for our heroine to journey all the way from England to South America to find herself a young man from Cambridge; it becomes less odd if we consider Rachel's pilgrimage as a fictionalized presentation of Virginia Woolf's own 'journey' from Hyde Park Gate to Bloomsbury" (Rose, *Woman of Letters* 58). The transition from her childhood home to a very different ménage in 1904 represented Virginia's entry into adulthood; it was also an escape from a traumatic, liminal place and time, Hyde Park Gate under the dual government of her father and her half-brother George Duckworth. Free from the latter's tyrannous conventionality, his insistence on proper Victorian dress and behavior, she and her sister Vanessa could finally devote themselves to art and the pursuit of uninhibited conversation with Thoby's Cambridge friends. More important, they were free of George's regular sexual advances; it is these predations, seemingly left behind at Hyde Park Gate, as Rachel Vinrace's stultifying girlhood with its ethos of repression and unspoken danger is apparently left behind in England, that infect the novel, forming its disturbing subtext. In the postcolonial ambiance of "Santa Marina," former tyrannies are still traceable in social relations: in Rachel Vinrace's case, such traces lead to tragedy; in Virginia Stephen's case, they may have led to considerable ambivalence about marriage, particularly to a former colonialist whose activities bore some resemblance to her half-brother's invasions.

In "A Sketch of the Past," the autobiographical memoir she wrote in 1939, Woolf relates the particular paradox of life at Hyde Park Gate: "The division in our life was curious. Downstairs there was pure convention: upstairs pure intellect. But there was no connection between them" (*MB* 135). In the ensuing paragraphs, Virginia reiterates this lack of connection almost compulsively. Her inability to solve the mystery—such bullhead-edness in the Duckworth realm, such clarity in Leslie Stephen's study, both encompassed in one house!—suggests a powerful mental blockage, and the insuperable, though often confused, boundary between upper and nether parts that is *The Voyage Out*'s most persistent motif.

A close reading of the memoir reveals another significance to the dichot-omy of upstairs and downstairs. In an earlier passage, Virginia describes what she calls her "looking-glass shame," her sense of "disconnect[ion from] my own body." Through a process of verbal self-therapy, she reaches back in memory for the origins of this sense of shame and arrives at an incident:

> There was a slab outside the dining room door [in the Stephens' summer house] for standing dishes upon. Once when I was very small Gerald Duck-worth lifted me onto this, and as I sat there he began to explore my body. I can remember the feel of his hand going *under* my clothes; going firmly and steadily *lower and lower*. I remember how I hoped that he would stop; how I stiffened and wriggled as his hand approached my private parts. But it did not stop. (*MB* 69; italics mine)

This incident might have had negligible effects on Woolf's adult sexual-ity had not George, the other Duckworth brother, begun to pay inappro-priate attentions to both Virginia and Vanessa during the girls' adoles-cence.[7] George Duckworth came to stand, in the sisters' eyes, for everything that was hateful and hypocritical about patriarchal, and espe-cially Victorian, society. Virginia consistently associates his narrow-mind-edness with his physicality: "What kind of material was George made of? ... He had very little brain, in the first place, and he had an abundance of emotion. He was poured into a perfectly adapted body. He was extremely handsome, perfectly healthy ..." (*MB* 131).

Being the daughter of Leslie Stephen, eminent editor, literary critic, and historian, and growing up in a Victorian household, Virginia was bound to rank brain over body. Brain was also what George Duckworth lacked, body what he and his brother forced upon her. To disjoin the two, to live inside thoughts and repudiate instincts, was partly a defense mechanism. If down-stairs and upstairs could be seen as different planes of being, only tenuously and illogically connected by the framework of a house, the memory of trauma could be kept at bay. Virginia need not remember that the lord of the downstairs had a nocturnal habit of climbing *up* the stairs and infiltrat-ing her own bedroom.

Yet Woolf was too clever, ultimately, not to sense that it is precisely such constructed divisions that perpetuate invasions, that the ideology of "purity" can veil the most savage predations. In her first novel, her maiden voyage, she embarked on a lifelong career of rending veils; if Rachel's death, as many readers feel, arises from a terror of defloration, this terror has formed itself behind the heavy curtains that enshroud her mental development, obscuring (and preventing) the "true relations" of men and women in her society. Far more frightening than the hymen's piercing is the unadmitted purdah of young Englishwomen in the early twentieth century; most appalling in George Duckworth's behavior was the mask of brotherly virtue he presented to the world, which kept that world from seeing what went on in darkness. At the end of "22 Hyde Park Gate," a memoir presented to friends in 1920 or 1921, Woolf describes the final part of an evening spent being presented to society by her half-brother. The whirl of mixed emotions, the desire for calm and solitude, the disruption of her privacy by a lustful older male, all recall the experiences of Rachel Vinrace, and the ending is no less stunning for its flippant tone:

> In a confused whirlpool of sensation I stood slipping off my petticoats, withdrew my long white gloves, and hung my white silk stockings over the back of a chair. Many different things were whirling round in my mind. . . . Ah, how pleasant it would be to stretch out in bed, fall asleep and forget them all!
>
> Sleep had almost come to me. The room was dark. The house silent. Then, creaking stealthily, the door opened; treading gingerly, someone entered. "Who?" I cried. "Don't be frightened," George whispered. "And don't turn on the light, oh beloved. Beloved—" and he flung himself on my bed, and took me in his arms.
>
> Yes, the old ladies of Kensington and Belgravia never knew that George Duckworth was not only father and mother, brother and sister to those poor Stephen girls; he was their lover also. (*MB* 155)

In the final chapters of *The Voyage Out*, when Rachel Vinrace is tossing in delirious fever, her fiancé enters the room and sits by the bed. He disrupts the curious sensations of her illness in a way she finds disturbing:

> [F]or long spaces of time she would would merely lie conscious of her body floating on the top of the bed and her mind driven to some remote corner of her body, or escaped and gone flitting round the room. All sights were something of an effort, but the sight of Terence was the greatest effort, because he forced her to join mind to body in the desire to remember something. She did not wish to remember. . . . (*VO* 347)

The act of joining mind and body suggests recuperation, yet Rachel clings to her dissociation. Memory and re-membering are synonymous here, and, as the one who "forces" Rachel to remember, Terence Hewet seems to embody a sexual threat; his entry into her bedroom, his interruption of her curious sensations, and his prevention of the escape she seeks, all recall George Duckworth at the end of "22 Hyde Park Gate." Although, in his behavior toward women, Hewet is overtly the most enlightened male in the novel, he is not above objectifying them sexually and has, by his own admission, had numerous affairs. As Rachel's husband- and sexual partner-to-be, moreover, he must inevitably be associated in her mind with her first sexual experience: on the voyage out, the smug, conservative ex-MP Richard Dalloway had seized Rachel and kissed her, evoking a powerfully ambivalent response, a rush of elation followed by hallucinatory dreams and fantasies so intense as to suggest an earlier, unmentioned trauma. Though Terence is younger and more progressive than Dalloway, Rachel has only this previous experience—and some glimpses of Hewet's surprisingly conventional attitude toward marriage and gender roles—to foreshadow the attentions of her bridegroom.

In her study of the evolution of *The Voyage Out* through a number of drafts, Louise DeSalvo identifies incest as the basis of Rachel's sexual terror. "Each time Woolf completed a draft of the novel," she writes, "each time she composed or revised or rewrote Rachel's delirium and death, she was staging her own punishment, delirium, and semi-suicidal death for having excited the lusts of an older man identified in the earlier version with the victim's father" (*Virginia Woolf's First Voyage* 159).[8] In a passage from *Melymbrosia*, the 1908–1909 draft of the novel, Virginia describes Rachel's father as "a sturdy man, more flesh than spirit"—the same type of man as George Duckworth. Though Captain Vinrace's "lusts" are no longer evident in the published version of *The Voyage Out*, he manhandles Rachel in small but significant ways—"enforcing his words" for example, "as he often did, when he spoke to his daughter, by a smart blow upon the shoulder" (28). Indeed Rachel's aunt Helen "suspect[s] him of nameless atrocities with regard to his daughter" (24). To understand these atrocities as literally incestuous, however, is vastly to simplify Woolf's message of social outrage. The real tragedy of Rachel's response to Dalloway is its unresolved ambivalence, the fact that desire, experienced as a wondrous new sensation, is compromised—worse, maimed—in the face of Dalloway's prim, cold behavior the evening after the kiss, when the seagoers reassemble for the civilized ritual of a communal English dinner.

The traumatic phasing of possibility into foreclosure is worth quoting in full. At first overwhelmed by an emotion characterized as fear and manifested in somatic disorder—a response to be expected in a young woman who, at the age of twenty-four, has been barred from all theoretical knowledge, let alone experience, of lust in another or herself—Rachel then feels

possessed with a strange exultation. Life seemed to hold infinite possibilities she had never guessed at. She leant upon the rail and looked over the troubled grey waters, where the sunlight was fitfully scattered upon the crests of the waves, until she was cold and absolutely calm again. Nevertheless something wonderful had happened.

At dinner, however, she did not feel exalted, but merely uncomfortable, as if she and Richard had seen something together which is hidden in ordinary life, so that they did not like to look at each other. Richard *slid his eyes over her* uneasily once, and never looked at her again. Formal platitudes were manufactured with effort, but Willoughby was kindled.

"Beef for Mr. Dalloway!" he shouted. "Come now—after that walk you're at the beef stage, Dalloway!"

Wonderful masculine stories followed. . . . (76–77; italics mine)

United in beefiness, Dalloway and Captain Vinrace represent the reasserted ideologies of empire and predation; while their carnivorousness metaphorizes aggressive carnality, that carnality is linked, as Michael Tratner has observed, to the other forms of rule in which they engage as "representatives of imperialism and the oppression of workers" (*Modernism and Mass Politics* 91).[9] In an earlier draft of the novel, Woolf designates Vinrace's business as the importing of goats from South America—a carnivorous neocolonial enterprise. Literally, however, "the beef stage" refers to Dalloway's full emergence from seasickness, and with it, the abrupt closure of an anarchic phase in which the prescribed boundaries of behavior between the sexes, between adult authority and youthful vulnerability, had been briefly transcended. While the transcendence necessarily takes a violent form—the kiss occurs in a collision of bodies caused by the lurching ship—more atrocious than that collision is the almost immediate repair of the oppressive curtain that was torn. The desire that felt like "infinite possibility" turns out to be finite, and, in the face of its repudiation, to have been sordid; the conversation that preceded the kiss, in which Richard had addressed Rachel as an equal, is buried away beneath "[w]onderful masculine stories." Lust is apparently a male prerogative, witheld from women in any form but imposition: the exclusive privilege of the colonizer, with his banal tales of adventure.

The Voyage Out is a novel of disjunction—so much so, according to E. M. Forster, who reviewed the book shortly after its appearance, that the eternal mind-body problem is rendered irrelevant. "In [Woolf's] pages," Forster claimed, "body v. soul—that dreary medieval tug-of-war—does not find any place. It is as if the rope has broken, leaving pagans sprawling on one side and clergymen on the other . . ." (Majumdar and McLaurin, *The Critical Heritage* 54). Forster's claim seems not only inaccurate but self-contradictory as well. The two sides are all the more conspicuously and problematically at odds for being far apart. Between them stands the figure of Rachel Vinrace, whose own sense of self is a site for tug-of-war—especially when what at times seems disjunction is, at others, sheer confusion. In the post-Victorian but as-yet unliberated milieu Woolf represents, shame still attends sexuality in the hypocritical form of the demeaning of women: a prostitute who inhabits the hotel in Santa Marina is banished from that edifice of propriety when her presence becomes too conspicuous—but the guests who do business with her go unnamed and unpunished. And Terence Hewet's nickname, Monk, heightens the confusion of values, suggesting as it does that his sexual activities have nothing at all to do with his spiritual life; sexuality belongs under cover and, like certain unidentified sea creatures invoked on the voyage out, vanishes—or must be made to vanish—in the light of day.

E. M. Forster probably did not know that in an early version of the novel, the heroine (*Cynthia* Vinrace) reads and is enthralled by Sir Thomas Browne's *Religio Medici*. DeSalvo notes that Cynthia is described at one point as " 'some restless amphibious creature,' " and that the adjective "amphibious" comes from Browne's description of human nature:

> We are only that amphibious piece between a corporeal and spiritual essence; that middle frame that links those two together, and . . . unites the incompatible distances by some middle and participating natures.
>
> . . . This is man that great and true amphibium, whose nature is disposed to live not only like other creatures in divers elements, but in divided and distinguished worlds. For though there be but one world to sense, there are two to reason. . . . (Qtd. in DeSalvo, *Virginia Woolf's First Voyage* 19)

Like Forster, Browne contradicts himself. In one breath, he represents the amphibian as a balanced mélange of air and substance (thus, incidentally, confusing air and water); in the next, he portrays a creature whose essence is division. The contradiction is perhaps unavoidable—particularly for a woman, like Rachel (or Cynthia) Vinrace, whose entrapment in her *lower* nature is constantly impressed on her by men. In *The Voyage Out*, Richard Dalloway explains his kiss by telling Rachel: " 'You have beauty. . . . You tempt me' " (76). And indeed, she does seem to have tempted him by answering his efforts to "communicate," his questions about herself and her interests, with the simple statement: "You see, I'm a woman" (66). Rachel's paradoxical, faltering assertion of her inability to voice subjectivity in a world where subjectivity is claimed by men gets lost in translation; to Richard, it is a reminder of her embodiment, his own sexuality, and the divorcement of body and brain in the relations between men and women. Later, Terence Hewet, perplexed because his initial attraction to Rachel is more intellectual than physical, finds that she "became less desirable as her brain began to work, inflicting a certain change upon her face . . ." (212)—he seems to prefer her to be purely physical.

Rachel's amphibious inner conflict—the effort to locate her true self between the sexual nature attributed to her by men and the intellectual consciousness she is just starting to possess—is manifested by her alternation between uplifting mental trances and disturbing, apparently causeless sensations of murky immersion. Her effort at balance is unsettled by the preoccupations of the men around her. *The Voyage Out* abounds with references to deep-sea creatures, including, early on, a description by the pedantic Mr. Pepper of "white, hairless, blind monsters lying curled on the ridges of sand at the bottom of the sea, which would explode if you brought them to the surface, their sides bursting asunder and scattering entrails to the winds when released from pressure . . ." (23)—a description that surely owes less to zoology than to poems like Alfred Tennyson's "The Kraken," with its Victorian subtext of fearsome sexuality. The ethos both exemplify is the "dreary medieval" fascination with and terror of women's lower parts, which provides the inexperienced Rachel with her own metaphoric bestiary. Later in the book, Terence Hewet presents a friendlier version of Pepper's krakens. Out on a walk the other day, he tells Rachel and his friend St. John Hirst, "I saw a sight that fairly took my breath away—about twenty jellyfish, semi-transparent, pink, with long streamers, floating on the top of the waves."

" 'Sure they weren't mermaids?' " asks Hirst, the intellectual and aesthete (204). Hirst himself is a decided misogynist who denigrates *all* of women's parts, upper, lower, and middle. Indeed, he denies them an upper, asking Rachel at one point, " 'Have you got a mind, or are you like the rest of your sex?' " (154) Apropos another English couple's engagement, he remarks to Hewet, " 'What I abhor most of all . . . is the female breast. Imagine being Venning and having to get into bed with Susan! . . . They're gross, they're absurd, they're utterly intolerable!' " (184) Here Hirst, modeled on Virginia Stephen's friend and day-long fiancé Lytton Strachey, echoes the rhetoric of that clever man's correspondence with Leonard Woolf in Ceylon, a correspondence containing regular expressions of disgust toward the body, sometimes male, more frequently female.

Virginia Woolf's suspicion of Hirst's Oxbridge-style posturings also shows itself in a 1907 letter to Violet Dickinson, in which she describes "the atmosphere of Oxford"—an atmosphere probably not unfamiliar from visits to Thoby at Cambridge—as "quite the chilliest and the least human known to me; you see brains floating like so many sea anemonies [*sic*], nor have they shape or colour. They are bloodless, with great veins on them" (*L* 1:319–20). Male intellection, rarefied as it pretends to be, is inseparable from male physicality; a "bloodless" thing that nonetheless harbors grossly phallic "great veins," the male brain is a repulsive sea creature, pretending away—like Hewet's nickname, Monk—its sexual drives. Virginia Stephen describes her own mind, in contrast, as absolved from physicality: "it floats," she writes, "in blue air; where there are circling clouds, soft sunbeams of elastic gold, and fairy gossamers—things that cant [*sic*] be cut— that must be tenderly enclosed, and expressed in a globe of exquisitely coloured words. At the mere prick of steel they vanish" (*L* 1:320). The fable suggests a fear of sexual violation, as well as an acute sense that female intellect is threatened by male sexuality—and not vice versa, as St. John Hirst would have it. But the contrasting visions, dialectically constructed, are also filled with playful mockery: of the universities' pretensions, of the system that keeps women pure by excluding them from "higher" education, and of the young female writer's dreams of transcendence in a material world. To be human—woman or man—is to be amphibious, a perverse condition only when one half of the amphibian pretends superiority or indifference to the other.

Hirst's mermaid fantasy foreshadows a subtly sinister exchange between Hewet and Rachel not long after their engagement. Hewet tells Rachel:

> "[W]hat I like about your face is that it makes one wonder what the devil you're thinking about—it makes me want to do that—" He clenched his fist and shook it so near her that she started back, "because now you look as if you'd blow my brains out. There are moments," he continued, "when, if we stood on a rock together, you'd throw me into the sea."
>
> . . . She sprang up, and began moving about the room, bending and thrusting aside the chairs and tables as if she were indeed striking through the waters. He watched her with pleasure; she seemed to be cleaving a passage for herself, and dealing triumphantly with the obstacles which would hinder their passage through life.
>
> . . . He caught her in his arms as she passed him, and they fought for mastery, imagining a rock, and the sea heaving beneath them. At last she was thrown to the floor, where she lay gasping, and crying for mercy.
>
> "I'm a mermaid! I can swim," she cried, "so the game's up." Her dress was torn across, and peace being established, she fetched a needle and thread and began to mend the tear. (297–98)

Rachel's self-designation as quintessentially amphibious is a gesture of both triumph and capitulation. Her lower half represents an independence, a physical vigor, and an unavailability that incite, at one and the same time, Terence's admiration and his desire for mastery. Like Richard Dalloway, Hewet denies his own volition and scapegoats Rachel: *her* face "makes me want to do that." And while he ascribes murderous desires to her, it is he who knocks her down and tears her dress—a synecdoche *both* for Rachel's fishy part, her disturbingly vital lower half, and for the brain, the autonomous thoughts, whose discreteness makes Hewet want to penetrate and possess them by force.

Woolf's persistent use of amphibian images, her portrayal of a young woman who finds herself, on the threshold of adulthood and self-realization, prey to the images others—men in particular—impose upon her, suggests not only a reworking of her own traumatic past but an attempt to grapple with the history of women's scapegoating. In *The Voyage Out*, she invokes the archetypal myth of woman as inherently sinful, registering her indignation and resentment at the Western narrative that has mired woman in her lower half and linked her to mud and serpents. In *The Voyage Out*, male sexuality is made the cause of *woman's* fall—not from grace, but from mental equilibrium and physical health. Near the start of their acquaintance, at a picnic organized by Hewet, the latter approaches Rachel in a peculiar manner: "Hewet crawled up to her on his knees, with a piece of bread in his hand" (135). Hewet's posture links him to a serpent: like Satan, he makes an edible offering. If Rachel is amphibious, this vignette seems to say, her Fall is initiated by a creature who is all bottom half, an earth-dwelling, phallic reptile.

A feminist revision of Western civilization's myth of origins, *The Voyage Out* is also a rereading of other versions of that story. Virginia's move to Bloomsbury from Hyde Park Gate is one explanation as to why Rachel Vinrace is made to travel to South America to meet a young Cantabrigian; another is the imperialist myth that locates all snakes in the jungle: to discover moral darkness, in other words, the protagonist must leave the drawing room for the colonies. Woolf adopts this topos as exemplified in Conrad's *Heart of Darkness* and parodies that novel's central voyage up a serpentine river in her own protagonists' much more genteel, Amazon journey. In *The Voyage Out*, the menace to civilization has no objective correlative in greedy cannibals or heads on pikes. The reader must glean it from a landscape whose threats are less overt—whose threats, indeed, are mostly in the protagonists' minds.

The crucial locus of *The Voyage Out*, the backdrop of Rachel and Terence's reenactment of the Fall, is a village in the jungle. The six English people who have traveled upriver with this village as their destination are the effete modern descendants of their Elizabethan imperialist forefathers. Mr. and Mrs. Flushing, the art-collectors, intend to purchase native crafts. Hirst, the aesthete, wishes he had brought his Kodak. The description of their journey mimics Conrad's rhetoric only to deflate it. Conrad's notion of the irresistible barbarity of the jungle is undermined by the trivial preoccupations of Woolf's characters:

> They seemed to be driving into the heart of the night, for the trees closed in front of them, and they could hear all round them the rustling of leaves. The great darkness had the usual effect of taking away all desire for communication by making their words sound thin and small; and, after walking round the deck three or four times, they clustered together, yawning deeply, and looking at the same spot of deep gloom on the banks. Murmuring very low in the rhythmical tone of one oppressed by the air, Mrs. Flushing began to wonder where they were to sleep. . . . She yawned profoundly. It was as Helen had foreseen; the question of nakedness had risen already. . . . With St. John's help she

stretched an awning, and persuaded Mrs. Flushing that she could take off her clothes behind this, and that no one would notice if by chance some part of her which had been concealed for forty-five years was laid bare to the human eye. (265–66)

As a parody of *Heart of Darkness*, the passage is highly entertaining. Evoking in one moment Conrad's famous "insistence upon inexpressible and incomprehensible mystery,"[10] in the next Woolf renders that mystery absurdly commonplace. The impression of "driving into the heart of the night" derives not from the sound of howling natives and beating tom-toms but merely from "the rustling of leaves"; and the "great darkness" has "usual" effects. Woolf also lampoons Conrad's constant emphasis on the penetration of unplumbed depths. The "deep gloom on the banks," all-pervasive in Conrad's narrative, here occupies a mere "spot"; its effect is to extract a "deep" yawn—later a "profound" yawn—from Mrs. Flushing. Finally, "the question of nakedness," absurd as it seems to the "pagan" Helen Ambrose, highlights the characters' resistance to the primitive rather than the latter's inexorable powers of seduction.

And yet the passage, read carefully and with the consciousness that Virginia Woolf was in no position to realistically describe the navigation of a jungle river, has sinister overtones. Mrs. Flushing's fears do not merely indicate her own prudishness (Mrs. Flushing is, on the surface at least, a rather daring person). They recall the customary restriction of women's lives back in England, to which Rachel alludes after Richard Dalloway's kiss, when she realizes that male lust is the reason " 'why I can't walk alone' " (82). Indeed, Rachel's conversation with Helen Ambrose on that occasion foreshadows the occurrences and effects of the river voyage, and suggests that Woolf's revision of Conrad is not all parody, nor her translation of London drawing room to South American jungle merely the gaucherie of an inexperienced writer striving for effect:

"So that's why I can't walk alone!"
By this new light she saw her life for the first time a creeping hedged-in thing, driven cautiously between high walls, here turned aside, there plunged in darkness, made dull and crippled for ever—her life that was the only chance she had. . . .
"Because men are brutes! I hate men!" she exclaimed. (82)

Here is the intensity, the sense of insidious evil, lacking in the passage more obviously evocative of Conrad—although the imagery anticipates the river-voyage description. The verb "drive" is used with apt forcefulness—all the more as the voice is passive. The reader senses Rachel's fury—and Woolf's—that Western women's enforced passivity "plunge[s their lives] in darkness." The images describing Rachel's life recall Milton's Satan ranting at his hellish lot—ironically, since Rachel's nemesis is not her own lower self but those hypocritical "brutes," men. Rachel's choice of word has at least two literary resonances. One, of course, is the dying inscription of Conrad's colonialist demon, Kurtz: "Exterminate all the brutes." The other occurs later in the text, at the very moment Rachel's fever begins, when Terence reads a passage from Milton's *Comus* describing, with sinister appropriateness, a mermaid:

> There is a gentle nymph not far from hence,

he read,

> That with moist curb sways the smooth Severn stream.
> Sabrina is her name, a virgin pure;
> Whilom she was the daughter of Locrine,
> That had the sceptre from his *father Brute*.

The words . . . seemed to be laden with meaning, and perhaps it was for this reason that it was painful to listen to them; they sounded strange; they meant different things from what they usually meant. Rachel at any rate could not keep her attention fixed upon them, but went off upon curious trains of thought suggested by words such as "curb" and "Locrine" and "Brute," which brought unpleasant sights before her eyes. . . . (326–27; italics mine)

As "Brute" evokes Rachel's earlier association of that word with rapacious male sexuality, the king's name naturally brings up "unpleasant" images—the more so as "Comus" tells the story of a virgin besieged by a wicked older man. Like Eve, the heroine of "Comus" is held responsible for her own downfall; she is a scapegoat in the making. Her ability to resist rape becomes the test of her virtue. In Virginia Woolf's revisionary text, Milton is yet another of the male figures who have besieged *Rachel's* body and, finally, assailed her sanity. It seems no accident that Rachel's fatal illness, wherever its seeds may have been sown, first manifests itself during Hewet's reading of Milton. And the Miltonian commandment "He for God, she for God in him" is of a piece with the nonethical ethic of imperialism; Milton's Adam-God who names the animals is the same brute who names the colonized Other.

For the actual source of Rachel's fever, readers as well as other characters in the novel predictably look to the jungle. But there is no empirical evidence that Rachel was contaminated on the river voyage. If her disease began in the jungle, it is a thing that, like the jungle, is ultimately unnameable; its "germs" lie in the imposition of a false and failed language, in an engagement that signals disengagement. The end point of the river voyage can be read as the end point both of imperialist positivism and of gender relations as dictated by English society. Two scenes parallel each other at the heart of the novel: the engagement of Rachel Vinrace and Terence Hewet, and the English party's encounter with native craftspeople. The former occurs between two hypercivilized people in an unchartable place, the latter between Europeans and natives in a jungle village. Each scene exposes, through contrasts of characters and setting, the empty heart of the myth of savagery vs. civilization.

The old idea of savagery has appeared already early in the novel when Helen Ambrose, on the voyage from England, is embroidering a tapestry:

> She was working at a great design of a tropical river running through a tropical forest, where spotted deer would eventually browse upon masses of fruit, bananas, oranges, and giant pomegranates, while a troop of naked natives whirled darts into the air. Between the stitches she looked to one side and read a sentence about the Reality of Matter, or the Nature of Good. (33)

This is a comical portrait of the woman who later chafes at Mrs. Flushing's prudery. Here Helen herself associates the naked body with wildness and aggression and is preoccupied with metaphysical questions. And when she actually encounters "native" life, she is profoundly disconcerted. At first, on their tour of the jungle village, the English people feel cumbersome and awkward among the graceful natives, whose savage beauty cries out for Hirst's camera.[11]

As their intrusive gaze is turned back upon them by the objects of their curiosity, the English people grow uncomfortable:

> Mr. Flushing . . . was engaged in talk with a lean majestic man, whose bones and hollows at once made the shapes of the Englishman's body appear ugly and unnatural. The women took no notice of the strangers, except that their hands paused for a moment and their long narrow eyes slid round and fixed upon them with the motionless inexpressive gaze of those removed from each other far, far beyond the plunge of speech.
>
> . . . Helen, standing by herself in the sunny space amongst the native women, was exposed to presentiments of disaster. The cries of the senseless beasts rang in her ears high and low in the air, as they ran from tree-trunk to treetop. How small the little figures looked wandering through the trees! She became acutely conscious of the . . . delicate flesh of men and women, which breaks so easily. . . . She kept her eyes fixed anxiously on the lovers, as if by doing so she could protect them from their fate. (285–86)

This scene briefly subverts the power dynamic of colonizer and colonized. The intense, shaming gaze of the native women is a refusal of objectification and an assertion of autonomy. Even the point of view is momentarily shifted so that it is the intruding tourists who become "strangers." Essentialist dichotomies seem to be collapsed with the simple remark that communication is impossible between two groups who don't speak the same language. But Woolf is actually describing only *one* gaze—that of the native women—as "the motionless inexpressive gaze of those removed from each other . . . beyond the plunge of speech." By denying them, in her pronomial slip, the capacity of speech, she seems to link them to the beasts: they are removed, not from the white visitors, but from "each other." Perhaps, however, her language precisely recognizes the violative nature of first-world designations. Any effort to communicate is a priori questionable: the English people visit in order to make purchases, a neocolonial enterprise in which the Flushings' excited interest in native crafts is the semibenign new version of earlier exploitations. Well-meaning is lost in translation, and native culture, too, is twisted in its passage to European hands—just as Rachel's "You see, I'm a woman" was twisted in the gulf between herself and Richard Dalloway. Most striking of all, perhaps, is the repetition of an earlier locution: the "sliding" eyes of the village women recall Richard Dalloway "slid[ing] his eyes over" Rachel at the dinner table on the evening after their kiss.

The text's subliminal consciousness here does not reflect any realization of Helen's; indeed, Helen has evidently gleaned nothing from her contact with strangers except a sudden fear for the bodily well-being of her friends. Her inability to communicate with the natives is only incidental, for she has reified them already as the naked, dart-throwing embodiments of human brutishness—an aesthetic brutishness, but still alien and terrifying. She herself remains trapped on the metaphysical plane, frightened at the body's capacity to elude control, its vulnerability to tear and destruction. Yet her dark mood at this moment suggests an inchoate awareness, an inkling of disaster that foreshadows her later, largely wordless battle with Hewet over the proper treatment of Rachel's illness—the battle of a woman whose loyalty to old customs prevents her from actively saving her niece, yet whose deep sense of systemic wrongs makes her suspicious of men's intentions, against a supposedly enlightened young man with a disturbing need to dictate the terms of engagement.

That engagement—the literal (though oddly undesignated) marriage engagement between Rachel and Hewet—has taken place the day before the party's arrival at the jungle village. The scene occurs in a tropical forest—a place both alien and familiar, with a path that "resembled a drive in an English forest" and exotic, unnamed flora. In that hybrid place, the prescribed and inevitable conversation is unmoored from its script and becomes, almost, a dialogue between aphasics. When Hewet "pick[s] up a red fruit" and throws it in the air "as high as he could," the primal Edenic scene is both suggested and subverted. His gesture initiates the strange catechism that follows:

"Does this frighten you?" Terence asked when the sound of the fruit falling had completely died away.

"No," she answered. "I like it."

She repeated "I like it." She was walking fast, and holding herself more erect than usual. There was another pause.

"You like being with me?" Terence asked.

"Yes, with you," she replied.

He was silent for a moment. Silence seemed to have fallen upon the world.

"That is what I have felt ever since I knew you," he replied. "We are happy together." He did not seem to be speaking, or she to be hearing.

"Very happy," she answered.

They continued to walk for some time in silence. Their steps unconsciously quickened.

"We love each other," Terence said.

"We love each other," she repeated.

The silence was then broken by their voices which joined in tones of strange unfamiliar sound which formed no words. Faster and faster they walked; simultaneously they stopped, clasped each other in their arms, then, releasing themselves, dropped to the earth. . . .

"We love each other," Terence repeated. . . . She said "Terence" once; he answered "Rachel."

"Terrible—terrible," she murmured after another pause. . . . (271)

The incoherent syntax of "Faster and faster . . . ," with its awkward repetition of pronouns and confusion of subject and object, suggests the pain and excitement that attend the expression of love between the sexes in a society whose conventions reify such expressions before they are fully grasped. On their return to the boat, the couple are assumed to be engaged—and the imminence of this return presses upon them already in the moments of declaration, so that exhilaration becomes instantly, indeed "simultaneously," constriction: that adverb, above, at first seems linked to "walked," so that the reader thinks the lovers are simultaneously hurrying through the woods and stopping still. Again, the imperfect language of a first novel reflects a disturbing subtext: the lovers are clasped in a Saint Vitus' dance, a spontaneous performance of joy that is instantly seized in the strictures of society. No "communication," however real and alive, is truly undictated: if, in this scene, Hewet seems disturbingly to declare the terms of love, Rachel to repeat them, both Hewet and Rachel are dictated to by conventions outside themselves. The literal dictator, in this instance, is the inexorable Flushing, who has demanded their return within an hour; and it is at the moment when "civilized" time reasserts itself that Rachel's disease seems to show its earliest signs: "She appeared to be very tired. Her cheeks were white." "The beef stage" is upon them once more; and with it, the first echo of Conrad's "horror": " 'I don't want to be late,' [Hewet] said, 'because—' He put a flower into her hand and her fingers closed upon it quietly. 'We're so late—so late—so horribly late,' he repeated." They are tragically late, for the Fall—not the sexual love of man and woman, but the Miltonic decree that love must be hierarchical and formalized once formulated—has already occurred.

The disjunction between English people and natives in *The Voyage Out* is a projection of the English characters' own alienation from their bodies. The novel deplores this alienation but refuses to escape or transcend it. The strange, syncopic dialogue of Rachel and Hewet, the tarantella that simultaneously possesses and liberates their bodies, enacts the schizophrenia of colonial relations even as it recalls the obscene divisions of the house at Hyde Park Gate. The very locus of Rachel's death inscribes those divisions in its name: Santa Marina, a postcolonial town, is a place of unintegrated distinctions. "Marina" denotes a sea-city, neither one thing nor the other, embodying the same paradox as "jungle village"; "*Santa* Marina" suggests that the saintliness of Victorian young women consists in their engulfment, their loss at sea. Rachel *has* been lost at sea, for the moment that sexuality is presented to her as possibility is also the moment it is wrested away; the gulf between herself and Richard Dalloway becomes the gulf between herself and Terence, which in turn reflects the loss in translation between English self and native Other. Mind and body, body and mind, she for God in him . . . There can be no true meeting of men and women as long as thesis and antithesis merely parrot one another.

VIRGINS/CONCUBINES

In an essay entitled "Virginia, Virginius, Virginity," Louise DeSalvo links Rachel Vinrace's death to Virginia Woolf's sense of herself as quintessentially virginal and of man as the enemy whose target is women's physical integrity (179–89). If Woolf felt this, and could not act against it, she surely felt it as a thing to be negotiated by wiser means than mere withdrawal. When Lytton Strachey wrote to Leonard in Ceylon, urging him to return home and propose to Virginia, he described her character in one phrase: "You see she *is* her name. . . ." A peculiar, amphibious ploy, and one that perhaps only Lytton Strachey, with his Wildean penchant for paradox, could carry off: to describe a woman as at once eminently marriageable and essentially impenetrable. It seems to have worked on Leonard, however. He returned to England, and the Virgin, strange to say, accepted him in marriage.

Perhaps it is too simple to understand the couple through the antithetical constructions of friends and critics: desiring virgin and ascetic sensualist.

Or perhaps one must understand them precisely through such chiasmic oppositions. Leonard's bodily experiences in Ceylon may have been enough to last him a lifetime. He wrote to Lytton often and in some detail about his "whoring"; gradually his accounts became statements of disgust toward the female body—a cathexis, perhaps, for the many more disturbing apparitions connected with his work: the bodies, for instance, of convicted men at whose hangings Woolf was compelled to preside, of murder victims, and of those afflicted with terrible diseases. Here is a letter written on November 25, 1908:

> It is my birthday today. I have been reading Forster's last book [*A Room with a View*] & as last year, at about the same time, it has just stirred the fringe of my brain [Woolf had read *The Longest Journey* in the summer of 1907]. It is almost a repetition of last year for do you remember the hanging [a gruesome, bloody quadruple-hanging described in a letter of September 29, 1907]? This time it came also upon a similar piece of "reality."
>
> As I suppose you know I am everything here: policeman, magistrate, judge, & publican. I was just going to begin breakfast when a message came that a murder had been committed at a place with the wonderful name Tissa-maharama. It is a wonderful place which one gets to through 20 miles of unin-habited jungle. . . . A man had kicked the woman with whom he lived to death because she had not got his dinner ready. They took me into the room of the hut where she was lying dead, & they stripped her naked for me to examine the wounds. Most women naked when alive are extraordinarily ugly, but dead they are repulsive & the most repulsive thing is the way the toes seem to stick up so straight & stark & dominate the room. But the most abominable thing was the smell. One gets accustomed to the smell of corruption and dead things here where the cattle are always dying of thirst & starvation & lie on the road-sides decaying: but I had no idea before that the smell of a decomposing human being is so infinitely fouler than anything else. Is that reality according to Forster? . . . [T]his book . . . is absolutely muddled isn't it?
>
> Isn't it dominated by a spectral Moore? . . . There is a curious twilight and pseudo mystery over his books. . . . (*LLW* 141–42)

This letter—along with several others like it—encapsulates Leonard's preoccupations during his stay in the tropics. His primary emphasis is on the "reality" of bodily experience; his criticisms of Forster, both here and in letters commenting on *The Longest Journey*, seem to call for a more natu-ralistic style of writing, and indeed Leonard's own letters are an odd mix of naturalistic description and almost flippant, curiously detached com-mentary. The tone of detachment is characteristic of Leonard, who often comments in his writings on his habits of psychic self-protection—habits nurtured by the need of "passing" in and through the various masculine, intolerant environments that made up the Victorian machine for churning out efficient, self-controlled governors of empire: public school, university, Civil Service. It was also a verbal habit of the Apostles, the secret Cambridge confraternity whose presiding genius was the philosopher G. E. Moore. Leonard's quiet disparagement of Moore in this letter signals the development that arose from the clash of his Ceylon "reality" with his earlier metaphysical concerns. Where a man is daily occupied with rotting corpses, diseased cattle, hangings, and the improvement of primitive sewage systems, he evidently becomes impatient with abstract rumination on "the Reality of Matter [and] the Nature of Good" (VO 33). Yet, for all his apparent contempt toward metaphysics, Leonard remains ambivalent: physical facts both engage and appall him. Side by side with chronicles of dysentery, his letters relate a fascination with the beauty and color of both landscape and people in Ceylon; while the bowels promote disgust, the poeticism of jungle villages with "wonderful" names like Tissamaharama incites a respect that phases gradually into an anti-imperialist conviction. This certainty, arising from initial ambivalence, became the foundation of Leonard Woolf's life's work as a political writer, activist, and Labour Party member.

Leonard's letter also illuminates the differences between his own writings on the colonial experience and Virginia's attempt to portray South American life in *The Voyage Out*. Helen Ambrose, while she embroiders her tapestry, is evidently reading George Moore's best-known book, *Principia Ethica*, and her sense of what she reads is far more "real" than her understanding of the naked figures she portrays on cloth. In Leonard's writings—his letters, his *Stories of the East*, and his novel, *The Village in the Jungle*—that dichotomy is reversed. Physical experience is more essential than philosophy; indeed, the mind-body question, which pervades Virginia's novel, is shown to be superfluous, a self-indulgent Western luxury, where the life of the mind is not a possible choice. Nor, indeed, is a life of liberation from social constraints, such as Helen and Rachel seek, where the power of the colonizer is to enforce constraint.

The most explicit illustration of this reversal of values occurs in one of the tales collected in Leonard's *Stories of the East*, "Pearls and Swine." The title itself indicates a classic dichotomy. The story is an attack on the imperialist mentality in both its supposedly beneficent and its obviously malevolent forms; its end is a subversion of the racist dichotomy that labels natives beasts and colonizers natural masters and enlightened redeemers. The initial first-person narrator, a colonialist on leave in England, repeats a story told by an older colonialist in the smoking-room of an English seaside hotel. The storyteller is provoked to his narrative by a discussion between two Englishmen about the proper mode of rule in the colonies. One, a clergyman, claims that the white man has "a duty . . . [to] spread the light" among the primitive races. The other, a stockjobber, fiercely maintains that " '[t]here's too much Liberalism in the East, too much namby-pamby-ism. . . . They want a strong hand. . . . I am a white man, you're black; I'll treat you well, give you courts and justice: but I'm the superior race, I'm master here' " (266–67). The storyteller, disgusted, interrupts the armchair colonialists in order to offset their "views" with what he calls "details, things seen, facts" (269).

The story he tells resembles Leonard's own account, in his letters and autobiography, of a pearl fishery he supervised in February 1906. Two characters, however, are added here, to parallel the two Englishmen whose conversation frames the story. One of these is the narrator's assistant at the pearl fishery, Robson, "a little boy of twenty-four fresh-cheeked from England . . . cocksure . . . of his 'views.' He was going to run India on new lines, laid down in some damned Manual of Political Science out of which they learn life in Board Schools and extension lectures" (270, 272). The political views of Robson—whose description recalls Leonard's criticism of Forster's naïveté, as well as the ignorance of Rachel Vinrace, herself twenty-four at the time of her voyage—parallel those of the clergyman. Robson believes that the unenlightened natives must be "taught how to live."

The villain of the story is a drunken brute called White who appears on the scene claiming to " 'deal' in pearls"—the stockjobber's counterpart and a new version of Conrad's Kurtz:

> He had views too, very much like Robson's, with additions. "The strong hand" came in, and "rule." . . . He talked a great deal about the hidden wealth of India and exploitation. . . . He would work for the good of the native, he'd treat him firmly but kindly—especially, I thought, the native women, for his teeth were sharp and pointed and there were spaces between each and there was something about his chin and jaw—*you* know the type, I expect. (273)

If Kurtz's surname is ironic and telling, White's needs no teasing out. Leonard's story debunks the ideology that still informs *Heart of Darkness*; despite Conrad's explicit condemnation of imperialism, he implies some correspondence between skin color and moral darkness and suggests that there are better and worse types of colonialism. White, like Kurtz, claims to have been seduced by the East: " 'India's got hold of me,' he'd say, 'India's got hold of me and the East' " (273)—implying that, before his entrapment, he was as pure as his surname might suggest.[12] But the storyteller depicts him as a brute from the beginning. He exposes White's hypocrisy by sarcastically calling into question the expression "firmly but kindly"— thereby also exposing the self-contradictory ethic of benevolent rule. And he reverses White's pseudoerotic portrayal of an India that relentlessly embraces him by suggesting that White is himself a sexual predator. When White, in his dying hour, is overcome with delirium tremens, he confesses "the horror" of his entire past life:

> I thought I had lived long enough out there to have heard without a shock anything that men can do and do—especially white men who have "gone under," but I hadn't. . . . It wasn't only that he had robbed and swindled himself through India up and down for fifteen years. That was bad enough for there wasn't a station where he hadn't swindled and bamboozled his fellow white men. But it was what he had done when he got away "among the natives"—to men, and women too, away from "civilization," in the jungle villages and high up in the mountains. God! the cold, civilized, corrupted cruelty of it. I told you, I think, that his teeth were pointed and spaced out in his mouth.
>
> And his remorse was the most horrible thing . . . the remorse of fear—fear of punishment, of what was coming of death, of the horrors, real horrors and the phantom horrors of madness. (276–77)

White makes his appalling confession while tethered to a stake in the middle of the night, surrounded by Arab, African, and Tamil pearl-fishers whom he mistakes for devils in the violence of his fever. In the moments before his death, he is "troubled by the flesh" and "scream[s] for someone to bring him a woman." He dies in midscream, and the narrator hastily covers "the horror of his face." The story ends with a moving description of an Arab funeral that takes place immediately after White's death. This event, which actually occurred under Leonard's supervision of the pearl fishery and impressed him so strongly that he narrated it in a letter as well as his autobiography, drives home the point of the story's title: that the "natives" are the pearls, the white colonialists who exploit them swine.

The story of White's fall emphasizes two concerns that recur in Leonard's novel, *The Village in the Jungle*. One is the uses and abuses of language, the other the victimization of women. White clearly dies for his own sins, the most heinous of which arise from an insidious combination of racism and sexual rapacity. The license to perpetrate his crimes itself derives from an ideology entrenched in the language of imperialism in both its "enlightened" and its purely tyrannous forms. The narrator of "Pearls and Swine" mocks the colonialist catchphrases essential to this language with an ironic vocal emphasis, conveyed in print by inverted commas. He calls into question the idea that the colonialist turns criminal only after he has "gone under" in the netherworld of a dark continent, along with the notion that "natives" represent the opposite of "civilization." By beginning and ending his tale with Tamil proverbs, the first of which he pronounces in the Tamil tongue, the narrator implies that the white man's language is an imposition on a people and a culture he can never understand. He stresses the arrogance and stupidity of his two listeners, who have remained unmoved by his narrative, with the second proverb: "When the cat puts his head into a pot, he thinks all is darkness" (279). The saying sums up a complete loss in translation: not only has the story been lost on the others, but the culture of "the pot"—the culture and continent intruded upon by a deluded and incapable predator—is translated by that predator into a place of darkness. Searching for his own values, the pearls he desires for himself, the colonialist sees only swine; the language with which he presumes to name unfamiliar beings is the vocabulary of blind imposition. Finally, the narrator's own reference to Tamil lore is a gesture of humility—as is the self-effacement of the initial narrator, who witholds final commentary, allowing the story to end with the proverb.

The connection between language and oppression—in particular the oppression of women—is one that Leonard recognized and emphasizes in his writings about Ceylon. In his autobiography he writes:

> I am afraid that I must often have irritated my staff . . . by allowing cases to drag on all the afternoon and witnesses to pour out their interminable stories, for if I encouraged them so that they forgot their fear and shyness . . . I would often get remarkable glimpses into [their] minds and domestic lives. . . . Also it was extraordinarily interesting that every now and again you learnt in one of these cases what it was so rarely that you heard in Ceylon, the woman's side of the case. (G 165)

In *The Village in the Jungle*, the novel Leonard began immediately on his return to England, the only white character is an English magistrate who displays a similar interest in the real stories of the Sinhalese. This magistrate, who, unlike the other characters, is never named, is sadly aware of the limitations of his role. In court, he must unjustly condemn the villager Babun for a theft he did not commit; the magistrate senses Babun's innocence but can do nothing for him, as according to the protocols of the courtroom, with which Babun is utterly unfamiliar, the latter has failed to prove his accusers false. The novel itself is a moving effort to rectify injustice by telling the story from the villagers' point of view. The narrator is omniscient; his language, however, is said to have the cadences and poetry of Sinhalese, and his sympathies are wholly with the Sinhalese natives. For this reason, perhaps, the novel came to be better known in Ceylon than in England, where it was published. In an article on *The Village in the Jungle*, Stephen Medcalf quotes the writer Mervyn De Silva's verdict that the novel is "the finest imaginative work based on life in [this] country," and goes on to say that

> people in Ceylon are apt to point out how naturally the dialogue can be rendered into Sinhalese, how it catches the rhythm of the villagers' talk. The achievement is perhaps more remarkable than that of any other colonial writer,

because the distance between writer and characters is so great. Forster, for instance, though he created a convincing character of another race in Aziz of *A Passage to India*, still does not move outside the educated middle classes ("The Village in the Jungle" 76).[13]

Leonard Woolf improves upon *A Passage to India* in another respect as well. Brenda Silver ("Periphrasis, Power, and Rape") criticizes Forster for his elision of the Indian woman's point of view, as well as the native woman's experience of sexual violation at the hands of either white or native men. The tragedies depicted in *The Village in the Jungle* all pivot upon the sexual coercion and abuse of women.

The novel begins with a description of the village Beddagama, "which means the village in the jungle," and its surroundings. The narrator emphasizes the mystery and danger of the jungle, its ultimate impenetrability even to those who think they know it intimately. In several pages of beautiful description, the jungle is portrayed as an inexorable, evil force against which human agency is powerless, which murders even its own animal inhabitants during seasons of drought. A general description of the village and its denizens follows, with sociological details. We are told that the villagers live by "cultivating chenas"—a form of subsistence farming. Each family clears a tract of jungle and plants grain, barely living from one year to the next on the meager harvest. In the course of the novel, we find out that the chena system also involves an annual payment by each family to the British government; thus the villagers are kept in a state of constant poverty. Many die of starvation and disease.

The actual story begins with the birth of the two heroines, Punchi Menika and Hinnihami. When their father, the half-mad hunter Silindu, discovers that his wife has borne female twins, he beats her severely "on the head and breasts"; she dies two days later. The incident is reported in an even tone, without pathos or judgment; its most significant result is "the beginning of Silindu's quarrel with Babehami, the headman; for Babehami, hearing the cries of . . . women, rushed up . . . and dragged Silindu from the house" (15). It is only later in the book, once we have come to know the characters, that their suffering is brought home to us.

The two girls, under the tutelage of the father who quickly begins to dote on them, grow up differently from others in the village; in English society, they might be called tomboys. Eventually Punchi Menika, the more docile of the two, marries Babun, the headman's nephew, against the headman's will. The family prospers for some time, until the Vederala, or medicine man, conceives an implacable lust for Hinnihami. When Silindu, unconventionally, honors his daughter's wishes and refuses to give her to the evil herbalist, the latter casts a spell on him. After all efforts to cure Silindu of his disease have failed, the anguished Hinnihami gives in to the

Vederala's coercion. She soon leaves him, however, and returns to her father's compound, where she eventually gives birth to a son. Silindu brings home a fawn from the jungle, whom Hinnihami suckles from her other breast, and who becomes her beloved companion after her child dies. The other villagers, who find Hinnihami peculiar, turn her into a scapegoat and attack her and the deer. They beat the fawn to death, and Hinnihami dies the next day.

Further misfortunes follow, initiated once again by a man's sexual rapacity. Fernando, a shopkeeper to whom the villagers owe money, moves into the headman's compound and decides to make Punchi Menika his mistress. Through blackmail and threats, Fernando and Babehami press Babun to give over his wife; when he refuses, they enact a sham robbery and accuse Babun of having stolen from the headman. Babun is jailed, and Silindu, in fury and desperation, murders both the headman and Fernando. He, too, is put in jail. Punchi Menika travels to the city to find her husband, discovers that he has died in prison, and returns to the village to perish alone. The other villagers have all left or died of disease and hunger; finally Punchi Menika is the only inhabitant of the village, which is quickly merging back into the jungle. She is killed by a wild boar that wanders into the hut where she lies ill. The jungle has won.

Like the amorphous "darkness" of Conrad's novel, the jungle is the central symbol of Leonard's book. Yet the reader is hard put to say precisely what it represents; more than anything else, it seems to *be itself*, an implacable natural force, the final nemesis of a people already oppressed by an imperial power and lacking tools for survival. While the narrator of *The Village in the Jungle*, unlike other narrators of colonial novels, speaks from a perspective of intimate knowledge—speaks, indeed, virtually in the tongue of the characters—he insists on the essential unknowableness of the jungle. His position seems, remarkably, ideologically innocent: he is not engaged in the construction of dichotomies, the projection of his own shame onto the Other. Elsewhere Leonard does, like Conrad or Virginia Woolf, represent an intimacy between "primitive peoples" and their habitat; yet even as he stereotypes, he attempts to bridge differences by negotiating the "gulf of speech" so troubling and irresolvable in the jungle-village scene of *The Voyage Out*:

> Our life [as urbanized Europeans] has normally nothing to do with the jungle where wild beasts . . . roam or even the human jungle where the human beast roams. If we have a tree in our back garden, there is no devil, no Yakko in it. Of course, very deep down under the surface of the northern European the beliefs and desires and passions of primitive man still exist, ready to burst out with catastrophic violence if, under prolonged pressure, social controls and inhibitions give way.

... I do not think that I sentimentalize or romanticize [the natives]. They are—or at least were in 1905—nearer than we are to primitive man and there are many nasty things about primitive man. It is not their primitiveness that really appeals to me. It is partly their earthiness, their strange mixture of tortuousness and directness, of cunning and stupidity, of cruelty and kindness. They live so close to the jungle . . . that they retain something of the litheness and beauty of jungle animals. The Sinhalese especially tend to have subtle and supple minds. . . . When you get to know them, you find beneath the surface . . . a profound melancholy and fatalism which I find beautiful and sympathetic— . . . something like it permeates the scenery and characters of a Hardy novel. . . . Few things have ever given me greater pleasure than, when I had learned to speak Sinhalese . . . discussing with the villagers their . . . problems, disputes, grievances. (*G* 55)

In the first paragraph of this reminiscence, Leonard describes the jungle as a thing of nature, a construct of primitive man (who associates trees with devils), and a source of primitive passions and aggressions. He alludes here to the theory he would develop two decades after *The Village in the Jungle*, in books such as *Quack, Quack!* (1935), relating fascist hero-worship to primitive mysticism and attributing the carnage of two world wars to an outbreak of "barbarian" instincts. In the next paragraph, however, he abandons these generalities about primitivism and concentrates on the particulars of the Sinhalese psyche. As if he knew that, as an outsider, even here he risked generalizing or imposing a false vision, he claims not to romanticize. He romanticizes nonetheless, translating Ceylon to Hardy's Wessex, transmuting the real into the literary. Yet in admitting that he had to learn their language in order to understand them, he acknowledges implicitly that English literature cannot capture the life of the Sinhalese. Thus he finally eludes us, his English readers, by receding into incomprehensible conversation "under a tree in a village or on the bund of a village tank" (55)—"disappearing," as Virginia would say, "into the tropics."

Virginia's depiction of Leonard as a savage among savages points up the difference between her first novel and his. What they share is a concern with the sexual victimization of women. Unable, in some sense, to do otherwise, Virginia partially projects this concern onto the primitive Other who represents the male body. Leonard did see himself in the Other, both as predatory male and as vulnerable fellow human. He had witnessed senseless violence against women and participated in their sexual exploitation himself; his disgust with the bodies of Sinhalese women sprang in part from self-disgust for his use of prostitutes—a form of exploitation mirroring the larger predation of imperialism.[14] Yet he also seriously considered marrying a Sinhalese woman and staying on in Ceylon—a consideration informed by a profound and, in some sense, admirable ambivalence, and one which demonstrates that, as Ann Stoler has eloquently argued in "Writing Post-Orientalist Histories of the Third World," "[c]olonial cultures were never direct translations of European society planted in the colonies, but unique cultural configurations, homespun creations in which European food, dress, housing and morality were given new political meanings in the particular social order of colonial rule" (Dirks, *Colonialism and Culture* 321).

Granted that most of these configurations were a form of assimilation that allowed rule to continue, paradoxically they also undermined that rule; the very arrangements that sprang up became—like Leonard Woolf's conversations beneath the village tree—threats to the larger arrangement of imperialism. Each small gulf bridged exposed the larger gulf, so that, as at the end of Forster's *A Passage to India* when Aziz and Fielding's horses prevent the friends' dialogue by rearing apart, the small bridgings themselves were finally untenable:

> [I]n December [1911, on his seven-year leave] . . . I had been feeling for some little time that I must make a decision about Ceylon. In October I began writing *The Village in the Jungle* and I realized that I was falling in love with Virginia. By the end of 1911 I had come to the following conclusions: (1) If Virginia would marry me, I would resign from Ceylon and try to earn my living by writing; (2) If Virginia would not marry me, I did not want to return to Ceylon and become a successful civil servant in Colombo and end eventually with a governorship. . . . But if I could go back and immerse myself in a District like Hambantota for the remainder of my life . . . I might welcome it as a final withdrawal, a final solitude, in which, married to a Sinhalese, I would make my District or Province the most prosperous place in Asia. At the back of my mind I think I knew that this last solution was fantasy. The days of paternalism . . . were over; I had been born in an age of imperialism and I disapproved of imperialism and felt sure that its days were already numbered. (G 247–48)

That he disapproved of "paternalism," though it was a more unabashed ideology than the "benevolent" hypocrisies of out-and-out imperialism, becomes clear when Leonard Woolf discusses the relations between his rejection of the latter and his move toward socialism on his permanent return to England. But "paternalism," characteristic of the first phase of British presence in India and Ceylon,[15] was not entirely exclusive of exchange between English and others, as Woolf's fantasy indicates. By the period of late colonialism, an untenable situation had become a pure fantasy, however, and is inscribed as such through Leonard's novel, a substitute for impossible communication and a compensatory gesture for the wrongs that he, bound to imperialism despite his sympathies, had inevitably committed against the bodies and lives of the Ceylonese. The story of Silindu's atonement for the murder of his wife through self-abnegating commitment to the autonomy of his daughters can be read as Leonard's own act of atonement for exploitation, affirming the right to independence of those he had formerly governed.

If Leonard represented savagery to Virginia, and was himself admittedly sensual, how could he wish to marry her, and she end by accepting him? He was doubly an outsider in Bloomsbury—not only by virtue of his Jewish birth, but also as a result of the colonial experience that merely made him seem *more* foreign to his acquaintances. He himself wrote in *Growing* that his return to England was

> a plunge—a slightly icy plunge—into an entirely different world, almost a different universe. But I was received by them all as one of themselves and slipped without much difficulty into the kind of place which I had occupied. . . . And yet . . . I think the seven years in Ceylon left a mark upon my mind and even character which has proved indelible, a kind of reserve or withdrawal into myself which makes me inclined always to stand just a little to one side of my environment. (246–47)

While his years in Ceylon unquestionably changed Leonard, this paragraph may be at least somewhat disingenuous. The "reserve" he speaks of had already, according to the first volume of the autobiography, *Sowing*, been developed in public school as a defense against his philistine peers who mocked any boy with intellectual inclinations. Certainly antisemitism must also have played its role in creating this "reserve," although Leonard constantly denied its impact on his life. It is hard, sometimes, not to feel that he protests too much. Very late in life he wrote a letter to the South African Jewish writer Dan Jacobsen, who complained in a review of the first three volumes of the autobiography about the relatively few words Leonard had devoted to the subject of his Jewishness. Leonard responded:

> As regards my Judaism, I know that it is strange that it should have had so little effect upon my life. I have always been conscious of being a Jew, but in the way in which, I imagine, a Catholic is conscious of being a Catholic in England, or someone of being of Huguenot descent, or even perhaps in the way a man is conscious of having been at Cambridge and not Oxford. I have always been conscious of being primarily British and have lived among people who without question accepted me as such. Of course I have all my life come up against the common or garden antisemitism. . . . But it has not touched me personally. . . . I cannot think of a single instance of it having the slightest influence on my own career or social life in Ceylon. (*LLW* 565–66)

Insofar as he repeats here what he wrote in *Growing*—that his English friends accepted him unconditionally—it is curious that Leonard should end his paragraph by saying that antisemitism never affected him in Ceylon. The sentence is something of a non sequitur at the end of several seemingly illogical statements. If Leonard's Jewishness had "so little effect" on his life, why was he always conscious of it? Were Jews regarded in precisely the same way as English Catholics?[16] Was Jewishness truly no less of a stigma than a Cambridge education—surely a "stigma" only to Oxonians, and even then hardly on the level of antisemitism, "common" or otherwise? And how could Leonard have felt so fully accepted if he was "all his life" coming up against this "common or garden antisemitism"? Presumably his friends, not being "common" themselves, were incapable of such lowly sentiments. And yet his eminent and intimate friend Lytton Strachey did *his* part, behind Leonard's back, to embody the primitivism beneath the curtain of genteel or drawing-room antisemitism.[17] And Leonard, on his return to England, was not long ignorant of Virginia's qualms about his "foreignness" (which she associated with his sexual drive)—indeed, it is impossible to imagine that he did not anticipate them.

Perhaps Leonard's remark about the absence of antisemitism in Ceylon is not so incongruous, after all, and the legends of his "disappearance" in Ceylon are not without a certain truth. Colonial culture was, as anthropologists and historians—including Leonard himself—have noted, both an exact reproduction and a restyling of economic and ethnic hierarchies in the metropole; "the resonance and reverberation between European class politics and colonial racial policies was far more complicated than we have imagined" (Cooper and Stoler, *Tensions of Empire* 9). As a Jew in the Civil Service, Leonard was ambiguously placed on the ladder of colonial relationships: rising up, on the one hand, with a rapidity that might have been stalled in a career at home; yet also drawn "downward," both through political sympathy with the natives and perhaps—one cannot know—through a sense of affinity with those not just at the bottom, but outside the categories of comprehension (even while comprehended by the jurisdiction), of white society.[18] Why option two—the marriage to a Sinhalese in a district of Ceylon—was impossible is, for the reasons Leonard himself states, a moot question; the more compelling question concerns the relationship between the two choices. What made Virginia choose to marry Leonard will be explored further in the next chapter; here I wish to establish the internal logic of Leonard's transition from sexual and political relationships in Ceylon to marriage with Virginia Stephen—how, in other words, did the former *translate* into the latter?

Two—or, technically, three—short narratives elucidate the translations and retranslations between the England Leonard left behind in 1904, the Ceylon he governed ambivalently for seven years, and the England he returned to in 1911. In 1901—the year Virginia was dreaming of "a colony where there shall be no marrying"—Leonard first met Virginia and Vanessa Stephen when they visited Thoby at Cambridge. He described that meeting in *Sowing*:

I first saw them one summer afternoon in Thoby's rooms; in white dresses and large hats, with parasols in their hands, their beauty literally took one's breath away. . . . They were at that time, at least upon the surface, the most Victorian of Victorian young ladies. . . . [They] were . . . very silent and to any superficial observer they might have seemed demure. Anyone who has ridden many different kinds of horses knows the horse who, when you go up to him for the first time, has superficially the most quiet and demure appearance, but, if after bitter experience you are accustomed to take something more than a superficial glance at a strange mount, you observe at the back of the eye of this quiet beast a look which warns you to be very, very careful. So too the observant observer would have noticed at the back of the two Miss Stephens' eyes a look which would have warned him to be cautious, a look which belied the demureness, a look of great intelligence, hypercritical, sarcastic, satirical. (S 184)

The correspondence of this description to Virginia's picture, largely concocted by Thoby, of the trembling, fist-shaking "savage" that was "her" Leonard in 1904, suggests, like the differences between their two first novels, the gulf between the young man and the young lady. To him, she was attractive on two, contradictory levels—he saw her as a being comprising surface *and* depth; while he, to her, was still a caricature concocted by another man, inaccessible and "foreign." Her depiction of him as wild and primitive belies, at this point, the wildness behind her own masquerade (that masquerade dictated by George Duckworth, who could not keep his hands off what lay beneath). His seven years in Ceylon taught Leonard to recognize the political content of that wildness in her; his experience as colonizer had converted him to feminism and taught him to reach out to the rebel behind the white veilings (veilings she had, in any case, discarded by the time of his return). And her own rebelliousness could meet, when they reencountered one another, with a sympathy unavailable among her effete English friends.

In *Growing*, the volume devoted to his years in Ceylon, Leonard describes another encounter, which, worlds away from Cambridge in 1901, nonetheless encapsulates a profoundly telling similarity in the dialectic between surface and depth in the subjectivity of female/colonized other:

In those days . . . no "natives" were members of the Jaffna tennis club. . . . The only Tamils admitted were the podyans, the small boys who picked up the tennis balls . . . and the great Sinnatamby. I used to watch Sinnatamby with some interest, a big stoutish Tamil in a voluminous white cloth and towering maroon turban. He was the keeper of the courts and served us the drinks. He was extremely respectful, but I sometimes thought that I caught in his eye a gleam which belied the impassive face when some more than usually outrageous remark . . . echoed up into the heavy scented immense emptiness of the tropical evening sky. He might have been a character in a Kipling story, and I could imagine generations of Sinnatambys standing respectfully behind their white masters in India right back to before the Mutiny—and some of them with that gleam in the eye getting their own back during the Mutiny. (G 45–46)

The white garb of servitude undercut by the gleaming eye, the deep though unspoken intent of "getting their own back"—the affinity between the conditions of middle-class womanhood in the English metropole and colonized subjectivity in Ceylon—observed cannily and without comment, come together in a third narrative, perhaps Leonard Woolf's most powerful allegory of imperialism, "A Tale Told by Moonlight." Another of his *Stories of the East*, "A Tale" compacts within the figure of a Sinhalese prostitute discarded by her English lover, both Virginia Stephen and Sinnatamby—and also recalls the divided subjectivity and terrible end of Rachel Vinrace in *The Voyage Out*. The character of Celestinahami, whose name points upward despite her earthy profession, embodies the entrapment of women and subalterns, the lies and false promises of imperialism; the story inscribes Leonard's own departure from an arena in which he could not but exploit, despite all his efforts at sympathy and his fantasies of marriage and benevolent government. The tale's tragic ending hints, too, at the challenges Leonard would face in reassimilating himself to English society—challenges that suggest a poignant, surprising alignment between the Jew in gentleman's clothing and the subaltern whose efforts at mimicry end in destruction.

Like "Pearls and Swine," "A Tale" has two narrators. The main narrator is a man named Jessop who bears a certain resemblance to Leonard himself. Like Leonard he is an outsider, "a dark reserved man" of notably un-English appearance. The story begins on a defensive note: "Many people did not like Jessop"—then makes its attack against such sissies. As well as anticipating a strand of Virginia Woolf's argument in *A Room of One's Own*, Jessop's words recall Leonard in his letter to Strachey criticizing E. M. Forster for failure to apprehend the "real":

> Many people did not like Jessop. He had rather a brutal manner sometimes of telling brutal things—the truth he called it. "They don't like it," he once said to me. . . . "But why the devil shouldn't they? They pretend those sorts of things, battle, murder, and sudden death, are so real—more real than white kid gloves and omnibuses and rose leaves—and yet when you give them the real thing, they curl up like school girls. It does them good, you know. . . ." (255)

On a sultry June evening, a group of male friends are reminiscing about their first loves when Jessop interrupts to give them a dose of reality. He maintains that "true love" is a construct of novelists and virtually never occurs in the lives of real human beings. Most love, he says, is merely an impulse of the body; "It's only when we don't pay for it that we call it romance and love, and the most we would ever pay is a £5 note" (257). Once in his life, however, Jessop had witnessed "the real thing." A novelist friend named Reynolds came to visit him in Ceylon, intent upon experiencing "life." Remaining introverted and unmoved through all his encounters with colonialists, he finally awoke one evening when Jessop took him to a brothel. There he fell deeply in love with the beautiful Celestinahami:

> It was the real thing, I tell you. . . . She was everything to him that was beautiful and great and pure, she was what she looked, what he read in the depths of her eyes. And she might have been. . . . But the chances are all against it. She was a prostitute in a Columbo brothel, a simple soft little golden-skinned animal with nothing in the depths of the eyes at all. (261)

The story of Reynolds and Celestinahami ends in tragedy when, after buying her from the brothel and living with her for several months, he realizes that she is not what he has made her out to be. "He was a civilized cultivated intelligent nervous little man and she—she was an animal, dumb and stupid and beautiful" (263). Celestinahami's love for Reynolds is "the love of dogs and women, at any rate of those slow, big-eyed women of the East. It's the love of a slave, the patient, consuming love for a master . . ." (263). Sensing Reynolds's disenchantment, Celestinahami "reasoned like a child that it was because she wasn't like the white ladies whom she used to see in Colombo. So she went and bought stays and white cotton stockings and shoes, and she squeezed herself into them. But the stays and the shoes and stockings didn't do her any good" (263). Reynold ends by sailing back to England, Celestinahami by drowning herself, attired in her pink-and-white costume.

While the spectacle of Celestinahami "squeezing herself" into the imprisoning accoutrements of white women is heartbreaking, and her death at the end of the story tragic, the "real" tragedy seems to be Reynolds's. He is the one, according to Jessop, who possesses deep and noble feelings; Celestinahami's own self-abnegation and loyalty are merely evidence of a slave mentality shared by beasts and children. He is "civilized cultivated intelligent," she, "dumb and stupid and beautiful," and while Jessop begins his story by seeming to question Reynolds's mentality, he tells us ultimately that Reynolds is a man and Celestinahami merely "a nice simple soft little animal like the bitch at my feet that starved herself if I left her for a day" (262). She, belying her name, is a creature of earth, while Reynolds, with his high sentiments, is far closer to the celestial element. Together, one might say, they make one amphibian. But the halves are unequal, and we are asked to pity Reynolds, whose great love has been wasted on a body without a mind.

But while Jessop seems to sympathize with Reynolds, his endorsement of Reynolds's ideals is finally questionable. Jessop's own relationship to the Sinhalese prostitutes is both less exalted and more clear-eyed than his "poor" friend Reynolds's love for Celestinahami; his insistence as narrator on calling the latter "the real thing," and the romantic streak in the style of his narration, are belied by his more sociologically observant portrait of brothel life—a portrait that presumably owes much to Leonard's conversations with Sinhalese women in their own language:

> Apart from anything else, it interested me. The girls . . . themselves interested me; I used to sit and talk to them for hours in their own language; they didn't as a rule understand English. They used to tell me about themselves, queer pathetic little stories often. They came from villages almost always, little native villages hidden far away among rice fields and coconut trees, and they had drifted somehow into this hovel in the warren of filth and smells we and our civilization had attracted about us. (260)

The emphasis on dirt neither created by the natives nor inherent in the bodies of the prostitutes[19] recurs in Jessop's description of Celestinahami: "She lay full length on the sofa . . . looking up into Reynolds' face and smiling at him. The white cloth had slipped down and her breasts were bare. She was a Sinhalese, a cultivator's daughter from a little village up in the hills: her place was in the green rice field, weeding, or in the little compound under the palm trees pounding rice, but she lay on the dirty sofa and asked Reynolds in her soft broken English whether he would have a drink" (260–61). As if to stress her condition of permanent enslavement, no less—indeed, more—virulent in her "romantic" idyll with Reynolds in a seaside bungalow than in her indentured brothel life, Celestinahami is wrapped in white both when Jessop first sees her and on his last encounter with her lifeless body. Her role as barmaid to the English, like that of the voluminously white-clad Sinnatamby, is void of subjectivity; unlike the latter, she will have no chance at mutiny, for as a young female without the phallic powers of revolt suggested by Sinnatamby's "towering maroon turban," she is literally smothered by the *increasingly* voluminous garments of colonial mimicry. "I never saw Reynolds again," Jessop ends his story, "but I saw Celestinahami once":

> It was at the inquest two days after the Moldavia sailed for Aden [carrying Reynolds away from the scene of his profound disappointment]. She was lying on a dirty wooden board on trestles in the dingy mud-plastered room behind the court. Yes, I identified her: Celestinahami—I never knew her other name. She lay there in her stays and pink skirt and white stockings and white shoes. They had found her floating in the sea that lapped the foot of the convent garden below the little bungalow—bobbing up and down in her stays and pink skirt and white stockings and shoes. (264)

The final words of Jessop's story, these also constitute Leonard Woolf's last words on colonialism—the final sentence of an imperialist repudiating the ideology he sustained for seven years. The repetitions and ambiguities of the description are rife with what Homi Bhabha calls the "ambivalence of colonial discourse." In his essay, "Of Mimicry and Man," Bhabha describes the self-defeating logic of just such mimicries as Celestinahami's: self-defeating because they deny the self of the mimic, but also because, precisely in exposing the subaltern's *lack* of subjectivity, they parody the spurious "self" of the colonialist, inscribing in the subaltern's defeat the expiration of the latter's rule: "The ambivalence of mimicry—almost but not quite—suggests that the fetishized colonial culture is potentially and strategically an insurgent counterappeal. . . . [T]he fetish mimes the forms of authority at the point at which it deauthorizes them" (Cooper and Stoler, *Tensions of Empire* 158). Jessop's repetitions are the stutterings of an authority in demise; within the story, they stand for his own, literal deauthorization—they are his last words—but they also stand for the end point at which the system collapses on itself. The precisely repeated phrase, "stays and pink skirt and white stockings and shoes," not only enforces the pathos of Celestinahami's end but mimes the very mimicry that indicates the emptiness—the lack of authority—in the original. Even more final and telling is the failure embodied in the tripartite sentence, "Yes, I identified her: Celestinahami—I never knew her other name." "Yes" is canceled by "never," and the center of contradiction is the name that fails to name a person: first, because it names a corpse; second, because it names only in the language of the (failed) namer. The white man "knows" nothing; his whiteness is a blank like the clothing and the ironically "pure" name that erase the self of "Celestinahami."

Jessop's presence at the inquest recalls Leonard Woolf's own position as a magistrate in Ceylon, his role as witness at inquests and as sentencer at trials and hangings, where he himself had to give the signal to the executioner. In *Sowing*, Leonard devotes four pages to his legendary manual tremor. With customary understatement, he writes, "In Ceylon it proved to be a nuisance in a curious way":

> When one sat on the bench as Police Magistrate or District Judge, one had to make notes of the evidence and write down one's verdict and the reasons for it. Normally the tremor does not affect my writing. . . . But if I found an accused guilty, almost always a strange, disconcerting thing happened. When all the evidence had been given and the lawyers had had their say a silence fell on the hot court, as I began to write my analysis of the evidence and my reasons for the verdict. I wrote away without difficulty, but again and again when I got to the words: ". . . and for these reasons I find the accused guilty of . . . and sentence him to . . . ," my hand began to tremble so violently that it was sometimes impossible for me to write legibly and I adjourned for five minutes in

order to retire and calm myself sufficiently to complete the sentence (in two senses of the word). (98–99)

In the end, Leonard completed the sentence by retiring permanently; he completed it by inscribing his refusal to go on, just as Jessop completes his story through a repetition that deauthorizes. On return to England, even before his official retirement, Leonard immediately began his first novel; *The Village in the Jungle*, he tells us in *Beginning Again*, was "the symbol of the anti-imperialism which had been growing upon me more and more in my last years in Ceylon" (47). His resistance is recorded in that novel through the story of an English magistrate compelled to sentence a Sinhalese man to an unjust punishment because the latter cannot defend himself in the language of English law. Morally, politically, it is a sentence that indicts itself. Leonard's "misanthropic" tremor was the sign of the self-hatred that undermines colonialism on both sides, a dialectic of ambivalence translated in his return to England and marriage with Virginia Stephen. The gleam in the eye of Sinnatamby—the vacancy of Celestinahami's eye, dead to the white men even before it was dead in fact[20]—became the challenge of a woman genius quivering with life but deeply resistant to male sexual imperatives. No sentence could make her "his," but she might answer his own will to action, his desire to write new, subversive sentences, by a complete intellectual and creative engagement. In turn, he might rectify past wrongs by daily justifying and encouraging her in her violation of imposed roles—her throwing off the veils of Victorian womanhood in the creation of a naked, vibrant modernism. And thus he might prevent her from ending like either Rachel or Celestinahami, victims of colonizing male sexuality and social hypocrisy.

But that engagement lay in the future.

CHAPTER II.

Incongruities; or, The Politics of Character

> Whether Leonard Woolf fell in love with a young
> woman of beauty and intellect, or . . . with a Stephen
> of beauty and intellect, will always be a formidable,
> and a necessary, question.
> (*Cynthia Ozick, "Mrs. Virginia Woolf:*
> *A Madwoman and Her Nurse"*)

> It is certain that Harry did feel that Camilla's presence
> there alone with him was in some curious way a
> proof of his value in the world, showed him to be finer
> and more of a man than all the other Toms and Dicks
> and Harrys. . . . It is just as certain . . . that Camilla felt
> no such reflection of her value in his presence.
> (*Leonard Woolf,* The Wise Virgins)

> [T]o be Anglicized is *emphatically* not to be English.
> (*Homi Bhabha, "Of Mimicry and Man:*
> *The Ambivalence of Colonial Discourse"*)

THE JOKE

In May 1912, Leonard and Virginia sent Lytton Strachey a note that read:

Ha! Ha!
Virginia Stephen
Leonard Woolf

Having been instrumental in their relationship, Lytton would have understood this note as an engagement announcement and shared the joke—a joke, perhaps, both on him and with him. He himself had been engaged to Virginia—for a day—in 1909; her new engagement might, in recalling that earlier fiasco, naturally evoke laughter. The laugh might also be one of conquest on the part of Leonard ("Ha! Ha! I did it!"), or a conspiratorial laugh between the two men, whose scheming had borne fruit.

To the reader not personally acquainted with either of the parties named in it, the note would pose some difficulties. It is the first cooperative literary effort of the couple, and it already seems to mock cooperation. If we didn't know what it was "about," how would we read it? Apparently the mere juxtaposition of these two names is supposed to be funny. Humor in juxtaposition generally arises from incongruity; therefore, we must look for the differences between the names. We see, first of all, that the two persons named are of opposite gender. The name on top—and its placement may also be significant—is a good, English name with a slightly aristocratic, rarefied ring. The name on the bottom is not so aristocratic, and although it has been anglicized by the addition of an "o," the patronymic is Jewish.

What to make, then, of the conjunction of these two different names? The difference of gender gives us a clue: a sexual union must be implied. Conventional engagement or wedding announcements, however, do not usually "imply" but state outright. This particular couple is obviously opposed to convention and strict definition. The mere thought of it makes them laugh. But it is not just the conventions of engagement and marriage that make them laugh, it is the fact that they of all two people should be embracing these conventions together . . .

BEGINNINGS: ESCAPE

Still mystified, perhaps, by this initial decision, both Woolfs wrote novels about their courtship within the first few years of marriage. While Leonard's *The Wise Virgins* is semiautobiographical, Virginia's *Night and Day*, which followed it a few years later, less obviously traces her own experience. The novel is dedicated to her sister Vanessa Bell, and the main character, Katharine Hilbery, was intended as a portrait of Vanessa.[1] In fact, the character of Katharine seems to be a conflation of Vanessa and Virginia; she shares more qualities with Camilla, Leonard's representation of Virginia in *The Wise Virgins*, than with his Vanessa-figure, also named Katharine. Ralph Denham, the young man who woos and eventually wins Katharine Hilbery, is not clearly based on Leonard Woolf but resembles him in certain ways, notably in his lower-middle-class background.[2] He is a decidedly milder version of Leonard than the abrasive protagonist of *The Wise Virgins*, Harry Davis: a self-portrait of almost cruel stringency.

The Wise Virgins was published in October 1914 and became an instant failure. Readers have taken against the book from the time of its inception. Both Leonard's mother and his sister, Bella, who are satirically portrayed in the novel, asked him not to publish it, less for their sakes even than to spare the feelings of the Rosses, family friends who appear in the novel as the narrow-minded, rather pitiable Garlands. Leonard went ahead and published the book as it stood. The production of *The Wise Virgins* seems to have been a psychological imperative, a willful gesture of rebellion on Leonard's part.

The book's kindest critic, in fact, was Virginia, who wrote in her diary on January 31, 1915:

... I started reading The Wise Virgins, & I read it straight on till bedtime when I finished it. My opinion is that its a remarkable book; very bad in parts; first rate in others. A writer's book, I think, because only a writer perhaps can see why the good parts are so very good, & why the bad parts aren't very bad. . . . I was made very happy by reading this; I like the poetic side of L. & it gets a little smothered in Blue-books, and organisations. (D 1:32)

It is curious that Leonard did not show the novel to Virginia earlier, and that she waited until four months after its publication to read it. Her portrait as Camilla Lawrence is not altogether flattering. In *The Unknown Virginia Woolf*, Roger Poole remarks that "the delineation of Leonard's bride before her marriage, and in her family surroundings, is not only brilliant, it is in many ways accurate to the point of being cruel" (79). Of Virginia's diary entry, Poole maintains that "the amount of repression here is massive," and attributes her hostility toward Leonard during her mental breakdown in 1915 to a "sense of betrayal" over his depiction of her in *The Wise Virgins*.

While Virginia may indeed have repressed angry feelings toward Leonard in her diaries, the elisions are generally more obvious. Her statement that she was "made very happy by reading" *The Wise Virgins* seems too positive to be a mask for fury and pain. And her own literary response to Leonard's novel does not suggest a bitter effort to turn the tables. It is, in fact, a far gentler book than Leonard's. *Night and Day* is a comedy of manners, quietly satirical on the subject of families and Victorian mores, but basically indulgent toward its two lovers, Katharine Hilbery and Ralph Denham. In fact, Virginia's treatment of Katharine is more critical, if also more thoroughgoing, than her depiction of Ralph. As a response to Leonard's novel, *Night and Day* is less a retaliation than a turning-the-other-cheek—and, perhaps, something of a self-explanation.

While it is easy to see Virginia's novel as good-natured and charming in contrast to Leonard's, a look at some of her letters from the time of the engagement amends this impression. In her announcements to various friends, she assumes a somewhat timid tone; she worries about their acceptance of Leonard and hinges a good deal of importance on it. She tells her oldest woman friend and confidante, Violet Dickinson:

I've got a confession to make. I'm going to marry Leonard Wolf [*sic*]. He's a penniless Jew. I'm more happy than anyone ever said was possible—but I *insist* upon your liking him too. May we both come on Tuesday? Would you rather I come alone? He was a great friend of Thobys. . . . (L 1:500)

And to Janet Case, Virginia's Greek teacher, she writes:

My Dear Janet,
    I want to tell you that I'm going to marry Leonard Wolf—he is a penniless Jew. He was a friend of Thoby's—and I'm so happy—Its not at all what people

say, but so much better. I dont think I'm nearly worth what he is. May we come and see you? You've always been angelic to me—no, much nicer than angelic, and I want you to like him. It has been worth waiting for. (*L* 1:501)

In her letter to Lady Ottoline Morrell, she finally remembers Leonard's other "o":

> This is to tell you that I'm going to marry Leonard Woolf. I'm very happy— and find him more necessary every day. Do you like him? I hope so, because I want to be a friend of yours all my life.[3] (*L* 1:501)

Another old friend, Madge Vaughan, is privileged with more information:

> . . . How am I to begin about Leonard? First he is a Jew: second he is 31; third he spent 7 years in Ceylon, governing natives, inventing ploughs, shooting tigers, and did so well that they offered him a very high place the other day, which he refused, wishing to marry me, and gave up his entire career there on the chance that I would agree. He has no money of his own. . . . We know each other as I imagine few people do before marriage. I've only known him 6 months, but from the first I have found him the one person to talk to. He interests me immensely, besides all the rest. We mean to marry in August. . . . We shall, I think, take a small house and try to live cheaply, so as not to have to make money. . . .
>
> At first I felt stunned, but now every day the happiness becomes more complete—even though it does seem a fearful chance—my having found any man who gives me what Leonard does. (*L* 1:503)

Ambivalence informs all these introductions. Virginia simultaneously glorifies Leonard and apologizes for him. As for their relationship, it both elates and frightens her. Her remark to Madge Vaughan that she first felt "stunned" corresponds to a curious statement in another letter to Violet Dickinson from the same time: "I've been rather headachy, and had a bad night, and Leonard made me into a comatose invalid" (*L* 1:502). Presumably Virginia means that Leonard—already assuming the duties that he would perform throughout Virginia's life—put her to bed, perhaps with medication; yet she also implies that he has deprived her of all physical and mental power. The statement that to have found a man like Leonard is a "fearful chance" also suggests mixed feelings.

Is it because Leonard had, in Virginia's eyes, awesome powers ("shooting tigers, governing natives") that she needed simultaneously to denigrate him as a mere "penniless Jew"? Or is it the other way around: acutely conscious that she was marrying a man of inferior class and peculiar creed, did she want to assure all possible critics of his credentials? One theme of these letters is vertical movement: Leonard has rejected a "high place" in order to marry Virginia; on the other hand, he is financially "low" to begin with, having "no money of his own." His *inherent* value, however, is far above Virginia's: "I dont think I'm nearly worth what he is." Twice, too, Virginia hastens to establish a link between Leonard and her deceased brother, the universally admired Thoby Stephen, thus making Leonard less of an outsider and perhaps elevating him in her readers' eyes.[4]

Reading over these letters, one observes Virginia constructing her description of Leonard according to priorities. Is her uncertainty about "how to begin" (in the letter to Madge Vaughan) genuine or feigned? She has settled this question twice previously and does so much the same way the third time—"First he is a Jew"—leaving his pennilessness this time for later in the paragraph. The issue of money is ultimately insignificant, as Virginia is apparently quite prepared to "live cheaply." What seems to nag her is Leonard's Jewishness. It is, for her, his defining characteristic, and instead of describing his qualities, she simply labels him. "He interests me immensely, besides all the rest": one is left wondering about "all the rest," and why it was not worth expounding upon. Virginia makes it essential *what* Leonard is, and not *how* he is (though old friends of hers who had never met him might be curious). Even after her marriage, Virginia referred to Leonard—this time in a letter to her friend Ka Cox—simply as "my Jew" (L 2:11).

It was Leonard Woolf's Jewishness that made him *un*like Thoby Stephen, for his Jewishness was a matter of family and heritage. Though he was an atheist, Leonard did not attempt to hide his background, and Virginia's most scathing epistolary commentary is reserved for her visit to his home in the suburb of Putney. To Violet Dickinson, she merely wrote that she still had a headache, as "[w]ork and love and Jews in Putney take it out of one" (L 1:502). She expounds in a letter to Janet Case:

> [S]uch a tea party at Putney.
> "A sandwich, Miss Stephen—or may I call you Virginia?".
> "What? Ham sandwiches for tea?".
> "Not *Ham*: potted meat. We don't eat Ham or bacon or Shellfish in this house."
> "Not Shellfish? Why not shellfish?".
> "Because it says in the Scriptures that they are unclean creatures, and our Mr Josephs at the Synagogue——and——
> It was queer— (L 1:502–3)

In *Night and Day*, Katharine Hilbery also goes to tea at the home of her fiancé, Ralph Denham. Struck at first by the house's "ugliness" and the unruliness of its numerous inhabitants (like Leonard, Ralph Denham has a large number of siblings), she gradually warms to the family and enjoys herself. Virginia's description of the tea party on Mt. Ararat Road lacks the satire of her letter to Janet Case.[5] She also, notably, does not make Ralph

Denham a Jew, though she emphasizes a certain "strangeness," even a "savageness" (19) about him. The tenor of *Night and Day*, purged of the distaste that Virginia had expressed privately, is genteel throughout: genteel and Gentile.

This link is an inevitable one: both Leonard's book and Virginia's establish that good manners are a product of, literally, good breeding. Nearly twenty years after the conception of *Night and Day*, Virginia wondered at Leonard's "despotic" behavior toward servants: "His extreme rigidity of mind surprises me. . . . What does it come from? Not being a gentleman partly . . . " (*D* 4:326). *Night and Day* opens with a description of Katharine Hilbery's ease of manner over tea, which contrasts with both this image of Leonard's "rigidity" and the later tea-scene at the Denhams' house:

> It was a Sunday evening in October, and in common with many other young ladies of her class, Katharine Hilbery was pouring out tea. Perhaps a fifth part of her mind was thus occupied. . . . But although she was silent, she was evidently mistress of a situation which was familiar enough to her, and inclined to let it take its way for the six hundredth time, perhaps, without bringing into play any of her unoccupied faculties. A single glance was enough to show that Mrs. Hilbery was so rich in the gifts which make tea-parties of elderly distinguished people successful, that she scarcely needed any help from her daughter, provided that the tiresome business of teacups and bread and butter was discharged for her. (*ND* 9)

As in the letters announcing her engagement, Virginia here gives priority to establishing her subject's social status. By the end of the first sentence, we know "what" Katharine Hilbery is. She belongs to that class whose members are called "ladies"; that the class consists of Christians probably goes without saying, but is also suggested by the fact that it is Sunday afternoon on which so many of these ladies are presiding over a leisurely tea. Moreover, she belongs by birth to this class, and her mother does, too. Both Katharine and Mrs. Hilbery are the descendants of a "distinguished" lineage that is "rich" in "gifts," social and material.

Even into this apparently straightforward description, however, Virginia inserts ambivalence. Though Katharine performs her tasks gracefully, she does them by rote. The duties of the tea-table neither interest nor challenge her. Moreover, denizen though she is of a household full of servants, she herself is servant to her mother: she takes care of the "tiresome business of teacups and bread and butter." The wandering of her mind suggests the desire for escape from this entrapment. The stage is set: Katharine requires a rescuer.

The figure who abruptly enters, however, is more a bull in a china shop than a knight in armor. Ralph Denham "flings" open the door; he "mutters" in answer to a remark; he sits "compressing his teacup, so that there was danger lest the thin china might cave inwards" (10–11). He is shy, nervous, and "strange"; he is "not easily . . . combined with the rest," and he strains Katharine's talents as a hostess. Katharine eventually grows to like Ralph, and he is portrayed sympathetically in the novel. But the consciousness that represents him is always essentially Katharine's—a consciousness defined in the book's very first sentence as one in opposition to Ralph's. For Ralph Denham's point of view, we must turn to his prototype, Harry Davis, in the book by his prototype's prototype, Leonard Woolf.

While the narrator introduces her heroine at the very beginning of *Night and Day*, Leonard solves this problem differently—as usual, with a framing device. *The Wise Virgins*'s first chapter is entitled "Begins with Words in a Garden"; the words belong to the Garland daughters, inhabitants of the suburb of Richstead. They fulfill the function Virginia alludes to in her rhetorical question to Janet Case, "How shall I begin?" The Garlands introduce and categorize Harry Davis to the reader, preparing us for our own first encounter with him. The unmarried daughters and their widowed mother are talking over the new arrivals in their neighborhood:

> "I don't expect they're gentlemen—they certainly don't dress like it." . . .
>
> "I thought the young man I saw looked rather nice," said Ethel. "Rather foreign looking and artistic. I don't know why you should say they aren't gentlemen. The father is a solicitor; it's absurd to say that solicitors aren't gentlemen." . . .
>
> "I only saw Mrs. Davis and the daughter. They both seemed very nice— rather foreign, I think."
>
> "I expect they're Jews," said May.
>
> "Do you know," Mrs. Garland said in her low, serious voice, "I believe, May, you're right; I think they may be. They don't seem to go to church."
>
> There was a silence. A feeling of disappointment came over Gwen.
> (*WV* 8–9)

Having begun the book with characters so obviously philistine, Leonard Woolf surprises the reader in the next chapter by actually conforming to the Garlands' prejudices in the narrator's own description of the Jewish family. His picture of Mrs. Davis is a catalog of stereotypes worthy of David Garnett:

> There was no doubt she had been a handsome woman—in fact, robustly and boldly, she still was a handsome, large woman. The big curved nose, the curling, full lips, the great brown eyes would have made a fine old woman of her, if she had been squatting under a palm-tree with a white linen cloth thrown over her head and drawn around her heavy oval face. The monotonous singsong of her voice would have sounded all right if she had sung the song of

Miriam which tells how the Egyptian horse and his rider were overwhelmed by Jehovah in the sea; it came incongruously through the large nose in her quiet, precise, voluble and thin-sounding English. (*WV* 19)

The narrator is peculiarly insistent: he emphasizes Mrs. Davis's physical size to the point of redundancy. Like the Garland sisters, who are reluctant to admit "foreign"-looking Jews to their neighborhood, he stresses Mrs. Davis's incongruity. Not only is she displaced in Richstead, she doesn't even seem to belong in present-day England; her English speaking is an act of encroachment. While her eloquence is impressive, the very precision with which she talks suggests that she is not at home in the language.

What motive could Leonard Woolf have had for creating such a carica-ture? Apparently the "real" Mrs. Davis, Marie Woolf, bore little resem-blance to her fictional counterpart. Leonard was on good terms with his mother throughout his life, as well as with his sister Bella, the astringent "Hetty" of the novel. Mothers, however, represent origins. Had Marie Woolf not been Jewish, Leonard Woolf would not have been born a Jew. Could this have been the grudge that made him publish *The Wise Virgins* despite the sad and angry protests of his family?[6]

In his book *Jewish Self-Hatred*, Sander Gilman ascribes this phenomenon to "outsiders' [Jews'] acceptance of the mirage of themselves generated by their reference group—that group in society which they see as defining them—as a reality" (2) Rather than see *The Wise Virgins* simply as a psy-chogram for Leonard Woolf's own self-hatred, we might also read it as his illustration of the phenomenon itself. The narrative progression of the first few chapters precisely illustrates the process Gilman describes. Small-minded as they are, the Garlands represent the Richstead mentality; they are the "reference group" that defines insiders and outsiders. In his stereo-typical representation of the Davises, Leonard Woolf may deliberately be following their lead.

In the third chapter of the novel, after the Garlands and the Davises have formally met in the second, Harry Davis's own perspective takes over. Harry has entered the studio where he spends his days painting, and we see its inhabitants through his eyes. A painter named Grayson has just finished a "study . . . faithful enough to show that the model had been a fat Jewess under the nun's dress which covered her" (*WV* 34). The remark is complex, exemplifying Harry's (and Leonard's?) self-hatred while also describing the broader phenomenon in all its subtleties. The notion that you can always tell a "Jewess," no matter what masquerade she dons to hide her identity, is highly questionable; yet it may also reflect a social truth, the impossibility of assimilation. A Woolf in sheep's clothing remains a Woolf. Why should a Jew want to put on Christian garments when he or she will inevitably be recognized? Why shouldn't she, instead, take pride in her specific attributes, whether or not these arouse the contempt of the "reference group"?

This question is embodied in Harry, who is a complicated mixture of pride, even arrogance, and self-contempt. "Every stereotype is Janus-faced," writes Gilman.

> It has a positive and a negative element, neither of which bears any resemblance to the complexity or diversity of the world as it is. The positive element is taken by the outsiders as their new definition. This is the quality ascribed to them as the potential members of the group in power. The antithesis to this, the quality ascribed to them as the Other, is then transferred to the new Other found within the group that those in power have designated as Other. For every "noble savage" seen through colonial power a parallel "ignoble savage" exists. (4)

In the polarities of *The Wise Virgins*, Harry's mother represents the "ignoble savage": vulgar, sexualized, incongruous. Harry, too, is conspicuous: the Garland sisters say he looks foreign. But they also nickname him "Byron," and his brooding, rebellious persona keeps him just this side of the noble/ignoble divide. Harry fascinates; by breaking social rules with seeming aplomb, he passes as exotic. Yet the very image that the Garlands dub Byronic could all too easily revert to "foreign," and thence to something worse. Knowing this, Harry still cultivates it with a vengeance. His determination to be seen and recognized for what he is makes him alternately defiant and painfully insecure. He does not resort to the sort of "passing" of which the Jewish art model is a cruel parody, but he does want to leave his family behind and join a different social group. His sense of self becomes a battleground in the course of the novel.

The group to which Harry aspires is represented by the Lawrence family, in particular Camilla Lawrence, a young woman Harry knows from the art studio. While the Garland family is the "reference group" for the suburb of Richstead, the Lawrences occupy a higher place in British society. They represent the antithesis of *both* Richstead and Harry himself. Contemplating Camilla in the studio, Harry reflects:

> She certainly did interest him, though he had very rarely spoken to her. Ever since he had been a child he had found the need of something romantic for the thoughts that were never spoken and for the dreams that he was accustomed to dream by day. . . . She was romantic, mysterious to him. He liked to recall the purity of her face and her voice: the remoteness of a virgin, he said to himself. When one knows the coarseness and ignobleness of one's own thoughts, he used to think to himself, such purity of beauty is almost frightening. One longs

to be intimate with it, but is there any point of contact? She seemed to be in another world from his, and that attracted him all the more. Sometimes in that sentimental quarter of an hour before sleep she seemed too to belong to two worlds, to bring, in what she said or might say, the fragments of . . . a stranger and more beautiful world into the stupid tangle of Sainthills and Graysons and Garlands. (*WV* 37)

It is worth comparing Harry's reflections on Camilla Lawrence to the earlier description of Mrs. Davis. The idea that Camilla belongs to "another . . . stranger and more beautiful world" acquires a double significance in the course of the novel. First and foremost, its meaning is sociological. Unlike Mrs. Davis, who is out of place not squatting under a palm tree and chanting in Hebrew, Camilla Lawrence belongs precisely where she is. And the world she belongs to is one whose denizens never squat: they lounge in "very comfortable chairs" (80), endlessly discussing life and art. This high-minded and articulate company is quite willing to admit Harry Davis on their own terms; it does not, however, make room for his differences. In Harry's nocturnal fantasies, Camilla enters *his* world and diffuses elements of her own; in actuality, she visits Richstead once in the course of the novel only to reject it. It is Harry who must climb into Bloomsbury, where the air is thin and alien, and accommodate himself as best he can.

During Leonard's courtship of Virginia, he wrote a series of sketches of his friends, including one of Virginia, which is labeled "Aspasia," the name by which he also referred to her in his diaries.[7] In one such sketch, he describes the atmosphere in which Aspasia resides:

The world may be divided into Olympus, Athens & other places. . . . If you wandered into [Olympus], you . . . would probably think you were still in Athens. You would see several large & small houses very much like other houses & inside would be rooms very much like other rooms except that there would appear to be an enormous number of books & sometimes some queer pictures. Inside the rooms would be sitting the Olympians. . . . You would be lucky if you ever saw them doing anything. . . . I should not be very surprised if you thought them rather dull. . . . I am describing to you Olympus as it would appear to you if you were not an Olympian & wandered into it one winter's day out of the Athens fog. But . . . I assure you that if the fog were not in your eyes you would see . . . that what you thought was a sitting room is a mountaintop, there is snow there & a great wind & upon all sides illimitable space. Below you are precipices & bottomless gulfs. It follows that to be an Olympian you must have . . . a clear & fearless eye to look out over the great distances, not dazzled by the snow, looking steadily into the heart of the sun. First then the Olympians have this quality, to see the truth fearlessly, to tear the truth out of the heart of each thing. . . . (LWP IID 7A)

Although they are easily confused with mortals, the citizens of the privileged world Leonard describes are gods. As narrator, Leonard occupies an ambiguous place in this description. The "friend" to whom he addresses himself is clearly an outsider: an Athenian perhaps, but not one of the elect who can see the Olympians clearly. The narrator, on the other hand, would seem to possess the vision the Athenian does not, for he is able to describe the noumenon behind the apparition of a Bloomsbury sitting room. Eventually, however, it emerges that he is more an outsider than the Athenian himself; he comes from one of those "other" places that are apparently too negligible to be named in conjunction with Athens and Olympus. In the final sketch of the series, the narrator reveals his origins:

> . . . I am a Syrian . . . & I am in love with Aspasia. . . . I was born at Jericho & like most of the inhabitants of Jericho I have a large nose & black hair. I wander between Athens & Egypt & sometimes I visit Olympus: that is how I came to know the Olympians. I should like to live on Olympus but all Syrians are wanderers, & I rather doubt whether any of them are really Olympians. There is some taint in their blood & blood you know has a great deal to do with the heart. You want a strong heart to live among the Olympians on Olympus. You want hot blood to keep the cold out, but Jericho where I was born is a hot place, & most of the inhabitants of Jericho have cold blood to keep the heat out. I daresay you have noticed all this & that I have a good brain & a bitter tongue. . . . I wonder what will happen if they ever read all this in Athens or Olympus. Shall I have to take the train to Jericho? . . . I expect that I will still be able to lie at the feet of Aspasia. (LWP IID 7A)

Here the narrator's identity explains his supposed objectivity about the Olympians: as a Wandering Jew, he is at home neither in his place of origin nor in the places he visits. He is not an Athenian; thus the Olympians are not his gods. Yet the "Syrian" subscribes wholeheartedly to the deification of Aspasia and her cohorts, even while the Athenian, who is closer to them, can see them as people like himself.

What made this mythology so necessary to Leonard Woolf? Like Virginia in her letter to Violet Dickinson, Leonard constructs a graph of vertical mobility. His own efforts, however, are all upward: he visits Mount Olympus, where he is allowed to lie at the feet of Aspasia. Whether he will be allowed higher—say, to eye level—is the central and defining question of the novel. This ruling desire to scale the heights of Camilla's society renders Harry Davis alternately reverent and resentful. The "frightening purity" he ascribes to Camilla both repels and attracts him. A perpetual reminder of Harry's own "tainted" blood, it occasionally rouses his "bitter tongue." Then he lashes out, as in an argument with a friend of the Lawrences named Trevor:

Harry turned on him. "You're a Christian," he said contemptuously, brutally.
"I hope not," Trevor smiled.
"I'm a Jew."
"Yes, I know. Well?"
"You can glide out of a room and I can't: I envy you that! But I despise you.
I like that big baby [Mr. Lawrence, Camilla's father] sitting all day long in his
arm-chair, but I despise him. I admire your women, your pale women with
their white skins and fair hair, but I despise them."
"Do most Jews feel like that?"
"All of them—all of them. There's no life in you, no understanding. Your
women are cold and leave one cold—no dark hair, no blood in them. Pale hair,
pale souls, you know. You talk and you talk and you talk—no blood in you!
You never *do* anything."[8]
"Why do you think it's so important to do things?"
"Why? Because I'm a Jew, I tell you—I'm a Jew!" (*WV* 51–52)

Harry here reworks Leonard's private description of Aspasia and Co. as
Olympians. These Christian gods, unlike their Hellenic counterparts, lack
human warmth. They do not descend from their ivory towers to mingle
with mortals and engage in either sexual or commercial transactions. Harry
defines Jews as people with "blood"—that is, physical vitality—who "do"
things. Elsewhere he indicates their propensity for business. Of Harry's
sister, Leonard writes, "She was not intelligent enough to see that life for
her was simply a business" (55). But Hetty is not stupid, either. Her social
observations are both shrewd and cynical. When Camilla comes to
Richstead and meets Harry's family, Mrs. Davis remarks privately that although Camilla's dress is plainer than Hetty's, it seems to suit her better.[9]
" 'I know exactly what you mean, mamma dear,' " Hetty replies. " 'I am a
lady and Miss Lawrence is a lady, but Miss Lawrence is rather more of a
lady than I am.' " When Mrs. Davis insists that she meant nothing of the
kind, Hetty replies: " 'I'm not a bit offended. Miss Lawrence is a Christian
lady and I am a Jewish lady' " (121).

Throughout *The Wise Virgins*, Leonard locates the defining traits of a
social group in its women. Harry's own right to the title "gentleman" has
already been disputed by the female Garlands in the first chapter of the
novel. But Harry, aware that he cannot escape either designation or assimilation by others, brashly insists on defining himself. When the good-
natured Trevor is quite willing to pass over the fact of Harry's background,
the latter hammers home the statement "I'm a Jew!" Harry does not allow
Gwen Garland, with whom he develops a friendship between his visits to
Camilla, to forget this either. When she begins to adulate him, he tells her,
" 'I'm the wandering Jew, the everlasting Jew . . . and proud of it too' "

(194–95). He does not want friends to like him *despite* his Jewishness, so he sets himself apart by insisting upon it.

Yet Harry rejects his background in his desire for acceptance into the "intellectual aristocracy."[10] He forgets that the Jews are the People of the Book, and constructs a mythology of Jewish primitivism and Christian high-mindedness that centers on the women of both groups. Here again his ambivalence is apparent. Harry is contemptuous toward *both* the squatting, fecund Jewess figure and the Gentile woman who is exactly what the Jewish art model in nun's garb pretends to be, a spiritualized virgin-by-vocation. But he claims descent from the one figure and desires access to the other.[11]

Camilla Lawrence's denial of this access arouses Harry's ire. She feels no elation corresponding to his sense of elevation, in her presence, above all other Toms, Dicks, and Harrys. The world contains legions of Harry Davises, but Camilla Lawrence, at least in Harry's eyes, is unique.[12] As such she is both infinitely desirable and ultimately unattainable. She is the wise virgin of the novel's title. Here, however, the New Testament dichotomy is reversed. The wise virgins are those who do not stoop to seduction and marriage; the foolish do, and cease to be virgins.

Yet the wisdom of the wise, while he recognizes and even at times applauds it, infuriates Harry. The "other world" that Camilla inhabits is not only the intellectual Olympus of Bloomsbury; she herself is otherworldly, inhabiting a private realm of dreams and visions. She is, to observers, the *quintessential* virgin, locked in an ivory tower of her own constructing. Camilla's sexual coldness is a constant theme of the novel. " 'She's a woman and a virgin,' " says Arthur, another character in love with her. " 'They don't know, they simply don't know what desire is' " (96). Arthur's concept of "woman" is absurdly Victorian: " 'They don't realize that we've got bodies,' " he says. " 'That's what makes it so intolerable: unless they are loose and vile they have no passions. What's noble in us is vile in them.' " Arthur's definition of Camilla as not only a woman but a virgin to boot sets her above and beyond even this simplistic dichotomy of the sexes. If "woman" is already virginal, then a virginal woman is in another realm altogether. In fact, Camilla is so redundantly asexual as to be, in Arthur's eyes, a would-be man: " 'What she really wants, only she doesn't know it, is to be a man . . .' " (97).

If to be a man is to possess freedom of movement and of choice, then Arthur's conjecture is not altogether off target. In fact, the sensual desires Camilla has—and she does have them—are not unwomanly at all but precisely too feminine for Harry's and Arthur's tastes. " 'I'm very affectionate, you know that, don't you?' " she asks her sister. " 'I like silk and kisses and soft things and strokings. I was told the other day that I was like hills with virgin snow on them; but that's nonsense, isn't it?' " (82).[13] Camilla's anxious query betrays an insecurity that has been fomented by men: the notion that she is sexually inadequate. She herself views her supposed inadequacy as a choice. Passion, at least as defined by men, seems to her an ensnaring thing. If she is like a man, it is in her wish to live life autonomously, and to forge her own adventure rather than be caught in someone else's.

A conversation between Camilla and Harry early in the novel reflects the clear-cut difference between their respective desires and ambitions. The two have been talking in a satirical vein about suburban spinsters, when Harry suddenly turns fierce and misogynist. " 'I daresay they're tragic,' " says Camilla,

> "but there *is* something fine, almost noble, in them. I like their point of view. It's alive, they're alive—so much more alive than those cow-like married women."
>
> "But they miss something immense; not only children, I mean, and child-bearing. The—the romance of life. It gives me the horrors sometimes to think of it. . . . It all seems so purposeless, so futile, idiotic. That's what dries them up mentally, just as their breasts and bodies are dried up. And little hairs sprout under their chins."
>
> . . . His dark view of life seemed to her to throw a gloom over the bright day. She fought in herself against that view. He had not said what those dried-up spinsters missed, what he was afraid for him and her missing. In his mind it had meant what the male wants, a certain fierceness of love, mental and bodily; . . . a flame that shall join and weld together and isolate from the rest of the world. She knew vaguely, felt vaguely what he meant. But it was not in her, a woman and unmarried, to know the want. . . . Among men, as among animals, it is the young male who is fierce and dangerous, and roars and bellows and makes all the noise. (41)

Here, Leonard links his mythology of Jew and Christian to a Victorian mythology of man and woman, representing them as opposite extremes. Just as Harry is physically "dark," his view of life is "dark" and casts a shadow over fair Camilla's civilized world. Camilla does not think him altogether wrong, nor can the reader: Harry desires romance, the stuff of which novels are generally made, and Camilla has a "vague" notion of what he means. Because, however, Camilla's concept of "romance" is quite different, *this* novel becomes a kind of dark joke on the comic tradition. Camilla idealizes spiritual independence, Harry mutual passion; it seems that the twain cannot meet.

The image Harry invokes in Camilla's mind, that of "what the male wants," represents precisely what, in this case, the female *doesn't* want. And because, on the social grid of the novel, the female in question occupies a high place and the male protagonist a lower one, her lack of desire determines his fate. In his frustration, Harry is briefly attracted to Camilla's more earthy and equally beautiful sister, Katharine. Ultimately, however, Katharine seems both too accessible and too much like Harry himself to present the challenge that Camilla represents. The two sisters are described following a mild argument in which Katharine takes Camilla to task for leading Harry on with no intention of marrying him:

> [Katharine] stood . . . looking down . . . and thinking of Camilla, who sat absorbed in thought on the arm of the chair. Katharine never worried about anything, but she came as near as possible to doing so about Camilla. In the East she would have sat with other women around the great tom-tom, tapping out the monotonous note every now and then and saying that fate is fate—only she would never have cried out and beaten the breast with them when misfortunes came. Having been born a European, she did not talk of fate; she merely saw life steadily without delusions or enthusiasms. One had only to look at the two sisters, each thinking now and silent, to see the difference of character, and, one might guess, of destiny. Katharine's great dark eyes . . . moved . . . slowly over the surface of things. . . . [S]he was dark and deep and beautiful. . . . By her side Camilla seemed stranger and fairer than she really was. Even when she was sitting now motionless and silent thinking, her eyes seemed to have to dart quickly to keep pace with her thoughts. . . . Harry was right, you did not think of innocence in Camilla's face; you thought perhaps of purity, coldness even, of hills and snow, of something underneath, below the surface, that might at any moment break out destructive of you—of her? (83–84)

Despite her birth, Katharine, like Harry, is fundamentally an alien—and thus, to Harry, not alien at all. Like him, she is "dark," and her very physical presence is primevally reassuring. The phrase "Harry was right" indicates that the two are, in fact, in collusion in their views about Camilla. Both of them adore her and are exasperated by her, and they communicate their opinions to one another. Camilla's potential volatility is a frequent theme of Katharine's ruminations, and is here explicitly linked to her chasteness. Paradoxically, both these qualities make Camilla attractive to Harry. The nervous energy and "enthusiasm" roiling beneath her placid surface resemble Harry's own perpetual restlessness. But his restlessness is physical as well as mental, while hers is only mental, and in this way her character is diametrically opposed to his. He approaches her at his own risk, for the repression of her physical desires lends intensity to her mental activity, and the combination might destroy both him and Camilla herself. This notion that Camilla's vivid intellectual and imaginative life renders her potentially unstable is invoked several times in the novel.

The paradox whereby Harry is attracted to Camilla by her very unattainability proves, in *The Wise Virgins* if not in Leonard's own life, irresolvable. Harry's incapacity to find a "point of contact" with Camilla gives rise to a further contradiction. By rejecting Harry's love, she forces him back into the world of stultified conventions and petit bourgeois sentiments whose very opposite she had seemed to represent. Harry could, of course, continue to visit Bloomsbury as Camilla's friend, but his own desires make this impossible. A doer rather than a thinker, Harry is ill at ease in the Platonic realm of the Lawrence drawing room. On his first visit to Camilla's home, Harry remarks that "[t]hese epicures in the art of the emotions and the emotions of art had emancipated themselves from the convention that there are some things that men and women cannot talk about. . . . It was perhaps their weakness, at any rate intellectually, that they never did those things . . ." (80).

In point of fact, the Lawrences are guilty of the same Victorian backwardness of which Harry accuses the stodgy citizens of Richstead. Worse still, the Lawrences are hypocritical: their daring is purely verbal. Unable to scale the icy Olympian heights, Harry returns to his suburb and attempts to raise Gwen Garland, the girl next door, to *his* level. In doing so, he proves his own hypocrisy. The unfortunate Gwen is Camilla's opposite. On adjoining pages, Harry reflects that Gwen "would bring no difficulty into the life of anyone else"; "for Camilla," on the other hand, "[t]here would never be any simplicity, any easiness . . ." (67, 68). The great irony is that Gwen ultimately lands Harry in the very difficulty that the contemplative Camilla so fervently avoids.

Gwen takes words literally. Like the proverbial impressionable female, she responds with a turmoil of emotion to the books Harry gives her to read. While Mrs. Garland is immersed in Mrs. Humphry Ward, Gwen devours Ibsen's *Master Builder*. She begins to think of herself as Hilda, the wild bird, of Richstead as a cage, and of Harry as *her* Master Builder. Like Hilda with Solness, Gwen brings about Harry's downfall by believing his word. He has preached the doctrine of free love and independence to her. The Garland and Davis families are on holiday by the seaside when she confesses her love to him and begs him to run off with her. Confused, desperately unhappy, and above all sexually frustrated, Harry asks her in an impulsive moment to marry him. She realizes his insincerity and reproves him. Overcome by her passion for him, however, the foolish virgin sneaks into his hotel room in the night and leaves it a virgin no longer. In the morning, the guardians of convention, Mrs. Garland and Mrs. Davis, descend upon Harry and compel him to propose to Gwen.

Himself evidently a virgin before this encounter, Harry is at first exhilarated by his sexual experience. He feels what he has never felt in Camilla's presence, an intense sensual self-awareness. "[H]e seemed to be all body. . . . He looked down upon his limbs, ran his hands down the firm flesh . . . and thought to himself, proud and half-amused: 'Thank God,

I'm a man!' "(221).[14] Harry's elation is soon destroyed, however, by the contemplation of the life that lies ahead of him as Gwen's husband.

In what is perhaps the most ironic moment of the book, Harry receives a letter from Camilla the next day. It is an abridged paraphrase of the letter Virginia wrote to Leonard on May 1, 1912:

Dearest Leonard,
. . . It seems to me that I am giving you a great deal of pain . . . and therefore I ought to be as plain with you as I can, because half the time I suspect, you're in a fog which I don't see at all. Of course I can't explain what I feel. . . . I feel angry sometimes at the strength of your desire. Possibly, your being a Jew comes in also at this point. You seem so foreign. And then I am fearfully unstable. . . . I'm half afraid of myself. I sometimes feel that no one ever has or ever can share something—Its the thing that makes you call me like a hill, or a rock. Again, I want everything—love, children, adventure, intimacy, work. . . . I sometimes think that if I married you, I could have everything—and then—is it the sexual side of it that comes in between us? As I told you brutally the other day, I feel no physical attraction in you. There are moments—when you kissed me the other day was one—when I feel no more than a rock. And yet your caring for me as you do almost overwhelms me. It is so real, and so strange. . . . But its just because you care so much that I feel I've got to care before I marry you. I feel I must give you everything; and that if I can't, well, marriage would only be second-best for you as well as for me. If you can still go on, as before, letting me find my own way . . . that is what would please me best. . . . (L 1:496)

Camilla writes to Harry:

"I told Katharine that I am an adventurer; she says I'm an adventuress. Perhaps I'm both. It's the romantic part of life that I want; it's the voyage out that seems to me to matter, the new and wonderful things. I can't, I won't look beyond that. I want them all. I want love, too, and I want freedom. I want children even. But I can't give myself: passion leaves me cold. You'll think I am asking for everything to be given and to give nothing. Perhaps that's true.

"And then there's so much in marriage from which I recoil. It seems to shut women up and out. I won't be tied by the pettinesses and the conventionalities of life. There must be some way out. One must live one's own life, as the novels say." (VW 231)

Camilla's letter to Harry is shorter and does not dwell on the themes that have already been emphasized and intertwined in the course of the novel. Virginia's letter clearly states the two main sources of her ambivalence toward Leonard: his Jewishness (an element unmentioned in Camilla's letter) and the sexual desire that he possesses in abundance and she lacks. The ultimate message of both letters is the same: Stay near me, be patient, and in time I may overcome my doubts. Virginia's letter decided Leonard Woolf to abandon his post in Ceylon and continue his courtship. In *The Wise Virgins*, Camilla's letter comes too late.

To the very end of the novel, the diametrical relationship of Harry and Camilla persists. He pays her one last visit, to tell her what has happened. " 'The romantic part of life is what you want—' " he says, " 'in your letter you said that. To me it's you, ever since I first saw you and your face—it's like a face in a dream to me . . .' " (235). Even Camilla's physical being appears to Harry purely spiritual. He, on the other hand, is so palpable to her that she cannot bear his glance, and his words seem like invasive touches. He accuses her of hypocrisy in declaring his relationship to Gwen ugly and cruel when he himself has heard her make witticisms over other people's heartbreaks. She is unable to answer: "It was as if Harry had taken her by the hand and was leading her up to touch something cold and hard" (236) Their meeting ends with a sad parody of the final moment in a marriage ceremony: "He just touched her hair with his hand and then kissed her on the lips without passion, as if it were a symbol, a ceremony, an act to be always remembered. It gave him pleasure even that she did not respond, that she lay back submissive, that, as he left her, she did not move or speak" (237).

Why did Leonard Woolf, so soon after his actual marriage to Virginia, write a novel in which that marriage fails to come about? Like Harry's final gesture toward Camilla, it seems an act of both renunciation and revenge. In his very passionlessness, Harry commits a figurative sexual assault. He forces a "cold, hard thing" on the woman who wanted only "soft things and strokings." The kiss he gives without her consent is also deliberately cold, and her posture beneath it is ironically like that of a Victorian virgin on her wedding night. Thus he combines passionlessness, which Camilla consistently upheld and represented, with the physical intensity she so much feared. It is the gesture of an angry man refusing to show his anger in order to come out, literally, on top. In doing so, he destroys Camilla's defenses and leaves her, finally, alone.

Perhaps Leonard meant *The Wise Virgins* as an admonition to Virginia, a reminder that had he not been willing to accept her terms, she would have been left, with her virginity, in the cold. Perhaps he even wanted, unconsciously, to punish her for sexlessness. The fact remains that, from all we know, Leonard sacrificed his sexual life for the spiritual and intellectual communion which Virginia embodied. In a love letter written late at night on April 29, 1912, Leonard begins by reassuring Virginia that his sleeplessness stems "not from desire but from thinking about you" (*LLW* 172). In denying his sexuality, Leonard renounced the sense of masculine superiority that a woman like Gwen would have given him. *Thinking*—and talking and writing—would become the predominant activity in his marriage:

an activity in which Virginia could outclass him, though on the whole they were evenly matched.

The Wise Virgins contains hints of the fallout from this alliance of minds. The novel describes the strange flightiness of Virginia's imagination, which could spin off into absurdities and profundities incomprehensible to others. It links this mental capriciousness both to genius and to madness, and shows it impeding Camilla's emotional as well as her sensual faculties. Katharine Lawrence at one point declares her pity for the man who will marry her sister. The marriage would be a one-way bargain, as Camilla loves to be loved but lacks the energy or desire to reciprocate.[15] It is this very passivity that makes her, to Harry, an object to be attained; when she does not give herself, however, Harry turns elsewhere. Leonard persevered.

Another cost of Leonard's perseverance was his strained relations with his family. His marriage into Gentility was a departure from his heritage; if he never actively repudiated his Jewishness, he tacitly submitted himself to the snobbish antisemitism of Virginia and her coterie. Like himself, those of Leonard's siblings who married all married Gentiles—without, however, making dramas of their exit from the fold. *The Wise Virgins* is such a drama, in its satirical portrayal of the author's mother and sister. If Leonard's treatment of Camilla is ambivalent, his delineation of Mrs. Davis and, to a lesser degree, Hetty, is decidedly hostile. Mrs. Davis is the savage who drives Harry to seek the Olympian heights of civilization. When he falls from the cold peaks into the arms of Gwen Garland, he returns home. Herself a self-hating Jew, Mrs. Davis can be satisfied by the Christian wedding ceremony as well as the suburban conventions that mark Harry's defeat. That he portrays it *as* a defeat suggests that Leonard saw marriage to Virginia as a means of escape. None of his family were invited to the wedding on August 10th, 1912.

ESCAPE, CONTINUED

In 1918, Leonard and Virginia's prime matchmaker debunked four icons of the nineteenth century. The method of Lytton Strachey's *Eminent Victorians* was not a frontal attack; in his preface, Strachey explains:

> Concerning the Age which has just passed, our fathers and our grandfathers have poured forth and accumulated so vast a quantity of information that the industry of a Ranke would be submerged by it, and the perspicacity of a Gibbon would quail before it. It is not by the direct method of scrupulous narration that the explorer of the past can hope to depict that singular epoch. If he is wise, he will adopt a subtler strategy. He will attack his subject in unexpected

places; he will fall upon the flank, or the rear; he will shoot a sudden, revealing searchlight into obscure recesses, hitherto undivined. (vii)

Strachey goes on to cite the lesson he has learned from the biographers of the past: "To preserve, for instance, a becoming brevity . . . [and] to maintain his own freedom of spirit" (ix). This is the method that Strachey, in contradistinction to those older writers, will use in the short biographies that follow.

Strachey's language is, characteristically, both ingenious and disingenuous. His paragraph begins with an inflated description of the Victorian legacy. Its adjectives and phrases suggest the burden beneath which the modern writer can only stagger. A mere child in the face of the epic achievements of his "fathers and grandfathers," he will have to use small and wily strategies to escape their authority: to run up behind them, as it were, and kick them in the pants. All the time he will pretend obedience and employ a "modest brevity" which suggests that he knows his own place. And by this very method he will transcend the place to which the fathers have consigned him: he will, by a brilliant twist, "maintain his own freedom of spirit."

Referring, in essence, to himself, Strachey uses the masculine pronoun for this modern biographer-*cum*-escape artist.[16] Strachey defines and carries off his project with the most jaunty self-assurance precisely because, while he deflates his fathers, he also follows in their footsteps. The technique he chooses may be guerrilla warfare, but it is still warfare, that eminently male occupation pursued by General Gordon himself. The fathers threaten but do not repress Strachey: he gets off scot-free. Indeed, for all the ambiguity of his title, suggesting reverence and asserting irony, Strachey ended by erecting *himself* into eminence. Deflater or not, he became one of the most feted of contemporary litterateurs.

Virginia Woolf's contemporaneous *Night and Day* is a far more uneasy, ambiguously victorious attack on her own nineteenth-century forefathers. Strachey succeeded because he was his fathers' son; Virginia was her father's daughter, and a daughter is not trained in warfare. She had her father's weapons at her disposal, but, as she would later say, a woman cannot comfortably deploy a man's sentence. While Strachey began *Eminent Victorians* with victory a foregone conclusion, Virginia Woolf's novel depicts the struggle itself. Even at the end, when Katharine Hilbery's father must literally turn his back and flee from the heroine's rebellious words, it is she who remains inside the room, and the novel's last scene shows her standing just within the threshold of *his* house.

Night and Day is a fiction of escape—or of attempted escape. It was Virginia Woolf's shot, in both senses of the phrase, at an older form of the novel. She wanted, by writing such a book, to have done with literary forebears. Without using Stracheyan tricks, she took on their cumbersome weight. The very lightness of *his* volume, in contrast to its forerunners, catapulted him into prominence. Virginia's book, at least by virtue of girth, is hard to distinguish from others on the sagging Victorian shelf. Yet it represents the rite of passage that enabled her transition to a new conception of the novel, embodied in the slimness of *Jacob's Room* and other later works.

The love affair that unfolds in the pages of *Night and Day* chronicles Virginia's efforts to slough off her Victorian legacy. Katharine Hilbery is the granddaughter of an eminent British poet, Richard Alardyce. She lives in her parents' home, runs the household, serves tea, shows visitors the poet's relics, and helps her mother to compile his biography. This work does not proceed apace, owing both to Katharine's lack of interest and to her mother's flightiness. Mrs. Hilbery's propensity for poetic sorties prevents her from writing the sort of "Standard Biography" described in Lytton's preface, while moral conventions as well as oedipal awe preclude a work of iconoclasm. Katharine is bored, frustrated, and engaged to a prig named William Rodney who represents precisely the stultifying life from which she wishes to be free. Ralph Denham, whom she meets in the novel's first chapter, offers an avenue of escape.

The two do not take to one another at first. Ralph feels the same mixture of insecurity and contempt toward the Hilbery family that Harry Davis feels toward the Lawrences. Like Harry, he is brash and judgmental; he unsettles Katharine—but her unsettling, unlike Camilla's, is ultimately positive. Their first discussion is a counterpoint that gradually crescendoes. Katharine takes Ralph to look at the family relics, which she catalogs mechanically. He, however, does not respond mechanically; unlike most visitors, he is conspicuously unimpressed, and this contrary reaction leads Katharine to observe him more closely:

> [S]he stopped for a moment, wondering why it was that Mr. Denham said nothing. . . . He had a singular face. . . . In his spare build and thin, though healthy, cheeks, she saw tokens of an angular and acrid soul. . . .
>
> "You must be very proud of your family, Miss Hilbery."
>
> "Yes, I am," Katharine answered, and she added, "Do you think there's anything wrong in that?" . . .
>
> "Isn't it difficult to live up to your ancestors?" he proceeded.
>
> "I dare say I shouldn't try to write poetry," Katharine replied.
>
> "No. And that's what I should hate. I couldn't bear my grandfather to cut me out. And, after all," Denham went on, glancing round him satirically, as Katharine thought, "it's not your grandfather only. You're cut out all the way round. I suppose you come of one of the most distinguished families in England." . . .

". . . I only help my mother. I don't write myself."

"Do you do anything yourself?" he demanded. . . .

"Nobody ever does do anything worth doing nowadays," she remarked. "You see"—she tapped the volume of her grandfather's poems—"we don't even print as well as they did, and as for poets or painters or novelists—there are none; so, at any rate, I'm not singular."

"No, we haven't any great men," Denham replied. "I'm very glad that we haven't. I hate great men. The worship of greatness in the nineteenth century seems to me to explain the worthlessness of that generation." (*ND* 16–20)

Indignant at first, Katharine gradually comes to see this young upstart as her rescue from massive anxiety of influence. Her fiancé in the early part of the novel is a hero-worshiper, a weak man preoccupied with appearances and insistent on social conventions. As Katharine's engagement to him comes to feel more and more like an ensnarement, her initial aversion to Ralph Denham grows into an attraction. The reader familiar with *The Wise Virgins* is struck by the essentially equal footing that these two lovers occupy. In the conversation above, Ralph's criticisms spring in part from a sense of his own displacement in the Hilbery house, but not from any feeling of inferiority. Virginia Woolf makes it easier for him: Ralph is not, at least as far as we are told, a Jew. In most other respects, however, his background resembles that of Harry Davis. Yet he is able to tell Katharine with a certainty, " 'I shouldn't like to be you' " (*ND* 19). The roles here are reversed: the poor young man awakens the sophisticated lady to the barrenness of her own life.

Not that Ralph's life is particularly fertile. He, too, feels trapped in his parental household, where he occupies a shabby attic room. From the moment he meets Katharine, he sets her up as an ideal of conduct and an object to be attained. Poring over his law books at night (he is a solicitor in a firm), he fantasizes about her. Curiously, it is not sexual desire that Katharine awakens in him. He sees her as statuesque, even marmoreal; Athena rather than Venus:

He possessed a book of photographs from the Greek statues; the head of a goddess, *if the lower part were concealed,* had often given him the ecstasy of being in Katharine's presence. He took it down from the shelf and found the picture. To this he added a note from her, bidding him meet her at the Zoo. He had a flower which he had picked at Kew to teach her botany. Such were his relics. (*ND* 385; italics mine)

Like Camilla in *The Wise Virgins*, Katharine appears to her lover as an object of purely spiritual worship, while he, like Harry Davis, represents the concrete side of life. To Katharine, however, this is refreshing. She is excited by Ralph's physical strength and his intimacy with the natural world. While her meetings with the effete William Rodney all take place indoors, her two most important rendezvous with Ralph occur in Kew Gardens and, in an amusing twist of drawing-room comedy tradition, at the zoo. She admires his adeptness with plants and animals. The first touch of sensuality in the novel occurs when Ralph gives Katharine a botany lesson:

> While she breathed and looked, Denham was engaged in uncovering with the point of his stick a group of green spikes smothered by the dead leaves. . . . She . . . asked him to inform her about flowers. To her they were variously shaped and colored petals, poised, at different seasons of the year, upon very similar green stalks; but to him they were, in the first instance, bulbs or seeds, and later, living things endowed with with sex, and pores, and susceptibilities which adapted themselves by all manner of ingenious devices to live and beget life. . . . (*ND* 330)

For perhaps the first time in her life, Katharine is able to "breathe." Her breathing, in conjunction with Ralph's activity with his stick, also suggests a sexual awakening. In uncovering the flowers' nakedness, he seems to be unveiling Katharine herself. In the next paragraph, when Katharine is obliquely likened to a flower, this metaphor appears to be borne out—and is instantly subverted:

> She wished he would go on for ever talking of plants. . . . Circumstances had long forced her, as they force most women in the flower of youth, to consider, painfully and minutely, all that part of life which is conspicuously without order; she had had to consider moods and wishes, degrees of liking or disliking, and their effect upon the destiny of people dear to her; she had been forced to deny herself any contemplation of that other part of life where thought constructs a destiny which is independent of human beings. As Denham spoke, she followed his words and considered their bearing with an easy vigor which spoke of a capacity long hoarded and unspent. (331)

Katharine's "vigor" is not sexual but mental; it is her mind, not her body, that has felt starved until her contact with Denham. His knowledge excites her because it is scientific, reasonable, ultimately masculine. It has nothing to do with the niceties of the tea-table, the duties of a good Victorian daughter whose first concern must always be the feelings of others. Ralph transports Katharine out of the feminine world of emotion. She has been studying mathematics in secret; now she has found a man to whom she can admit her desire, not for love as it is generally understood, but for intellectual freedom. Paradoxically, Ralph's discourses on the sexual life of plants transport Katharine into an ecstasy of abstract thought. Here is the rationality she has dreamed of alone in *her* room, the ability to name, classify, and order, not the relics of a dead hero, but the world outside the Hilbery household. Ralph is, ultimately, as much of an abstraction to Katharine as she is to him. He is her vehicle to self-fulfillment.

Yet Ralph idealizes Katharine with a difference. To her, he represents a means to an end. To him, however high and mighty she may appear, she is an end in herself. This difference in purpose and vision leads to the main trouble in their relationship. With all the levelheadedness of the most modern lovers, they sit and discuss "what in their common language they had christened their 'lapses' ":

> What was the cause of these lapses? Either because Katharine looked more beautiful, or more strange, because she wore something different, or said something unexpected, Ralph's sense of her romance welled up and overcame him either into silence or into inarticulate expressions, which Katharine, with unintentional but invariable perversity, interrupted. . . . Then the vision disappeared, and Ralph expressed vehemently in his turn the conviction that he only loved her shadow and cared nothing for her reality. If the lapse was on her side it took the form of gradual detachment until she became completely absorbed in her own thoughts. . . . It was useless to assert that these trances were originated by Ralph himself. . . . The fact remained that she had no need of him and was very loath to be reminded of him. How, then, could they be in love? (473)

Despite the narrator's "if," the "lapses," at least the ones considered to stand in the way of the lovers' union, are Katharine's. If Ralph is faulted for originating them, it is only because he voices his adoration. This seems to disturb Katharine; why, the two are unsure. Perhaps it is the abstractness of Ralph's desire, his glorification of Katharine, that alienates her. Perhaps it is his desire itself that, in its forcefulness, frightens Katharine as, in *The Wise Virgins*, Harry Davis's desire frightens Camilla Lawrence. In any case, we find ourselves once more on a vertical plane, with Katharine the indifferent object of Ralph's adoration. The lovers' troubles of *Night and Day* are merely a more genteel version of those in Leonard's novel. Katharine's indifference springs neither from an explicitly stated, inherent sexual coldness nor from objections to Ralph's background. Paradoxically, it derives from the same source as her *attraction* to Ralph: namely, her ability to be mentally autonomous, to think her own thoughts, in his presence.

Because this complicated relationship so little resembles romantic love as previous generations have represented it, Katharine doubts whether marriage is desirable. She has already struck a blow at convention by breaking her engagement to Rodney in favor of a man of somewhat lower class. Virginia Woolf strikes two further blows at the conventions of romantic fiction by making her heroine not only loath to marry but willing to live with her lover outside wedlock. This way, if the "lapses" continue, the relationship can be broken off. However, convention reasserts itself at the novel's end, in what some critics consider a capitulation on Virginia Woolf's part.[17] After defying her father, who has railed against her abnormal behavior, Katharine falls under the sway of Mrs. Hilbery. Returning at a crucial moment from a visit to Shakespeare's tomb, Katharine's mother descends upon Ralph at his office, whisks him to her house, and persuades the two lovers to marry.[18]

Of the novel's resolution, Janis Paul writes that "Katharine is a Modernist spirit trapped in a Victorian novel, and the question of her independence resolves into the question of whom she will marry. She cannot reject tradition herself; the best she can do is marry a man who rejects it. . . . [Virginia Woolf] creates characters who question the limitations of traditional social forms, but her novel ultimately follows the traditional social forms of English fiction by ending in marriage" (*The Victorian Heritage* 84–93). While Paul's analysis is astute, it requires qualification. Biography, in this case, cannot be left out of the picture. *Night and Day* is not an autobiographical novel, but it follows on the heels of a book by the writer's husband that *was* semiautobiographical, and implicitly refers to this predecessor. Moreover, the novel was written within a few years of Virginia Woolf's own decision to marry.

To say that "the best" Katharine Hilbery "can do" is marry a man who rejects tradition implies a negative decision, a failure of independence. Yet the very peculiarity of Katharine's relation to Ralph is the fact that in his presence, even more than when she is alone, Katharine feels autonomous. Paul goes on to remark that "Katharine and Ralph's final exchange, 'Good night,' perhaps acknowledges their special cognizance of their inner world, but only symbolically. In that other world, the external world, they speak standing on the threshold of the Hilbery house. . . ." She concludes that in *Night and Day*, "Woolf had not yet integrated vision and form" (98–99). We must ask, then, why she was able to achieve such an integration *after* writing *Night and Day*.

I believe that the marriage of Katharine Hilbery and Ralph Denham, however problematic to some critics, represents a transition to modernism. The autobiographical elements of *Night and Day* are more symbolic than factual. By the time she reencountered Leonard Woolf in 1911, Virginia Stephen's father had died, and the various Stephen children were living independent, adult lives. Virginia, unlike Katharine, did not technically need a deliverer. What she wanted was productive companionship. The creative autonomy that Leonard afforded her was itself an escape from patriarchy; the further escape of unmarried cohabitation would have been redundant. Moreover, the "lapses" that occur between Katharine and Ralph might be read as gaps in the conventional romance plot which dictates that love is an enthrallment. These lapses represent brief escapes, moments of freedom from engagement with the other's personality; and it is precisely the ability to achieve such moments that makes marriage with Ralph desirable for Katharine Hilbery.

I do not mean to dismiss the element of Victorian nostalgia in either Katharine Hilbery's or Virginia Stephen's decision to marry. I believe, however, that it was precisely Virginia Woolf's marriage to a man of different background and radical politics which helped her in later works to explore unconventional themes in a new style—that this intercultural alliance was more productive for being, paradoxically, reified in a most conventional fashion. Describing the final scene in *Night and Day*, Rachel Blau DuPlessis writes in " 'Amor Vin,' " "[Ralph and Katharine] kiss on the limen between love and quest": they are on the threshold of new discoveries and, as DuPlessis goes on to say of later novels, "heterosexual romance and marriage are set aside precisely in being achieved" (Homans, *Virginia Woolf* 124, 133). Katharine's own deviation from literature to mathematics is an allegorical representation of Virginia Woolf's literary escape from her "fathers and grandfathers."

Both *The Wise Virgins* and *Night and Day* are fictions of escape that end, ironically, as fictions of *engagement*. The two protagonists, seeking to elude "the family system," finally perpetuate the family foundation.[19] Harry Davis finds himself married to the wrong woman; Katharine Hilbery finds herself a second time, quite suddenly and unexpectedly, on the threshold of marriage. In both novels, the heroine has responded reluctantly while the hero has pursued hotly. Camilla's reluctance ends in absurd tragedy for Harry; Katharine's, defeated by her mother, in the questionable triumph of the lovers. Together, the two books illuminate Virginia and Leonard's conception of their engagement as a joke.

Yet this conception, for a pair so attuned to the nuances of both language and social convention, is entirely fitting. That a penniless Jew, in a society that did not readily accept his kind, would snare an intellectual aristocrat, is funny because unexpected. That the aristocrat herself would cooperate in her ensnarement is a joke on the forefathers. That two iconoclasts would perpetuate an ancient social ritual is absurd. Finally, however, the joke is against the convention itself. To *engage* is not only to become entangled but also to challenge. Neither Leonard nor Virginia conceived of marriage passively. Theirs was to be an ongoing intellectual counterpoint in which each challenged the other, and both challenged the norms of art and society. "We both of us want a marriage," Virginia wrote to Leonard on May 1, 1912, "that is a tremendous living thing, always alive, always hot, not dead and easy in parts as most marriages are. We ask a great deal of life, don't we? Perhaps we shall get it; then, how splendid!" (*L* 1:497). What remained for both to "get" was a release from their own escape fictions, dependent as these were on a vertical definition of their relationship. To achieve a sense of balance, of mutual recognition across the lines of difference, and to construe these lines as horizontal—like a hyphen rather than a ladder—was their lifelong engagement.

DEPARTURES

Five years after their marriage, in 1917, the newly founded Hogarth Press issued its first publication. The Woolfs saw their press as an opportunity for creative and intellectual freedom, and as a respite from mental labor. It would enable Virginia to publish what she chose—and thus, more easily, write what she chose—and provide a forum for avant-garde writers whom more conservative publishers might turn away. Its first production was a pamphlet-size volume containing a short story by each member of the couple.

Two Stories encapsulates the fraught dialectic of imagination and sociological fact that informed the Woolfs' marriage as well as their fiction. Leonard's story, "Three Jews," is so laden by its theme of sociological destiny as to imply the impossibility of imaginative transcendence; its central character is a grave-digger, and the story ends with a figurative burial that might be read as Leonard's self-burial as Jewish writer. Hermione Lee calls "Three Jews" "a signpost pointing down a road [Leonard] would not take— as a fiction writer, as a Jewish writer"; Virginia's "The Mark on the Wall," on the other hand, signaled "a completely new direction, the beginning of a new form and a new kind of writing" (*Virginia Woolf* 359). The yoking of these stories is powerfully suggestive; like the engagement notice to Lytton Strachey, they comprehend a union tugging in two directions. Leonard Woolf's departure from fiction and increasing involvment with "real world" politics and history shadowed Virginia's literary flights, her development of a fictional style at first quite fantastical, and gradually more and more deft in its interweaving of fantasy and fact. The Hogarth Press was the spawning ground of those parallel trajectories, and its first publication contained them in embryo.

Both Woolfs were snobs, but her snobbery, directed at people recognizably different from herself, energized her fiction: the energy was compounded of both the snobbery itself and the desire to overcome it. Virginia saw that objectifying others is a way of objectifying the self—for better and for worse—and also that the boundaries between self and other are finer than class politics and entrenched prejudice allow. It is easier, however, to ignore the boundary beneath oneself, attempt empathy for the person lower down, than to recognize one's real identification with that person— to feel, in fact, that one is something of an imposter on the higher rung.

For Leonard, snobbery lurked dangerously near self-hatred, just as his acceptance by elite groups, a form of tokenism, bordered on rejection. He was a Jew in England: a species Theodor Herzl described as fundamentally self-divided when he referred, in an 1897 article, to "the efforts of amphibious-minded men to combine ancient tradition with an exaggerated imitation of national customs" (qtd. in Finestein, *Jewish Society in Victorian England* 177). It is this amphibiousness that informs the family caricatures in *The Wise Virgins* and constitutes the subject matter of "Three Jews."

If, as Homi Bhabha has written, the subaltern's mimicry parodied the colonialist original, the early-twentieth-century metropolitan Jew in English masquerade was in a trickier position, both less and more of a parody. He was allowed to don gentleman's clothing—he was, in fact, enjoined to do so as a condition of membership in English society, barred him if he maintained orthodox garb or Eastern European customs; yet, this entrance once permitted, he often exposed himself by the *way* he wore his clothes. His masquerade could not function as satire, for he was always in the minority in a land that defined itself—despite universalist rhetoric—as both Christian and insular; when the gentleman-Jew served as parody, it was himself he mocked. The balancing act British Jews performed in the early and mid–nineteenth century, which won them their political emancipation—a victory with "the aura of a bargain" (Finestein, *Jewish Society in Victorian England* 147)—involved the insistence on difference in religious belief only. Socially and culturally, English Jews declared themselves to be thoroughly English; though never persecuted for their religion, they became a new sort of crypto-Jew, adopting all the customs of the host society while keeping their Jewish habits for home and family.

An antiessentialist philosophy was at work in the insistent self-Anglicization of British Jews through the late nineteenth century and into the early twentieth. That philosophy assumed no racially or even culturally inherent Jewishness, but instead that individuals of Judaic background and persuasion could be molded into perfect and wholehearted citizens of their new nation. The process of molding was to be performed as quickly and efficiently as possible on new immigrants; it was carried out by Jewish organizations that mimicked, even down to name, clubs and organizations of the larger society: the Jewish Working Men's Club, the Jewish Lads' Brigade, the Jewish Soup Kitchen, and so on.[20] Those very names embody the division that made Anglo-Jewish identity so vertiginous: the prefix suggests separateness, particularist or parochial considerations, but the purpose of these "Jewish" organizations was, almost exclusively, an acculturation in Englishness. At the same time, the names expose the ambivalence behind the apparently antiessentialist, liberal ideology of acculturation: if immigrant Jews were publicly incongruous only by virtue of Polish customs or Yiddish speech, and these groups had no religious purpose, why call them

"Jewish"? Jews *were* a separate group in English society, and it was as a separate group that they formed smaller groups to expedite and prove their assimilability and loyalty to the new nation—a distinctly paradoxical enterprise.

The bifurcated nature of Anglo-Jewish identity, and the antialienism that formed the particular English quality of English antisemitism, provide the subject matter of "Three Jews." It is a story about the failure of Anglicization, a failure the author seems to ascribe on the one hand to an essential Jewishness that will out despite masquerades (or that will *not* out despite efforts at eradication), and on the other to tenacious Jewish exclusivism. The story neither represents nor apparently indicts British antisemitism; yet the narrator, even as he exaggerates Jewish incongruity, places such unflattering emphasis on the norms of English respectability as to suggest yet a third reason for the unassimilability of the Jews: a distinct, almost laughable (if one dared laugh aloud), even pathetic (if one dared say so) lack of magnetism in British ways.

It is here—on the subject of English uptightness—that Leonard's story both joins and parts ways with Virginia's "The Mark on the Wall." The short stories—"Mark," "Kew Gardens," "An Unwritten Novel," and various others—that adumbrate Virginia's first stream-of-consciousness novels (*Jacob's Room* and *Mrs. Dalloway*), also read like sketches leading up to her famous modernist pronouncement on "reality" of character, the 1924 essay "Mr. Bennett and Mrs. Brown." All are concerned with transcending demarcation; the eponymous mark on the wall transmutes, in the essay, into the "markers" of character so clumsily deployed by Edwardian realists, and the entire corpus of short prose from the period between *Night and Day* and *Mrs. Dalloway* is an experiment in conveying character from within rather than marking it from without. A principle of Woolf's modernism, this idea was also central to her politics: in *A Room of One's Own*, she would expound her repugnance toward all forms of categorization and measure, the tools of territorialization and of the colonizing of women and others.

But Virginia Woolf was not marked in the way Leonard was. To be her father's daughter was both advantage and disadvantage; it was not a stigma. Wearing the masquerades of upper-middle-class femininity (white hats, white drapery, tea-table decorum) did not mean inviting disdain—although inhabiting a woman's body did mean categorical exclusion from public life. Virginia's examination of exclusion and inclusion led her to conclude in *A Room of One's Own* "how unpleasant it is to be locked out; [but] it is worse perhaps to be locked in" (24), and the conviction that there was more space on the outside—space in which to question, parody, and reconceive the inside—informs the early articulations of her modernism. Leonard's firm position as a man, a Cambridge graduate, and an ex-imperialist, was always undermined, potentially if not in fact, by his precarious station as English

Jew; this tenuous identity made it more difficult to choose the outside, for the stigmatized cannot really escape.

The very structure of "Three Jews" nails home the fact of Leonard's entrapment, while the structure of "The Mark on the Wall," inclusive, inconclusive, and suggestive, opens out into Virginia's further flights. Her story embodies possibility even when it rails against containment, while his shows up alternatives as vain fantasy. As in some of his other short fictions, the main story of "Three Jews" is encased in a double frame, and the awkwardness of this construct echoes the story's theme: the ill-fittingness of Anglo-Jewish identity. Each of the story's three speakers occupies a different position on the spectrum of that identity: the narrator who begins the tale is evidently the most assimilated, but as the story unfolds, the idea of progressive assimilation is complicated. Is it a ladder, on which the most Anglicized is most priviliged? Or is the most Anglicized also most self-deluded, most thoroughly self-parodying, and thus most profoundly uncomfortable? Answers suggest themselves but are never proposed, and the identity of the first narrator is never fleshed out, so that it is tempting to find in his character signs of Leonard's stance toward the questions he raises.

Like Virginia in "Mr. Bennett and Mrs. Brown," Leonard concerns himself with character as seen through the eyes of another. Here the encounter arises from an explicitly escapist desire: on a Sunday in early spring, the first-person narrator chafes at the sooty airlessness of his city environs. He boards a train to Kew Gardens (the scene of another of Virginia's early stories), which provides at least the taste of nature amid excessively ordered and regulated grounds. So far, the plot gives a foretaste of *A Room of One's Own*, in which imagination is both vivified by the lawns and streams of Oxbridge and constrained by its sexist strictures. But the strictures in "Three Jews" are not imposed by an identifiable authority, arising instead from a general aura both less definite and more ubiquitous than Virginia's Oxbridge beadle. The first indication that the narrator is not at home in Kew comes with the surprising national characterization of the season and weather: "It was spring there, English spring." Once invoked, the adjective recurs, and recurs again, accompanied by other repeated modifiers:

Yes, the *quiet orderly English spring* that embraced and sobered even the florid luxuriance of great flowers bursting in white cascades over strange tropical trees. . . . And the spring had brought the people out into the gardens, the *quiet orderly English people*. . . . They looked at the flaunting tropical trees, and made jokes, and chaffed one another, and laughed not very loud. They were happy in their *quiet orderly English way*. . . . They did not run about or shout, they walked slowly, *quietly*, taking care to keep off the edges of the grass because the notices told them to do so. . . . I watched them eating plum-cake and drinking tea *quietly*, *soberly*, under the gentle apple-blossom. (*TS* 6–7; italics mine)

The narrator's cool, sarcastic, half-admiring distance from the "English" people implies that he is a foreigner, a tourist, perhaps, culling observations to repeat at home. But the description of "florid . . . strange tropical trees" (so perplexing to the English), incongruously set against "gentle" apple-blossom, metaphorically indicates the narrator's identity: he is not a tourist, but a transplant—one whose alien roots inevitably "show." The luxuriant blossoms of imported flora are analogized almost instantly in the floridity of the second Jew, a man who appears in the tea gardens with a good deal more than the conspicuous energy of Ralph Denham arriving to Sunday tea at the Hilberys'. That second Jew, whose narrative will shortly take over, is a veritable catalog of orientalist and antisemitic stereotypes: his movement is "bustl[ing]," his face "dark fat . . . and inscrutable," his mouth "sensual" and eyes "mysterious" and heavy-lidded, and, says the narrator, "I noticed the slight thickness of the voice, the over-emphasis, and the little note of assertiveness in it" (7). But he is recognized almost immediately by the way he wears his clothes—as though they belonged to another.

Whose side are we on? The story presents the reader with a narrator who is both native and excluded, who measures the man opposite by an alien standard that we know already to be alien to himself, as well. The story that follows concerns a third Jew, whose tale the second man recounts only once he and the narrator have compared notes on the subject of their own conspicuousness and the question of "belonging." Both feel entitled to possess or claim their surroundings; both feel, however, that their surroundings would never claim them; and, as nonbelieving Jews, both feel deracinated. The third man, however, though also a skeptic, is not deracinated; his tenacious Jewish parochialism gives him a rootedness-despite-transplantation that the story conveys as at once enviable and primitive.

The third man is a grave-keeper and, though he presides over a dusty Jewish cemetery, represents a spirit that, far from dying out, thrives ever more stubbornly in the face of opposition and adversity. "By Jove!" says the second Jew, whose idiom distinguishes him from the third he is about to describe—and, presumably, from the first as well, whose locutions are more highbrow—

> You couldn't mistake him for anything but a Jew. His arms hung down from his shoulders in that curious, loose, limp way—you know it?—it makes the clothes look as if they didn't belong to the man who is wearing them. Clever cunning grey eyes, gold pince-nez, and a nose, by Jove, Sir, one of the best, one of those noses, white and shiny, which, when you look at it full face, seems almost flat on the face, but immensely broad, curving down, like a broad high-road from between the bushy eye-brows down over the lips. And side face, it was colossal; it stood out like an elephant's trunk with its florid curves and scrolls. (11)

This eloquent description seems implausible, overdetermined—a fabulistic flight that almost touches the fantastical digressions of "The Mark on the Wall" and other early stories by Virginia. But *her* fantasies are the deliberate meanderings of a narratorial imagination refusing to be pinned down, a mind willfully defying rules and roles, refusing simple plots. The satirical fervor that seizes the second Jew in his description of the third marks an ugly confinement at the very moment of imaginative flight: it is imagination in the service of self-hatred, creativity immured in textbook racism. Sociological entrapment defeats the desire for transcendence; prejudice strangles a potentially original mind: the Anglo-Jewish writer, this passage seems to suggest, is damned both ways. If he chooses the questionable universalism of "Englishness," he denies his particular origins; if he seeks his origins, he becomes an anachronism, a displaced particularist; caught between the two impossibilities, he is forced to tell self-defeating stories.[21] Incongruous in the tea gardens, he takes up residence in a graveyard.

The third Jew's story is simple enough, though its ending exposes the ambiguity of the entire tale. Having failed in business, he has taken a job as grave-keeper, an inglorious position but sufficient to provide a comfortable living for his wife and two sons. When the second Jew visits the grave of his first wife, he converses with the grave-keeper on matters of belief and concludes, " 'He isn't a Jew now any more than I am. We're Jews only externally now. . . . Even *he* doesn't believe, the keeper of Jewish graves!' " (14). But the ending of the story proves this wrong; the second Jew returns to the graveyard some time later and finds the third in a state of defiant misery, Job-like and gloriously stiff-necked. The ultimate disaster has occurred: his son has married a Christian woman. The grave-keeper's condemnation of his son in fact mingles two kinds of stiff-neckedness, one that might be called Jewish, the other, perhaps, classically English—for in the end, it seems, he is more disturbed by the son's crossing of class borders than he is by his departure from the fold:

> "That eldest boy of mine, he's no longer my son— . . . I had a servant girl here working in my house, a Christian serving girl—and he married her behind my back. He asks me to sit down to meat with a girl, a Christian girl, who worked in my house—I can't do it. . . . Times change: I might have received his wife, even though she was a Goy. But a servant girl who washed my dishes! I couldn't do it. One must have some dignity."
>
> He stood there upright, stern, noble: a battered scarred old rock, but immovable under his seedy black coat. I couldn't offer him a shilling; I shook his hand, and left him brooding over his son and his graves. (17–18)

Thus the story ends, contradicting some of its earlier elements: the point of view has changed, a piece of the frame has dropped out—the last words, without quotation marks, belong to the second Jew rather than the initial narrator—and what had seemed ludicrous now appears sublime. The incongruous English Jew is a figure of biblical pathos, and assimilation, represented up to now as an inevitably failing gambit, the performance of a monkey in a top hat, appears as a tragedy. The description seems unambivalent; the characterization derives from Sholem Aleichem rather than a proto-Nazi textbook. But this Tevye, rooted in his eternal displacement, recalls the specifically displaced previous narrators; the story, after all, is about "Three Jews." The title lumps them together, even as each is at pains to distinguish himself from the next, and the ending signals a fading out in two directions: the loss of distinctive Jewishness in intermarriage (and the inevitably non-Jewish offspring), and the loss of distinction the first narrator undergoes through seeing himself in the other.

The recognition, after all, is mutual: the grotesque Jewish businessman gravitates to the narrator's tea-table even as the latter labels him Other. They speak the same language, though each notes the "distinctive Jewish speech" of the next man. Therein lies the story's irony: the very distinctions that the first Jew notes in the second, the second in the third, would be noticed by a fourth in the first; not even the most assimilated is exempt.

That the word "distinction" has a particular English connotation, one that will never apply to these three figures, is the tragic irony of Anglo-Jewish identity. Leonard Woolf could never be "distinguished"—wherein precisely lay his attraction for Virginia Stephen, whose hand is in this text as in the whole slim volume. Virginia, in fact, set the type for the story of a Jew marrying a "Goy"; it was her first typesetting venture and resulted in some quirky errors, mostly in punctuation and spacing. The last line of the story is half-effaced by a sloppily printed woodcut, one of three illustrations commissioned for the volume from the painter Dora Carrington. The story is thereby given an additional valence, for Carrington, like Virginia, had a fraught alliance with a Jew. Her much-documented relationship with Mark Gertler (possibly alluded to in the grave-keeper's reference to his faithful, second son, a painter?) ended in a breakup, supposedly because his sexual demands were too much for her, conceivably also because they combined with his East End background and notorious unwashedness to make him seem deeply alien.

The shadowy textual presence of Mark Gertler highlights the issues of class, nationality, and religion that Leonard's story raises. Gertler belonged to that group of Jewish immigrants who were simultaneously seen as an embarrassment, and aggressively cultivated and Anglicized, by the more prosperous, more rooted and more "Western" British Jews whose own continuing acceptance depended upon "civilizing" the recent arrivals.[22] Yet he came late enough, with the great influx of the last two decades of the nineteenth century, to belong to that generation which changed the profile of

English Jewry and exposed its paradoxes: ten years younger than Leonard Woolf, he grew up in squalid East End poverty, speaking Yiddish, unashamed of his background—yet nonetheless wishing to escape it for airier, brighter spaces in which he might cultivate a modernist art. He never rejected his class or his family, though he did leave his religion behind; his Orthodox parents, like the grave-keeper in Leonard's story, were surprisingly tolerant—indeed, proud—of a son whose vocation violated the biblical law against creating images.

This universal desire for escape, which constitutes a fundamental trope of early English modernism—escape from parents, forefathers, British philistinism, traditional realism—informing the rebellious outcries of Carrington as well as Gertler, Virginia as well as Leonard, represents both the suture and the split between "Three Jews" and "The Mark on the Wall." Insofar as Leonard's English Tevye seems finally to reject his new daughter-in-law on the basis of class rather than religion, he aligns himself, however unconsciously and coincidentally, with English values: class values *both* Leonard and Virginia consciously rejected even as their lives and livings depended upon them. The dependence was somewhat different in the two cases, however: Virginia, as the next chapter will note, relied on others' service for her own creative freedom—and sometimes just shied clear of including Leonard in the servant category: "Poor devil," she wrote flippantly to her friend Jacques Raverat in 1923, "I make him pay for his unfortunate mistake in being born a Jew by discharging the whole business of life. This induces in me a sense of the transitoriness of existence, and the unreality of matter, which is highly congenial and comfortable" (L 3:58). That Leonard's psychic comfort also depended upon class-consciousness is underscored by Virginia's remark. Ironically, it was precisely such prejudices as hers against which his own snobbery was erected, in order to align him with English insiders rather than immigrant newcomers; yet his position as potential target of these prejudices helps explain his deeply principled egalitarianism. This lifelong stance comprehended the realms of gender, economic, and imperial relations; if, when it came to the relations between Jews and the Gentile majority, he was ambivalent and ultimately passive, perhaps he may be forgiven, considering the double bind of Anglo-Jewish identity and the aversions of those he most loved and admired.[23]

But Virginia Woolf's remark about confining Leonard to "business" while she pursues her fantasies casts light on more than the failings that formally characterize and thematically inhabit Leonard's story of closed possibilities; it also elucidates the contradictions inherent in Virginia's early modernist experiments, superficially universalist in ethos yet undergirded (and, to a critical eye, undercut) by a form of deeply rooted particularism. "The Mark on the Wall" echoes the structure of "Three Jews" in containing three encounters; each is a frustrating convergence between a narrator desiring complete freedom and some other figure or figures, real or imaginary, trying to impose confinement. Like the indecorous shatterings and willful obscurities Woolf attributes to Messrs. Joyce and Eliot—though not, curiously, to herself—in "Mr. Bennett and Mrs. Brown," the demonization of those jailers and the textual meanderings that seem intended to confound them arise from a counterreaction that energizes her early prose. Hermione Lee cites a 1930 letter to Ethel Smyth in which Virginia describes her early experimental work during her long illnesses of the early teens:

> I used to make up stories, profound and to me inspired phrases all day long as I lay in bed, and thus sketched, I think, all that I now, by the light of reason, try to put into prose (I thought of the Lighthouse then, and Kew and others, *not in substance but in idea*)—after all this, when I came to, I was so tremblingly afraid of my own insanity that I wrote Night and Day mainly to prove to my own satisfaction that I could keep entirely off that dangerous ground. I wrote it, lying in bed, allowed to write only for one half hour a day. . . . I shall never forget the day I wrote The Mark on the Wall—all in a flash, after being kept stone breaking for months. The Unwritten Novel was the great discovery, however. That—again in one second—showed me how I could embody all my deposit of experience in a shape that fitted it. . . . I saw . . . when I discovered that method of approach, Jacobs Room, Mrs. Dalloway etc—How I trembled with excitement; and then Leonard came in, and I drank my milk, and concealed my excitement, and wrote I suppose another page of that interminable Night and Day (which some say is my best book). (*L* 4:231; in Lee, *Virginia Woolf* 370; italics mine)

The structure of confinement—the body in bed, the mind constrained to function on traditional lines—pierced through by flights of imagination is a founding trope of the early fiction. It is a dialectic that works through the later fictions in ever subtler, more formally complex *and* sociologically astute fashion: as Woolf grows more and more alert to social conditions and prejudices, she seams the material and the metaphysical more closely, illuminating their interdependence. The sickbed was a prison, which paradoxically liberated her fancies.[24] This was the case in an extreme sense during her long illness of 1913–1915; for the rest of her life, briefer stints in bed would function as periods of fertilization, during which Leonard, nursing her, would appear less as warden, more as nurturer. But in the early fictions, written, as it were, straight from the prisoning bed and the recent experience of young womanhood as itself an imprisonment, the ambivalence is more intense. It shows itself in her conception of character, whose development can be traced through "The Mark on the Wall" to "Mr. Bennett and Mrs. Brown" to *Mrs. Dalloway*, in which compassion toward the ill-treated mental sufferer is at last diametrically balanced with a condemnation of social villainy.

From the start, Woolf's modernism was based on the idea of character, bound up with questions of empathy, of the precise distance between self and other. Thomas Caramagno describes the process both critics and therapists must undergo to comprehend texts or symptoms that elude their conventional notions of order—a process of understanding, and liberating themselves from, their own countertransference: "What is essential, in understanding both literature and manic-depressive illness, is the ability to open oneself up to experiences, reactions, emotions, and ideas that do not slavishly reinforce our defensive, narrow, entrenched strategies for coping with self-world transactions" (*The Flight of the Mind* 76). It is a process Woolf herself underwent in the early modernist experiments, with an important difference: rather than seeking authorization and reinforcement, she strove vehemently *against* all figures who might represent such authority—so vehemently that she came close, at times, to reincorporating the exclusivist attitudes they represented.

This fraught paradox of liberation founded on enclosure, rebellion compromised by resentment, animates the two texts in one volume that together signal three important developments: the incorporation of "the Woolves" as a working team, the ultimate demise of Leonard's fictional enterprise, and the launching point of Virginia's bold literary experiments.[25] The founding of the Hogarth Press freed Virginia to write what she chose, as she chose—and "The Mark on the Wall" is a chronicle of that liberation. It sits oddly next to Leonard's story of essentialism and entrapment, and challenges the reader's capacity for maintaining tension in the face of seeming breakdown[26]—thus mimicking the very challenge Woolf was facing in the early fiction. Again, Caramagno's discussion of Woolf's anti-countertransference illuminates both her development and the stance required of the reader of the Woolves' only dually (but not co-) authored volume:

> Can we . . . possibly read what the writer writes? Woolf thought we could, if, paradoxically, we tolerated disorder while detecting patterns; by combining disorder and pattern . . . we might see something new. What, exactly, would that new thing be? It doesn't matter, just as long as we start seeing what previously could not be seen, the *différance* of the text, the voice of the Other, which urges us to question every assumption we hold sacred. . . . (*The Flight of the Mind* 86)

The voice of the Other does not inhabit "The Mark on the Wall," which is, in a sense, a univocal text. But it is also a text of *différance* par excellence, in which the principle is never to mark, always to see—and always to see differently. The narrator, who never leaves her chair during the story,

builds her defiantly senseless narrative around a mark on the wall, a kind
of Rorschach blot, which is neither one thing nor the other but whatever
the narrator (and, implicitly, the reader) wishes it to be. This is the principle
and the plot of the narrative, in whose course various conclusions—definitive ideas—are rejected in favor of inconclusion. The other persons who
appear in the story are engaged, it seems, solely to embody those rejected
notions: first, the former inhabitants of the room, a wife and a husband
met so fleetingly as to make clear that we are not in the realm of realism—
"he was in the process of saying that in his opinion art should have ideas
behind it when we were torn asunder, as one is torn from the old lady about
to pour out tea and the young man about to hit the tennis ball in the back
garden of the suburban villa as one rushes past in the train" (20); second,
a "house-keeper, a woman with the profile of a police-man . . . [who] talks
always of art . . . [who comes] nearer and nearer" until she nearly compels
the narrator to get up and examine the mark on the wall—"But no. I refuse
to be beaten. I will not move. I will not recognise her" (22); and third, an
imagined group of people in a room, who spawn elaborate reflections:

> "And then I came into the room. . . . [I]t is curious how instinctively one pro-
> tects the image of oneself from idolatry or any other handling that could make
> it ridiculous, or too unlike the original to be believed in any longer. . . . It is
> a matter of great importance. Suppose the looking glass smashes, the image
> disappears, and the romantic figure with the green of forest depths all about
> it is there no longer, but only that shell of a person which is seen by other
> people—what an airless, shallow, bald, prominent world it becomes! A world
> not to be lived in. As we face each other in omnibuses and underground
> railways we are looking in the mirror; that accounts for the expression in our
> vague and almost glassy eyes. And the novelists in future will realise more and
> more the importance of these reflections, for of course there is not one
> reflection but an almost infinite number; those are the depths they will
> explore, those the phantoms they will pursue, leaving the description of reality
> more and more out of their stories . . . but these generalisations are very
> worthless. . . . Generalisations bring back somehow Sunday in London,
> Sunday afternoon walks, Sunday luncheons. . . . How shocking and yet how
> wonderful it was to discover that these real things, Sunday luncheons, Sunday
> walks . . . were not entirely real, were indeed half phantoms, and the damnation
> which visited the disbeliever in them was only a sense of illegitimate freedom."
> (24–25)

Talking to herself, the narrator addresses in this one long passage both
the socio-/psychological questions of Leonard's story and the ideas of intersubjectivity that will inform all Virginia Woolf's further work. The conventions of the Sunday afternoon walk, so stultifying, so dictatorial, and
yet so easily dispensed with, mark the boundary between Leonard's identity

and Virginia's; from here on in, that boundary will also define the progress of their respective careers. For Leonard, the convention was not so easily rendered unreal: recognition of the customs of the Christian sabbath was the price he paid for admission in non-Jewish society. Had he denied the substantiality of those customs, he would have been ghettoized, reconfined, as it were, to the soot and chimney pots his narrator flees at the start of "Three Jews." For all their worldliness and bohemianism, his set were also parochial—parochial, indeed, in the name of worldliness. It is this conflict between the imposition of one's own vision on others and the validation of another's mode that defines the narrator's mental convolutions in "The Mark on the Wall." Trying to find her way between definition and discovery, she is not yet comfortable in the realm of intersubjective relations; seeking freedom, she paradoxically confines herself to a room, an inanimate sign, and a misanthropy arising from *fear* of confinement. Others disturb her because they raise questions about the relation between narcissism and mutual understanding, prejudice and self-realization. Encounters are dangerous because the other so often sees us as a shell, a mere projection of his or her own fears and preconceptions. Not to engage with others, however, is to elude the self—to elude, also, the moral and political questions so pressing in a society that defines most encounters between people as encounters between *types*, either harmonious (because homogenous) or hierarchical (because incongruous). In this instance, the narrator settles for a tree, advancing from the inanimate stain to an organic object with which, in an almost ludicrously beautiful final fancy, she intensely empathizes, imagining the feel of cold, the song of birds, the feet of insects, from the tree's point of view. It is an engagement that falls short of activism; but the final moment of the story, with the sudden intrusion of a second presence, begins to imagine an affirmative relation toward an Other that will be elaborated and complicated in Woolf's work henceforth:

> Where was I? What has it all been about? A tree? . . . I can't remember a thing. Everything's moving, falling, slipping, vanishing. There is a vast upheaval of matter. Someone is standing over me and saying—
> "I'm going out to buy a newspaper."
> "Yes?." (30)

Thus the story ends, having raised a complex set of questions about the relations between character and "reflection," with the latter word punningly deployed to suggest the ways in which two beings can either glassily refract or thoughtfully illuminate each other. The intruding presence in the final paragraphs, which both stanches overwhelming flux and suggests future possibilities, might be that of a husband. Both Leonard and Virginia seem to inhabit their respective narrators; both stories are intensely personal, chronicles of decision, and the figure who leaves the room for the world of action and headlines suggests Leonard himself, leaving behind the fiction-writing venture in favor of an engagement with the real world that might lead to real change, if not for English Jews specifically, then for all those oppressed by conventions and hierarchies.[27] The figure who remains in the room, half-denying, half-answering the voice of the Other, is the narrator/writer who will favor, more and more, a starting point of stability-in-flux. Already in this story, and wholeheartedly in "An Unwritten Novel" and "Mr. Bennett and Mrs. Brown," Woolf employs the metaphor of vehicular travel as a way of conceiving character: face-to-face in a railway carriage, author and character partake of one another; if the author, ultimately, is the one who *creates* character, and is thus hierarchically in a position of power, the idea of movement past an ever-changing landscape and the image of two people in the same carriage[28] is a corrective reminder that we're all, for better or worse, in it together.[29]

On this recognition, Virginia Woolf's future fictions were founded. The limits of her capacity to empathize and equalize define her early prose experiments as much as the ideal of free travel fuels them. No terrain is undemarcated, and Woolf's attitude toward character—like her attitude toward Others—negotiates between the desire to liberate trapped souls and a tendency to redraw the lines of engagement. Snobbery is in almost mortal conflict with the ideal of empathy, making for a particularly turbulent train journey for narrator and character in "An Unwritten Novel," the story that most clearly adumbrates the narrative and theory of "Mr. Bennett and Mrs. Brown." Acutely observing the woman opposite, the narrator realizes time and again that the watcher is also watched, also in danger of construction and misconstruction. To take another's life in one's own hands is potentially an act of hubris. Yet the imagining of that other life is also the supreme act of social empathy; in a sense, all our lives depend on the capacity of others to imagine us. The story plays ceaselessly with this idea, moving beyond the endless play of "A Mark on the Wall" by carrying fantasy out of the compartment of one brain and into another. That crossing rebounds, however, with the narrator's recognition that all such games are determined by the self's preconceptions; the ending of the story is a surprise and a lesson, as the narrator learns that "her" "old woman opposite" is really quite a different character from the one she'd imagined all along. The story concludes, however, with a new beginning, as the narrator readjusts to her discovery. It is such perpetual new beginnings that from here on characterize Woolf's writing, in its refusal to draw character simply as caricature and its continual pursuit of what remains elusive. To mark, she realizes, is to kill the spirit.

The capacity for such ceaseless pursuit is a luxury that characterizes Woolf's modernism. From the point of view of her imaginative privilege, the author conceives herself as a transparent vehicle, conveying the dreams and desires of the disenfranchised to a readership privileged like herself. In "Mr. Bennett and Mrs. Brown," this relationship among author, character, and readers is made explicit, again via the metaphor of railway carriages: author and character occupy one carriage, with the readers next door. As Rachel Bowlby reminds us, carriages in that period had no corridors; they were entered from outside, not within, the train (*Feminist Destinations* 4). It is thus the author's responsibility to penetrate the dividing walls, a performance with profound social implications, and one that can be achieved only through an imaginary disembodiment.

But the author, as a social being, is never disembodied—this is the paradox of Virginia Woolf's empathy. "Mr. Bennett and Mrs. Brown" enshrines a new definition of character. The responsible, the imaginative, writer conveys character by conveying the world seen through that character's eyes, rather than describing the character as seen through her own (the writer's) eyes. The writer is a transparent eyeball, taking in another's vision without imposing her own. This is an impossible act, but one worth striving to achieve, and it is in such perpetual striving that Virginia Woolf's art of empathy succeeds. The counterpoint of failure and success is itself instructive. At one point in the essay, Woolf makes a surprising distinction: "[T]he men and women who began writing novels in 1910 or thereabouts," she tells her audience, "had this great difficulty to face—that there was no English novelist living from whom they could learn their business. Mr. Conrad is a Pole; which sets him apart, and makes him, however admirable, not very helpful" (*CE* 326).

Of all possible discriminations, surely this is the least legitimate.[30] Is not the lecture's central idea the importance of understanding and learning from those who are "set apart," through a valiant effort to penetrate differences? The insularity at work in such a statement is contradicted by many others; it was contradicted by Woolf's own marriage. In the essay "On Being Ill" (1930), she wrote, as so often, of the creative value in sickness, comparing it to a strange country: "In illness, with the police off duty . . . if at last we grasp the meaning, it is all the richer for having come to us sensually first . . . like some queer odor. Foreigners, to whom the tongue is strange, have us at a disadvantage. The Chinese must know the sound of *Antony and Cleopatra* better than we do" (*M* 19). Thus a Pole, it seems, especially one repatriated, eloquent in at least three tongues, using language all the more brilliantly for its late acquisition, could teach young English writers a great deal . . .

The Jew, unlike a true foreigner, was doubly stymied, both a part of and apart from the country that denied him the very acculturation it insisted upon. This dual vision hampered Leonard Woolf's autobiographical fiction, whereas Virginia Woolf's work, even when the subject matter was far from her own daily life, always arose from her unusual capacity to leave the self behind even when the self was speaking. ("When the self speaks to the self," asks the narrator of "An Unwritten Novel" near the end of the story, thus encapsulating its central questions about intersubjectivity, "who is speaking?") "I'm amphibious," Woolf wrote in a diary entry whose flow of fancies evokes the early fictions, "in bed & out of it" (*D* 3:40); able to inhabit two realms, she was never hobbled in either. But—and the conjunction is of utmost significance—she was a woman, neither schooled nor wanted for public action. Thus she became a deeply political writer of fiction and essays, while her husband turned to traditional genres of political writing: the tract, the history, the argument from hard facts. Between them, they shared contemplation and action, prejudice and understanding.

CHAPTER III

Links into Fences

And there is the girl behind the counter too—I would
as soon have her true history as the hundred and
fiftieth life of Napoleon or seventieth study of Keats
and his use of Miltonic inversion which old
Professor Z and his like are now inditing.
(*Virginia Woolf*, A Room of One's Own)

To expect us, whose minds . . . fly free at the end
of a short length of capital to tie ourselves down
again to that narrow plot of acquisitiveness
and desire is impossible.
(*Virginia Woolf*, "*Introductory Letter*," Life as
We Have Known It)

When one gave up seeing the beauty that clothed
things, this was the skeleton beneath.
(*Virginia Woolf*, The Voyage Out)

VIRGINIA WOOLF'S grand stream-of-consciousness debut was *Mrs. Dalloway*, the novel whose polyphonic style sweeps up characters, and readers, too, in an exhilarating flow of impressions. The famous web technique, linking the minds of disparate people, seems to defy barriers between subjectivities; indeed, the whole book seems founded upon Clarissa Dalloway's philosophy that the self is unbounded and inheres partly in other people, other things. "Odd affinities she had with people she had never spoken to, some woman in the street, some man behind a counter—even trees, even barns" (*MD* 153). The idea of affinity with a barn, though not unthinkable, strikes such an absurd note that the appended clause calls the first one into question. And indeed, as I will argue, Woolf means her web to be a paradox, in which the links are the very things that divide. One can talk across a counter; one can never communicate—if by communication we understand an authentic exchange. The high-society hostess's "affinity" is a fiction; the gossamer web belies an iron grid, the skeleton of class division beneath the novel's fabric.[1] This novel about a conservative woman of the English upper class, who engages the reader's sympathies by the vivacity of her imagination and the wholeheartedness, if not always the warmth, of her relationships with friends, family, and servants alike, suggests that egalitarian wishful thinking is just that—thinking, not action, a form of passivity enforced by inescapable social structures.

Since 1913, at least, Woolf had been thinking in political terms about issues of social class. That year she accompanied Leonard to a congress of the Women's Co-operative Guild in Newcastle and was much impressed—and alienated—by the assembly of working-class women ascending one after another "like marksmen" to the podium to voice their political concerns and demands. In 1914, during her recovery from a nervous breakdown, she distracted herself by reading Co-operative manuals, and from 1916 on she ran the Richmond branch of the Guild. In 1931, the Hogarth Press published *Life as We Have Known It*, a volume of short autobiographies by working women, collected by Margaret Llewelyn Davies, the Woolfs' good friend and general secretary of the Guild for many years. Virginia Woolf wrote the "Introductory Letter," addressed to Davies, which is now well-known to most Woolf scholars but bears a closer examination than it has yet received. Although it was written five years after *Mrs. Dalloway* appeared, it chronicles observations harbored over seventeen years and helps elucidate how, in fact, Woolf's first "major" novel enacts her stated intention to "criticise the social system" by "showing it at work, at its most intense."

Woolf's introduction to *Life as We Have Known It* is deeply affecting in its concern for the women described, but above all in its relentless honesty about the unbridgeable distance between herself and them, even the hostility she feels toward these stolid, angry, "half-articulate" women. The essay is also a narrative of the distance Woolf has traveled between 1913 and 1931, and by its end one feels that, paradoxically, in exposing her alienation, she has come somewhat closer to the lives and emotions of the authors of these memoirs. The voyage from alienation to greater sympathy and solidarity is registered in various ways, including the abandonment of the martial imagery with which she initially describes the women's ascent to the podium, and the subtle recognition that their "stiff" postures are the sign, not of unimaginative militancy, but simply of overworked bodies. Despite these realizations, it remains clear to Woolf that the ladder of social class permits little real exchange between herself and them.

In *Mrs. Dalloway*, the imagery of horizontal motion represents vertical stasis. It is a novel full of vehicles, perambulations, threads; more often than not, the vehicles are stalled, crossings are interrupted, threads snap. These disengagements in part suggest what we today would call the "glass ceiling"; while vertical motion, in the increasingly capitalist economy of postwar England, may have seemed a given—thus Septimus Warren Smith has left a working-class home to rise in an office, and Sally Seton's industrialist husband has shaken off his beginnings as a miner's son—the rags-to-riches plot is largely a fiction. Sir William Bradshaw, the symbolic police-man of this economy, exposes that fiction with his chilling talk of propor-tion. When his patients think of suicide, Sir William "replied that life was good. Certainly Lady Bradshaw in ostrich feathers hung over the mantel-piece, and as for his income it was quite twelve thousand a year. But to us, they protested, life had given no such bounty. He acquiesced. They lacked a sense of proportion" (101).

If Dr. Bradshaw is the guardian of the narrow plot behind the fiction of upward mobility, Septimus Warren Smith is the prisoner of that plot. The narrator first introduces him as "Septimus Warren Smith, who found him-self unable to pass" (14); ironically, the ambulance that carries his corpse away near the end of the book *is* allowed to pass, prompting Peter Walsh to consider "the triumph of civilisation . . . the efficiency, the organisation, the communal spirit of London" (151). The communal spirit, as always, has asserted itself too late; the passing ambulance, which briefly links Septi-mus to Peter, is an echo of the royal or ministerial motorcar that initially connected him to Clarissa in the central of three sentences—"Mrs. Dallo-way, coming to the window with her arms full of sweet peas, looked out with her little pink face pursed in enquiry. Everyone looked at the motor car. Septimus looked." (15)—only to symbolize disconnection: for the car, like the area railings onto which Septimus will suicidally plunge, and like the "low, grey, powerful car" of Dr. Bradshaw that it anticipates, represents a social system based on the power of property. Between Septimus and Cla-rissa, too, is the pane of that window which, like the French doors at Bour-ton through which she never *really* plunged, preserves and protects her life of privilege—and, ultimately, ignorance.[2]

Septimus's grisly death has multiple resonances, all of them painfully ironic. The word "railings" itself suggests Smith's own ineffectual ravings about universal love: " 'Communication is health; communication is happi-ness, communication—' "—the sentence is broken by a dash, as communi-cation is cut by a fence. That fence enforces proportion, acting as an imper-meable border between plots—land plots and story plots, the delineated properties of neighbors and the life stories of rich and poor—and precipi-tating Septimus to that narrowest of all plots, his grave. The railings recall, too, a phrase with which an impersonal voice designates Septimus in a description Alex Zwerdling describes as an "almost clinical scrutiny—as pitiless in tone as a medical report not designed for the patient's eye" (*Vir-ginia Woolf and the Real World* 90):

> To look at, he might have been a clerk, but of the better sort; for he wore
> brown boots; his hands were educated; so, too, his profile—his angular, big-
> nosed, intelligent, sensitive profile; but not his lips altogether, for they were

loose; and his eyes (as eyes tend to be), eyes merely; hazel, large; so that he was, on the whole, *a border case*, neither one thing nor the other; might end with a house at Purley and a motor car, or continue renting apartments in back streets all his life; one of those half-educated, self-educated men whose education is all learnt from books borrowed from public libraries, read in the evening after a day's work, on the advice of well-known authors consulted by letter. (84; italics mine)[3]

"Border case": the phrase bears considerable weight. The Bradshavian second term evokes both criminology and medicine, implying, on the one hand, threatening deviance; on the other, an easily categorized, containable scientific "specimen."[4] "Border" has a similar double resonance: interpretation rests on the question of whether Septimus is *on* a border or *in* it. Does it mean a narrow space outside the dominant plot, like the border of a page, the grass around a building, or the "shore of the world" on which Septimus is said, at one point, to lie? Or does it denote a middle ground, as the next phrase, "neither one thing nor the other," would suggest? To be "neither one thing nor the other" is also, of course, to be both one thing *and* the other—for how can one inhabit a border without, in fact, having one foot on either side? Such an image would imply possibility, even fertility, rather than limitation; but Septimus's end, his body pierced by an iron border, counters that vision. This harrowing paradox—Septimus's potential as his destruction—is encompassed in his "scientific" perception of himself, earlier in the novel:

His body was macerated until only the nerve fibres were left. It was spread like a veil upon a rock. . . . He lay very high, on the back of the world. The earth thrilled beneath him. Red flowers grew through his flesh; their stiff leaves rustled by his head. (68)

Septimus is already living his death: the "back" of the world is a precarious spine (evocative of Clarissa Dalloway's rigid backbone), and the flowers (poppies of Flanders? Clarissa's roses?) foreshadow the bloody spears of the area fence; the stiff leaves, the railings that will surround him.

The word "railings" first occurs in connection with Evans, Septimus's lost war comrade. Hallucinating in the park, Septimus sees "white things . . . assembling behind the railings opposite. . . . Evans was behind the railing!" (25) It is the loss of Evans—another victim of territorial rapacity, the rapacity of war—that is behind Septimus's railings, the desperate desire to recover him that prompts them; the last mention of Evans occurs minutes before Septimus's death, as he sits facing a screen, trying to recapture vision. "Where he had once seen mountains, where he had seen faces, where he had seen beauty, there was a screen. . . . 'Evans!' he cried. There was no answer" (145). Seeking communication, perhaps (but also, spitefully, to punish his doctors Holmes and Bradshaw with the very melodrama their bounded brains conceive), he hurls himself at a barrier—and is impaled upon it.

In addition to the railing and the screen, the text contains numerous other images of Septimus blocked off from sounds, sights, other living beings—hopelessly encased. Another example of blockage occurs in the description of Lady Bradshaw waiting for her husband in the car, "thinking sometimes of the patient, sometimes, excusably, of the wall of gold that was mounting between them and all shifts and anxieties" (94). Shifts and anxieties are, of course, among other things what Bradshaw's patients suffer from; the money he takes from them is the bar to his compassion; in short, he extracts payment for their imprisonment in "*my* homes, Mr. Warren Smith" (97). Snobbery and greed, or "Class and Money," as Alex Zwerdling entitles a chapter in *Virginia Woolf and the Real World*, throw up the screens that halt communication; Septimus's speech is mere railing *because* Bradshaw and his like have "shut [him] up" (102). ("He shut people up," the narrator declares, foreshadowing Woolf's description of the fascist dictator in *Three Guineas*.)

Both Zwerdling, in the social context, and Caramagno in that of psychology, quote the striking passage from Woolf's diary in which she uses the image of a screen to denote class alienation:

> Two resolute, sunburnt, dusty girls, in jerseys & short skirts, with packs on their backs, city clerks, or secretaries, tramping along the road in the hot sunshine at Ripe. My instinct at once throws up a screen, which condemns them: I think them in every way angular, awkward & self assertive. But all this is a great mistake. These screens shut me out. Have no screens, for screens are made out of our own integument; & get at the thing itself, which has nothing in common with a screen. The screen making habit, though, is so universal, that probably it preserves our sanity. If we had not this device for shutting people off from our sympathies, we might, perhaps, dissolve utterly. Separateness would be impossible. But the screens are in the excess; not the sympathy. (*D* 3:104)

This passage comprehends profound social and psychological issues. Among other things, it suggests that Septimus Warren Smith is damned both ways: at times his screens dissolve, and he loses the ego boundaries that might preserve him from engulfment; at others those very boundaries (his "integument") render him tragically isolated from fellow human beings and cut off even from himself.[5] The very notion that screens are made of "our own integument" suggests self-alienation, for if we are surrounded in rind, then our senses don't meet our inner selves, and the entity we call "I" is merely that middle ground, a "border" space, where neither self nor other is truly felt. Woolf's seemingly illogical grammar in the second sentence supports this vision of self-alienation, by making the screen the agent of condemnation: the shell has taken over the functions of subjectivity.

More than one critic has noted the frequent cutting imagery in *Mrs. Dalloway*, and feminist analysis often focuses on Peter Walsh's knife as a phallic weapon. That Peter, who loved Clarissa in her youth, is a pursuer of women, and that his purported desire for mental interpenetration sometimes conceals a darker impulse to cross into Clarissa's mind and annex it, is indisputable; justice, however, requires that we reconsider both Peter's knife and Clarissa's nunlike self-preservation in the light of Woolf's theory of screens. My reading treads the ground between earlier denotations of Clarissa as frigid and feminist celebrations of her mental chastity: her relationship with Peter, as well as her tendency to "contraction" and martial "stiffness," consistently suggest an inclination toward "cutting off" rather than connecting, and weight her vaunted capacity to be in two places at once[6] ("She sliced like a knife through everything; at the same time was outside, looking on") more heavily on the side of detachment. Clarissa herself reflects that "she lacked . . . something central which permeated; something warm which broke up surfaces" (31). Peter links this "coldness" (8, 80) with her "conventionality" (49)—always a bugaboo in Virginia Woolf's vocabulary—and that in turn with the proprietary impulse that makes her call her daughter "my Elizabeth" (in something of the spirit, perhaps, that informs Bradshaw's "*my* homes"). Thus Peter's knife-play (which Clarissa, tellingly, associates with his "silly unconventionality") is not merely aggressive but also suggests the desire to slice past integument, to be rid of screens—as when, at Clarissa's party, he disagrees with Sally Rossiter's rather clichéd observation that "we [are] all prisoners":

> She had read a wonderful play about a man who scratched on the wall of his cell, and she had felt that was true of human life—one scratched on the wall. Despairing of human relationships (people were so difficult), she often went into her garden and got from her flowers a peace which men and women never gave her. But no; he did not like cabbages; he preferred human beings, Peter said. . . . Peter did not agree that we know nothing. We know everything, he said; at least he did. (193)

This light philosophical exchange masks a moral content, for Sally's preference for cabbages over people echoes Clarissa's greater interest in roses ("the only flowers she could *bear to see* cut" [120; italics mine]) than in massacred Armenians. Indeed, between the effeteness and moral reprehensibility of such a trivializing attitude, and the telling evocation of a screening image—Clarissa closing her eyes against others' suffering—Mrs. Dalloway, for the moment at least, loses much of her authority as a representative of human connection. Nor is this the only such moment;

"he made her feel the fun," her famous interior declaration at the news of an unknown young man's suicide, seems to me a phrase far more condemning of Clarissa (on Woolf's part, consciously or unconsciously) than many critics maintain.

Peter's pocketknife, like so many of the novel's metonymies, thus becomes a symbol of desired communication as well as one of sharp division. In the scene where that knife is parried by Clarissa's needle as she sits sewing, Woolf choreographs the battle in a perfect, chiasmic balance: for the needle, used to heal rifts, also stands for its wielder's prickly integument.[7] Taken together with her continual stiffness of posture, it compels us to wonder whose stance is the more phallic. Interrupting Clarissa's erotic colloquy with Sally Seton at Bourton, Peter had been "like a granite wall" (36); equally painful, however, is Peter's memory of the moment Clarissa rejected him: "She seemed contracted, petrified. . . . He felt that he was grinding against something physically hard; she was unyielding. She was like iron, like flint, rigid up the backbone" (64). This ramrod spine divides her down the middle, preventing internal as well as external communion— or, as Zwerdling puts it, conceiving her division as horizontal and multiple rather than vertical and singular: "Clarissa's is essentially a laminated personality, made up of distinct layers that do not interpenetrate" (139).

Shutting his pocketknife on the street after his midday visit to Clarissa, Peter finds himself at a curb—"Here he was at a crossing" (80)—where, ironically, his ruminations on women's lack of passion are interrupted by the passionate song of the vagrant woman at the mouth of the subway. Like this and other moments and images of intersection in the novel, Peter and Clarissa's crossed swords point to the questions of class that Woolf deals with in her introduction to *Life as We Have Known It*. Both Peter's knife and Clarissa's needle, the wielding of which places her momentarily (and superficially) with the class of women who work for a living, recall the passage in which Woolf introduces a key concept, that of "fictitious" or "aesthetic" sympathy:

> [I]f it were possible to meet [the working classes] not as masters or mistresses or customers with a counter between us, but over the wash-tub or in the parlour casually and congenially as fellow-beings with the same wishes and ends in view, a great liberation would follow, and perhaps friendship and sympathy would supervene. . . . But, we said, and here perhaps fiddled with a paper knife, or poked the fire impatiently by way of expressing our discontent, what is the use of it all? (xxvii–xxviii)

Like Clarissa's sympathy for Septimus at the end of the novel, or her notion that she bears affinities to shopkeepers, this sympathy of the educated lady for the working class is "defective" (xxix). "It differs from real sympathy," Woolf writes, "because it is not based upon sharing the same important emotions unconsciously" (xxix). It is "the sympathy of the eye and of the imagination, not of the heart and of the nerves" (xxvi). Thus the fluid narrative form of *Mrs. Dalloway*, while seducing the reader into believing in the connection between Clarissa and Septimus, thinly masks rigid class boundaries. In turn, Woolf's own writing (metonymized, above, in the form of a paper knife) "detached" though it may seem, is founded on the work of others—just as Clarissa's party is founded on what takes place below stairs. Without servants, without her inherited income, Woolf's life would have been filled with the menial duties others performed for her.[8] The narrator's nervous knife-play arises from that recognition and, like Peter Walsh's, seems to have a double valence: the desire to ward off and the desire to cut through.

The horizontal counter invoked in the "Introductory Letter" and in Clarissa's reflections on affinity, though a locus of exchange, in fact signifies hierarchy, differentiating even as it links. Clarissa could achieve a true "affinity" with the shopkeeper only if she were to take his place (a substitution the tutor Miss Kilman fervently imagines: "With all this luxury going on, what hope was there for a better state of things? Instead of lying on a sofa . . . she should have been in a factory; behind a counter . . . " [124]). As for washtubs and parlors, these, of course, are where people of the same class meet; it hardly needs noting that Clarissa's party includes no one of the working class, and almost no one from the middle class. Even the supposed bohemians—Sir Harry, whose "bad pictures . . . were always of cattle" (175); Jim Hutton, "a very bad poet" (176)—are inferior artists, as if to uphold a class allegiance that good art might call into question. But the arbitrariness of class, its complete disjunction from character, appearance, or bearing, is emphasized by a sentence about the prime minister: "You might have stood him *behind a counter* and bought biscuits—poor chap, all rigged up in gold lace" (172; italics mine). The important difference between the prime minister and a shopkeeper is, however, enforced a line or two later in a phrase denoting the former as "majesty passing" (172)—a direct echo from early in the book, and a reminder that the shopkeeper is trapped behind his counter while the customer can enter and exit freely. The prime minister's free movement, "rigged up" as he is, is precisely what inhibits *true* fluidity, for passing majesty is, to the party guests, a "symbol of what they all *stood for*, English society" (172; italics mine)—the symbol, in other words, of that society's stasis. But the participle bears a double meaning, for majesty is also passing away, to be superseded by new forms of government.

Though Clarissa's party is undergirded, even largely orchestrated, by servants from the basement, the upper rooms allow no place for their class (the fact that Septimus "plunges" from his window, while Clarissa can stand serenely at hers contemplating the Bradshaws' description of his death drives this home with tragic force). Through Clarissa's fraudulent egalitarianism, Woolf gently mocks herself, the upper-crust, educated lady pursing her face in inquiry at the Guild congress and practicing a mere fictitious sympathy. ("I am a benevolent spectator," Woolf writes. "I am irretrievably cut off from the actors. I sit here hypocritically clapping and stomping, an outcast from the flock" [19].) Indeed, sympathy at times gives way entirely to fictionalizing, or "scene-making," as Woolf called her irresistible writer's impulse in "A Sketch of the Past." Her portrayal of Miss Kidd, the secretary guarding the doors of the Guild offices, as a kind of strangely dressed human bulldog embodies her penchant for Dickensian caricature, a penchant she sometimes indulged at the expense of empathy:

> [O]ne could not enter and go upstairs without encountering Miss Kidd. Miss Kidd sat at her type-writer in the outer office. Miss Kidd, one felt, had set herself as a kind of watch-dog to ward off the meddlesome middle-class wasters of time who come prying into other people's business. Whether it was for this reason that she was dressed in a peculiar shade of deep purple I do not know. The colour seemed somehow symbolical. She was very short, but, owing to the weight which sat on her brow and the gloom which seemed to issue from her dress, she was also very heavy. An extra share of the world's grievances seemed to press upon her shoulders. When she clicked her typewriter one felt that she was making that instrument transmit messages of foreboding and ill-omen to an unheeding universe. But she relented, and like all relentings after gloom hers came with a sudden charm.[9] (xxiv)

But the "Introductory Letter" is also a narrative, one whose form resembles an allegory, at the end of which the narrator/protagonist has learned a lesson by passing through a series of doors. In the innermost room, figuratively the space of the working women's own lives, the caricature Miss Kidd turns into an all-too-human Miss Kidd; on the threshold of that room—at the end of her introduction, that is, before granting the reader passage into the actual memoirs—Woolf exposes the memory that lies behind the receptionist's purple integument:

> And then there is a fragment of a letter from Miss Kidd—the sombre purple figure who typed as if the weight of the world were on her shoulders. "When I was a girl of seventeen," she writes, "my then employer, a gentleman of good position and high standing in the town, sent me to his home one night, ostensibly to take a parcel of books, but really with a very different object. When I arrived at the house all the family were away, and before he would allow me to leave he forced me to yield to him. At eighteen I was a mother." Whether that is literature or not literature I do not presume to say, but that it explains

much and reveals much is certain. Such then was the burden that rested on that sombre figure as she sat typing your letters, such were the memories she brooded as she guarded your door with her grim and indomitable fidelity. (xxviii–xxix)

Certainly this story compels a revised comprehension of Miss Kidd's fervent gatekeeping and adds an extra poignancy to the "charm" of her earlier "relenting." Woolf presents a crossing within and between the two passages: in one, Miss Kidd guards a threshold; in the other, traumatic urtext, the threshold of her body is violated upon her passage through the door of an upper-class house. Her story suggests a brutal moral: that the crossing of class barriers can only be violent—just as the traversal of national borders is commonly an invasion of one country by another, as in the war that destroyed Septimus.[10]

But can there be a middle ground: a border that, instead of rending (or being rent by) the migrant, accommodates the peaceable meeting of two sides—even, perhaps, their mingling? In the introduction to *Life as We Have Known It*, that middle ground is represented architecturally as the central of three rooms, where the dialogue between Guild and outsiders occurs; whether, however, that room lets *equally* onto outside and inside, remains questionable. Having been granted safe passage by Miss Kidd, the narrator proceeds up a stair and encounters a second person, the middlewoman Miss Lillian Harris:

[A] very different figure . . . indeed, who, whether it was due to her dress which was coffee coloured, or to her smile which was serene, or to the ash-tray in which many cigarettes had come amiably to an end, seemed the image of detachment and equanimity. Had one not known that Miss Harris was to the Congress what the heart is to the remoter veins—that the great engine at Newcastle would not have thumped and throbbed without her—that she had collected and sorted and summoned and arranged that very intricate but orderly assembly of women—she would never have enlightened one. She had nothing whatever to do; she licked a few stamps and addressed a few envelopes—it was a fad of hers—that was what her manner conveyed. It was Miss Harris who moved the papers off the chairs and got the tea-cups out of the cupboard. It was she who answered questions about figures and put her hand on the right file of letters infallibly and sat listening, without saying very much, but with calm comprehension, to whatever was said. (xxiv–xxv)

Who is this odd, oddly attractive figure, Miss Harris? A hybrid, she seems, of the worker and the lady; hostess and servant (she receives, but she also tidies and arranges); Miss Kidd and Mrs. Dalloway. Her anteroom has the aura of a stage set, designed to convey the right combination of industry and leisure to the middle- or upper-class visitor who must not be put off, whose patronage, indeed, is highly desirable. She herself is an actress, conveying to the visitor an illusion of ease and comfort, transforming her office into a drawing room. Neither one thing nor another, she, and her space, seem self-fashioned for purposes of rhetorical seduction: for easing the passage from downstairs to up, from the outer organs to the intellectual repository of the Guild.

The fashioning, however, was Woolf's own fiction—wrung out of her, ironically, from a perceived need to mollify the *workers'* sensibilities. The "real" Miss Harris, undersecretary as well as companion to Margaret Llewellyn Davies, was a solid human figure who smoked a pipe and read detective novels; Mrs. Eleanor Barton, Davies's successor as general secretary, had censored these details in Woolf's earlier description of Harris, as well as certain physical descriptions of the women themselves. Davies had evidently supported this censorship, to which Woolf replied, in the first of at least two bemused letters:

> What rather appals me (I'm writing in a hurry . . . dont please take my words altogether literally) is the terrific conventionality of the workers. Thats why— if you want explanations—I dont think they will be poets or novelists for another hundred years or so. If they cant face the fact that Lillian smokes a pipe . . . and can't be told that they weigh on average 12 stone—which is largely because they scrub so hard and have so many children—and are shocked by the word "impure" how can you say that they face "reality"? (I never know what 'reality' means: but Lillian smoking a pipe to me is real, and Lillian merely coffee coloured and discreet is not nearly so real.) What depresses me is that the workers seem to have taken on all the middle class respectabilities which we—at any rate if we are any good at writing or painting—have faced and thrown out. . . . [I]t is that to my thinking that now makes the chief barrier between us. One has to be "sympathetic" and polite and therefore one is uneasy and insincere. And why, with such a chance to get rid of the conventionalities, do they cling to them? However . . . if you want me to make them sylphs I will. (*L* 4:228–29)

Aestheticization serves diplomacy in the anteroom, the space between readers and characters. We cannot know if the working women's objections had to do with vanity, suspicion of Woolf's stance toward them, or the image they wished to project to potential sympathizers; while Woolf questions their desire for prettification, a later letter to Davies makes clear, once again, her own inclination to fantasy. "I made too much of the literary side of my interest," she writes; "its partly a habit, through writing reviews for so many years. I tried to change the tone of some of the sentences, to suggest a more human outlook, and also, I brought in a few cigarettes in Lilians ash tray—do they matter? A little blue cloud of smoke seemed to me aesthetically desirable at that point" (*L* 4:287). In fact, no such cloud appears in the text; rather, the considerably less aesthetic cigarette butts suggest, as a corpse does, an earlier spiritual/ethereal presence. The metonymic ploy both reverses and obeys the process of beautification imposed on Woolf by the working women's wishes—the dead cigarettes substituted for the twelve-stone bodies of the women are no prettier but are meant to draw attention away from less appealing "realities." Here, as in "Mr. Bennett and Mrs. Brown," that theoretical essay on character written as Woolf was embodying her theories in *Mrs. Dalloway*, Woolf deals in creating corridors between character and readers; her method obeys the express wishes of the former and caters to the prejudices of the latter.

To cater is, of course, to play hostess—as does Mrs. Dalloway, as does Miss Harris, in the description that may or may not be true to life. Resenting this role at first, Woolf ends by embracing the middle ground, the blurring of fact and impression that, to her, constitutes the best politically committed stance for a writer who stands outside the lives she describes. Her final letter to Margaret Llewellyn Davies on the subject of the introduction stresses her gratitude to the working women who had written appreciative letters in response to it, and ruminates ultimately: "I doubt that I was the right person to make people interested in the womens stories, because if one is a writer by profession, one can't help being one. It would be far worse to pretend not to be" (*L* 4:341).[11]

Yet Lillian Harris's anteroom, and Woolf's compromise between mirroring and beautification in portraying that space, raise a question about middle ground, a locus in danger of neutralizing rather than cross-fertilizing opposing energies. Is the blue smoke dynamic, a conduit; or is it static, a smoke*screen* in the service of existing divisions? The workers, Woolf laments, have disarmed themselves by taking on the complacent, stultifying attitudes of the middle class. That very class, however, are described at the start of *Mrs. Dalloway* riding on top of omnibuses, the most powerful and visible moving vehicles in the novel, displacing the motorcars of obsolescent nobility—and thus, it would seem, heralding change rather than reinforcing stasis. Those middle classes with their symbol, the omnibus, bear a closer look: "with parcels and umbrellas, yes, even furs on a day like this . . . more ridiculous, more unlike anything there has ever been than one could conceive; and the Queen herself held up; the Queen herself unable to pass" (17). Clarissa, whose voice this is, belongs to the older, royal/feudal order, that hierarchy of land ownership being rendered obsolete, in 1923, by the steady growth of a commercial economy. This economy, despite its injustices, effects a blurring of lines that threatens Clarissa's way of life; as embodied in the omnibus, it represents a dynamic and inevitable forward movement and the stalling of rigid authoritarianism. If there is hope for the future—and Woolf, setting her novel only months before Labour was to take power, must have thought there was—that hope rides on the omnibus. Stopped only momentarily by the hand of the policeman, the omnibus, or one just like it, reappears late in the novel to carry off the next generation in the person of Clarissa's daughter Elizabeth Dalloway: "She took a seat on top. The impetuous creature—a pirate—started forward, sprang away" (note that "pirate" momentarily confuses passenger and bus, and the word's powerful suggestions of both liminality and class aggression)—"she had to hold the rail to steady herself, for a pirate it was, reckless, unscrupulous, bearing down ruthlessly, circumventing dangerously, boldly snatching a passenger, or ignoring a passenger, *squeezing eel-like and arrogant in between*, and then rushing insolently all sails spread up Whitehall" (135; italics mine).

Will this bold progress continue or be halted? Rachel Bowlby has written compellingly in *Feminist Destinations* on the question of Elizabeth's possible future—on whether she will break the bounds placed around her by class and gender, or assume her legacy as a marriageable upper-class woman and lose this rebellious energy. For the time being, she pivots indecisively, thinking less of destination than of vehicles: "Buses swooped, settled, were off—garish caravans, glistening with red and yellow varnish. But which should she get on to? She had no preferences" (135).[12] Momentarily, at least, she chooses flux, democracy: "She liked the geniality, sisterhood, motherhood, brotherhood of this uproar. It seemed to her good" (138)—and the imagery that follows her ride and accompanies her subsequent perambulations suggests a fertile inconclusiveness, a "neither one thing nor the other" that is all promise and no fixity: "this vow; this van; this life; this procession, would wrap [people] about and carry them on, as in the rough stream of a glacier the ice holds a splinter of bone, a blue petal, some oak trees, and rolls them on" (138). These images of solid objects caught and breaking into liquid flow carry on in Woolf's description of the sky's changing light:

> [A]lthough the clouds were of mountainous granite so that one could fancy hacking hard chips off with a hatchet, with broad golden slopes, lawns of celestial pleasure gardens, on their flanks, and had all the appearance of settled habitations assembled for the conference of gods above the world, there was a perpetual movement among them. Signs were interchanged, when, as if to fulfil some scheme arranged already, now a summit dwindled, now a whole block of pyramidal size which had kept its station inalterably advanced into the midst or gravely led the procession to fresh anchorage. Fixed though they seemed at their posts, at rest in perfect unanimity, nothing could be fresher, freer, more sensitive superficially than the snow-white or gold-kindled surface; to change, to go, to dismantle the solemn assemblage was immediately possible; and in spite of the grave fixity, the accumulated robustness and solidity, now they struck light to the earth, now darkness. (138–39)

No passage in *Mrs. Dalloway* is more political than this description of clouds. The imagery speaks for itself: everything is poised on the balance and could collapse back into stasis or move forward into new articulations. "Nothing is what it seems," as Woolf will later write in *Orlando*. *Between the Acts* is here anticipated, too, for this description takes place between two bus rides (and is allied with the bus "squeezing eel-like . . . in between"), the second of which will return Elizabeth to her home and her destiny. As in *Between the Acts*, everything rests on an interval; and that interval inevitably ends. Unlike the novel's many linking/separating metonymic objects—motorcar; knife; needle; counter—the interval represents a space in the grid rather than a piece *of* it.[13] Has that space brought new energy to the other side?

Elizabeth's appearance at the party, dressed in pink, the color associated with Clarissa's "contraction" and conservatism, the darling of her father ("it was his Elizabeth" [194], Richard thinks, suddenly recognizing the lovely young woman), suggests not. The escaped filly is corralled at novel's end; in whose hands, then—to borrow Peter Walsh's phrase[14]—does the future lie? Not, certainly, in the "great hand" of Miss Kilman, from whom Elizabeth has fled; that extremity, which endlessly opens and shuts over Cclairs at the Army-Navy Stores, signifies the faultiness of Kilman's socialism: at heart she is acquisitive, lusts after other people's parcels, and would rather switch roles than erase them.[15]

This question about the future leads, finally, to Lucrezia Warren Smith, the war bride from Italy, and her heterogeneous hats. Only in a work of art—and Rezia is the one real artist of the novel[16]—do disparate things come together. The "ribbons and beads, tassels, artifical flowers" and other effluvia from which Rezia composes her hats evoke the fluent clouds and cloud-icebergs of Elizabeth's walk; they also recall St. Margaret's "lap full of odds and ends, lap full of trifles" (128). These trifles are contrasted throughout the text with Big Ben's booming "bar of gold" (128), so that, by analogy, the artist Rezia becomes the opposite of the capitalist prison-warden Bradshaw. Most significant, St. Margaret's bells represent neither an interval nor an authoritative marker: they step forward again and again to ring changes on, and call into question, the voice of masculine authority; refusing to recede or be muted, theirs are the first notes of a future music.

Rezia's story, like the hat she'd begun before her husband's suicide, breaks off shortly after that terrible disruption. The reader feels compelled to wonder what may become of her when she awakens from her drug-induced reverie of stepping through long windows into a garden. That reverie, of course, is an echo of Clarissa's youthful memory in the opening paragraphs of the novel: the difference being that Rezia exits, while Clarissa never did. This suggests a possible new beginning; however, the actual window in Rezia's room was the launching pad for Septimus's suicide, and it is now obscured by the dark silhouette of the rapacious Dr. Holmes. The text has already hinted at Holmes's predatory interest in Rezia; alone and poor, her escape blocked by the doctor's body, she might well find herself in the position of Harriet Kidd on the threshold of her employer's home. If, like Miss Kidd, she were also to find herself pregnant, her dream of motherhood will have been as brutally and ironically fulfilled as were Septimus's dreams of reconnecting with Evans.

But Woolf, uninterested in retelling the ancient story of woman's fall (having told it for good in *The Voyage Out* and chosen a man literally to fall in *Mrs. Dalloway*),[17] leaves Rezia's plot open. She may still finish the hat. In that case, she'll make ends meet through hats for ladies with more money than herself, ladies who won't know to value her found objects as metonymies of the disparate human race. For though they may enjoy the product, its maker will remain behind a screen. Like Virginia's web, the artwork will present a unity as yet unattainable in real life.

Rezia's hat, finally, is a truer ideological analogue to the novel *Mrs. Dalloway* than is Clarissa's party. Like the novel, the hat represents its maker's attraction to aesthetic (and therefore upper-class) finery and her commitment to scattered remnants. In "Solid Objects," a short story first published in the *Atheneaum* in 1920, Woolf created a more admirable counterpart to Clarissa Dalloway, the self-encased lady who is less disturbed by the murder of Armenians than by the lopping of flowers. The story begins with two sturdy young men, college friends, perhaps, and presumably both well-off, arguing vehemently on a beach. Having ended the discussion by declaring, "Politics be damned!" (*CSF* 96), the young man called John burrows in the sand and comes up with a curious piece of glass. This moment spawns an obsession with the collection of found objects and a decreasing interest in politics. Having intended to stand for Parliament, John eventually abandons his political career and devotes himself entirely to his hobby. The story ends with a visit from his former friend, Charles, and a complete disjunction in understanding between the two men, now much older. Charles barely takes note of John's collection; he is appalled at the latter's hermitlike existence and ends by leaving John's flat, never to visit again.

Yet if John has abandoned his official political career, the "solid objects" he collects are invested by the narrator with a significance that cannot be divorced from politics—the social politics of class and gender. The objects are metonymies of the people who once owned them. They are not precious stones; on the contrary, they are discards, marginalia, discovered in "the neighborhood of waste land where the household refuse is thrown away," or in "one of those little *borders* of grass which edge the bases of vast legal buildings," and on "commons in the neighborhood of London" (98–99; italics mine). There is some lovely subversive punning here: "household refuse," for instance, suggests John's refusal of the Houses of Parliament, a favoring of "commons" over "Commons" or "Lords"; "edging the bases," a quiet nudging and unsettling of authority's center. John's objects represent society's border cases, excluded from that center and ignored by the powerful. Charles, who glances briefly at John's treasures and labels them "pretty stones," is the politician as power-monger—an upholder and worshiper of "divine Proportion, Sir William's goddess" (*MD* 99). That which defies categories—like John's treasures, neither objets d'art nor utensils—is beneath his notice.

But the dissolution of edges, the blurriness that prevents classification, is precisely what fascinates John from the start. The first object he finds, smoothed by the sea, edges the border of class: "[I]t was impossible to say whether it had been bottle, tumbler or window-pane; it was nothing but glass; it was almost a precious stone" (97). Like Rezia, he considers combining it with finer materials to make an ornament:

> You had only to enclose it in a rim of gold, or pierce it with a wire, and it became a jewel; part of a necklace, or a dull, green light upon a finger. Perhaps after all it was a gem; something worn by a dark Princess trailing her finger in the water as she sat in the stern of the boat and listened to slaves singing as they rowed her across the Bay. Or the oak sides of a sunk Elizabethan treasure-chest had split apart, and, rolled over and over, over and over, its emeralds had come at last to shore. (97)

The entire historical plot of exploitation and enslavement, of rapacity and division, upon which the social system of England in 1920 (or '23) was built is here encompassed or suggested. Through the softening of borders accomplished by nature, and the recombination of objects imagined by John, that plot may be revised. If not, finally, in John's (for he seems destined to remain a hermit, touching no one), or in Rezia's, or in Virginia Woolf's, in whose hands does that revision lie?

Tentatively, skeptically, with the most restrained optimism, *Life as We Have Known It* posits a linking of the privileged woman writer's hand with the hardened hands of working women. Both kinds of hands have wielded the pen to make this book, this assemblage of plots. Contrasting her leisured capacity to engage in fictions and abstractions with the workers' bondage to the material, Woolf writes: "No, they were not the least detached and easy and cosmopolitan. They were indigenous and rooted to one spot. Their very names were like the stones of the fields—common, grey, worn, obscure, docked of all splendours of association and romance" (xxii). Patronizing though that final sentence is, Woolf used her patronage to lift the stones from their undiscovered margins and present those women's names and words in a broader forum than the Newcastle convention. That strange hybrid of elegant prose opening into stories told simply, often ungrammatically, and utterly unfacetiously remains class-bound, dependent on a lady's openhandedness. But that lady's hands set type as well; and though this work, like Mrs. Dalloway's sewing, is purely elective, it was work in service of social change rather than static demarcation.[18]

Thus one might call the flow and tumble of Woolf's prose radical—in the sense that it unsettles roots to shift plots.[19] Woolf's own grounding in her class, however—and her honest acknowledgment of that grounding, and refusal to act the proletarian as she would later accuse the "leaning tower" poets of the thirties of doing—keep her aware of her fictions. This awareness makes *Mrs. Dalloway* a brilliant and extraordinary border case, an enacted oxymoron in which the very emblems of possibility are also the signs of stasis. Just as Woolf's unflinching engagement with her alienation from the women of the Co-operative Guild led paradoxically to a better understanding of their lives and psyches, the book's representation of what *is* beneath the surface of what is hoped for makes the latter more plausible: "we" (citizens of class-based societies) know what barriers we're up against and can begin considering the revision of fences into links.

In "The Prime Minister," a set of preliminary notes for *Mrs. Dalloway*, Woolf allowed herself a fantasy in which the tightly woven social grid is briefly unmade, and a loophole appears. "If the Prime Minister," she wrote, "yielding to a sudden impulse to look at the sky, had dawdled away an entire afternoon, there wd have been a hole in the fabric of history. So an old woman knitting a comforter drops a stitch, + her work falls into chaos."[20] As if she were God unwriting Genesis, this "common" goddess in one careless moment disposes of the ur-plot of property and oppression: no walled gardens; no male proprietor on high, guarding fruits he'll never need for sustenance; no women bringing children forth in pain.[21] So Mrs. Scott, J.P., author of the memoir called "A Felt Hat Worker," organized a boycott at her factory and brought about, through her creative idleness, the restitching of one tiny plot in the historical fabric: "Everyone put down their work and two . . . went down to see the head of the firm. They all sat there until I was sent for . . . I always feel proud of the way they all stood by me."

CHAPTER IV

Translations

An agreement or obligation of whatever sort—a promise, a
marriage, a sacred alliance—can only take place, I would
say, in translation, that is, only if it is *simultaneously* uttered in
both my tongue and the other's. . . . In order for the
contract or the alliance to take place, in order for the "yes,
yes" to take place on both sides, it must occur in two
languages at once. . . . Thus the agreement . . . has to imply
the difference of languages, rather than transparent
translatability, a Babelian situation which is at the same time
lessened and left intact.
(*Jacques Derrida*, The Ear of the Other)

Copia is that figural capacity of discourse which allows man to
express the diversity of his nature, as well as that of
surrounding nature, and even to inaugurate mutations in its
being. Without *copia*, there is only repetition.
(*Eugene Vance, ibid.*)

Copia: Plenty, a plentiful supply; now chiefly in the L. phrase
copia verborum abundance of words, a copious vocabulary.
1713, ADDISON, *Guardian* no. 155[:] Since they [women] have
such a *copia verborum*, or plenty of words, it is pity they should
not put it to some use.
(OED)

I snuggled into the core of my life, which is this complete
comfort with L., & there found everything so
satisfactory & calm that I revived myself, & got a fresh start;
feeling entirely immune. The immense success of our life,
is I think, that our treasure is hid away; or rather in such
common things that nothing can touch it. That is, if one
enjoys a bus ride to Richmond, sitting on the green
smoking, taking the letters out of the box, airing the marmots,
combing Grizzle, making an ice, opening a letter, sitting
down after dinner, side by side, & saying, "Are you in your
stall, brother?"—well, what can trouble this happiness?
(*Virginia Woolf*, Diary, *June 14, 1925*)

SMOKE AND COBBLESTONES

In a diary entry in August 1924, Virginia described what she saw as the difference between Leonard's mind and hers. She begins by noting that yesterday's mood, which she describes as "my silver mist," is dissipating; and today

> L. has been telling me about Germany, & reparations, how money is paid. Lord what a weak brain I have—like an unused muscle. He talks; & the facts come in, & I can't deal with them. But by dint of very painful brain exercises, perhaps I understand a little more . . . of the International situation. And L. understands it all—picks up all these points out of the daily paper absolutely instantly, has them connected, ready to produce. *Sometimes I think my brain & his are of different orders.* Were it not for my flash of imagination, & this turn for books, I should be a very ordinary woman. No faculty of mine is really very strong. (*D* 2:309; italics mine)

Here, as elsewhere, Virginia pays homage to what she considers Leonard's superior capacity for facts. The point, however, is not one of superiority or inferiority but of a difference that appears to Virginia virtually insurmountable. Her brain and Leonard's are simply not of the same "order." Virginia's operates in "flashes" and "silver mists," Leonard's precisely by the ordered grasping of solid facts. How, then, did they mediate the differences between them?

In her memoir of a Bloomsbury childhood, Virginia's niece Angelica Garnett recalls a typical visit from "the Woolves," and the curious counterpoint of two very different minds and characters. Virginia was fantastical, she observes, and Leonard "was made of different material from the rest of us, something which, unlike obsidian, couldn't splinter, and inevitably suggested the rock of ages" (*Deceived with Kindness* 108).[1] The contrast emerged particularly in their respective methods of narration:

> Virginia . . . poured out tea . . . waving the teapot to and fro as she talked. . . . Before tea was over she would light a cigarette in a long holder, and as her conversation took fire, she herself grew hazier behind the mounting puffs of smoke. She would . . . rise to heights of fantasy unencumbered by realism. . . . Leonard would wait, and then describe the same incident in terms that were factual, forthright and objective. (110)

Garnett's words suggest that Leonard and Virginia's radically different relations to reality—or relations *of* reality—stemmed from an actual constitutional difference. Her metaphors imply that these two people were composed of different elements: Virginia of air and fire, Leonard of solid rock. She inhabits "heights"; he is firmly grounded. Garnett recalls that Leonard would take command after tea and Virginia's performance were over: he organized "the ritual game of bowls . . . pac[ing] the doubtful distances with large, thick-soled feet placed carefully one before the other, sometimes attended by Pinka [his dog], who adoringly sniffed each mark on the grass, only to be gruffly told to go and lie down. Leonard's word was law, his judgment final . . ." (110–11). The contrast, again, is clear: having described Virginia, in talk, dissolving upwards in smoke, Garnett distinctly recalls Leonard's *feet* defining distances that to others seem doubtful. If the order of precedence—Virginia, the literary genius, presiding at tea, Leonard, the man of action, at bowls—places him second, his aura of command provides a counterweight to her compelling but airy storytelling. Not only is Leonard body to her mind; his connection with the earth, with the world of "facts," makes his word "final." To what extent, one might wonder, was this finality merely literal, and to what extent was it sometimes a revision and an obliteration of Virginia's own version of the truth?

That Leonard was not only a stickler for accuracy but positively obsessed with it was attested by numerous contemporaries and is evinced by his own writings. Throughout his life, he recorded the number of words he wrote each day; it was this same efficiency that made him so effective as a colonial administrator. It also made him, depending on whose opinion one consults, either the perfect nurse or a forbidding father figure in his management of Virginia's health and daily regimen. "Management" is perhaps the key word ("husbandry" might also be invoked): for better or for worse, Leonard was good at taking over. And his preoccupation with strict government could sometimes reach levels of absurdity. At the Hogarth Press, he was apt to fly into rages if an employee arrived two minutes late. Unintentionally, Virginia paints a perfect satirical miniature of her husband when she describes him, minutes before a solar eclipse, continually checking his watch. While everyone else gazes raptly at the heavens, Leonard looks downward, measuring time (see *Diary* 3:147).

The irrational length to which Leonard could sometimes carry his preoccupation with rationality and accuracy appears to perfection in a passage in *Beginning Again* that deliberately revises an entry in Virginia's diary. The passage, to which a long footnote is attached, is worth quoting:

> I am going to relate another conversation with the Webbs because it is the best thing I ever heard them say. . . . I can vouch for the accuracy of what follows. In September, 1918, we boldly, if not recklessly, asked Beatrice and Sidney to come to us for a week-end . . . and were rather astonished and a little dismayed when they accepted. . . . They arrived on a Saturday. . . . On Sunday afternoon the Webbs, Virginia, and I went for a walk. . . . Even a walk with the Webbs tended to become regularized or institutionalized and organized, like the municipal bricks, and therefore on the way out I walked with Beatrice

and Virginia with Sidney, and on the way back we changed partners. Sidney and I walked rather faster . . . so we stopped on the top of a small hill. . . . When they came into view some distance away, Sidney said to me: "I know what she is saying to your wife; she is saying that marriage is the waste paper basket of the emotions." In the evening . . . I asked Virginia whether on the road from Southease to Asham Beatrice Webb had told her that marriage was the waste paper basket of the emotions. She said she had. As soon as Sidney and I had started off ahead of them Beatrice had asked Virginia what she intended to do now that she was married. Virginia said that she wanted to go on writing novels. Beatrice seemed to approve and warned Virginia against allowing her work to be interfered with by emotional relations. "Marriage, we always say," she said, "is the waste paper basket of the emotions."[1] [Superscript in original.] To which, just as they came to the level crossing, Virginia replied: "But wouldn't an old servant do as well?" "We were entangled," Virginia writes in her diary, "at the gates of the level-crossing when she remarked: 'Yes, I daresay an old family servant would do as well.' "

1. [Footnote in original.] It is a curious fact that in Virginia's diary she records this conversation as follows: "One should have only one great personal relationship in one's life, she said; or at most two—marriage and parenthood. Marriage was necessary as a waste pipe for emotion, as security in old age when personal attractiveness fails and as a help to work." This shows how difficult it is to be certain of any accuracy in recorded conversations. I am absolutely certain that Sidney used the words "waste paper basket of the emotions" in speaking to me, and I am almost certain that those were the words that Virginia agreed Beatrice used to her. But did Beatrice in fact say "waste pipe" and not "waste paper basket"? It is impossible now to know. Virginia was never an accurate recorder of what people said, and it is quite possible, if not probable, that when she came to write her diary, three days after the events, she dashed down (inaccurately) waste pipe. But it is, as I say impossible to know. (116–17)

This passage, from beginning to end, is both unintentionally hilarious and fascinating for the light it sheds on certain quirks of Leonard's character, and on his sense of self. Like many of his other personal statements, it contains significant contradictions. While he reiterates the "impossibility of knowing" what Beatrice Webb said, or indeed what anyone said in a past conversation, he claims at the very start of his narrative that he "can vouch for the accuracy of what follows." To vouch for something is to guarantee its truth or worth—but how, if the conversation was never recorded except in Virginia's questionable transcription, does he intend to do so? And whom does he expect to question him? It is true that Leonard's autobiographical volumes, appearing serially, elicited a number of correspondents. But Leonard Woolf was an old man by the time he wrote his life; the last volume was published in 1969, the year that he died, and most of his readers have not been able to question him. Nor, for that matter, could his wife question or dispute his own somewhat petulant disputation of a text *she* left behind. Since Virginia's notation was made three days after the event, and Leonard's transcription forty-five *years* later, common sense would dictate that we believe *her*. But Leonard insists upon his wife's inaccuracy. One could, of course, subject the phrases "waste pipe" and "waste paper basket" to a Freudian analysis and determine what stake Leonard had in insisting on the drier metaphor, and Virginia in dwelling upon a cloacal one. But this would obscure what I think is the central issue raised by the passage: namely, the tremendous importance ascribed by Leonard not so much to the phrases themselves as to accuracy in recording them—and particularly to his own accuracy and Virginia's supposed flightiness.

Leonard Woolf was sometimes remarkably blind to the ironies of his own phraseology. Satirizing the Webbs, he maintains that a walk with them "tended to become regularized or institutionalized and organized, like the municipal bricks." Doesn't this very metaphor, however, characterize Leonard's own tendency, particularly in his writing? In his recollection of the Webbs' visit, Leonard builds up petty external details as if these constituted essential truth. Tones of voice are elided, as are description and characterization. Ironically, the most original touch in the passage is Leonard's brick metaphor.

The differences in style of perception and narration that Virginia Woolf highlights in her 1924 diary entry, Garnett in her memoir, and Leonard, half-inadvertently, in *Beginning Again*, constitute the theme of Virginia's 1927 essay "The New Biography." In this review of Harold Nicolson's book *Some People*, she uses her well-known metaphor of granite and rainbow.[2] The former term characterizes an old-fashioned style of life writing, typical of the Victorians, that emphasizes fact, or "truth in its hardest, most obdurate form; . . . truth as truth is to be found in the British Museum" (*GR* 149). The latter suggests a kind of biography built on personality and all the less tangible facets of its subject's life. Though we can deduce a link between granite and masculine, rainbow and feminine, such a link is not explicit; and indeed, the essay concludes that Nicolson (the husband of Virginia's intimate friend of this period, Vita Sackville-West) errs in his writing too much on the side of rainbow.

This very conclusion, however, indicates Woolf's concern with unsettling the definitions of gender even as she elsewhere posits such potentially essentialist notions as the existence of a "woman's sentence" whose shapes and sounds differ from male formulations. Both men and women contain the elements of rainbow and granite, and the trick is to find their best balance. This is extraordinarily difficult "[f]or though both truths are genuine, they are antagonistic; let them meet and they destroy each other. . . . Let it be fact, one feels, or let it be fiction; the imagination will not serve under two masters simultaneously" (154). Here is the great dilemma faced by the modern biographer, for although "truth of fact and truth of fiction are incompatible . . . he is now more than ever urged to combine them" (155). And here Woolf becomes enmeshed in her own metaphors, shuttling back and forth, in the course of a page, not only between granite and rainbow, but between images of union and images of destruction, until oppositions become so entangled as to seem spurious. First, she imagines the mere "meeting" of the two "truths" as a battle in which one is sure to obliterate the other. And such an obliteration means ultimate failure, for if, for instance, the biographer goes too far in his use of "the novelist's art . . . he loses both worlds; he has neither the freedom of fiction nor the substance of fact" (155). The favoring of one method or discourse over another brings about a loss on *both* sides rather than the triumph of the dominant one. Here Woolf would seem to be suggesting that granite and rainbow cannot exist without one another; each in equal measure affirms the other; and a perfect combination of the two is the ideal to be striven for. Volatile as they are when brought together, we are beginning to think that with great care and gingerliness, a union might be achieved—when, suddenly, Woolf ends the paragraph by declaring that in fact "the mixture of the two is abhorrent."

Just as suddenly, then, in her next and final paragraph, she gestures once again toward possibility. The essay, like other works by Woolf, in particular *A Room of One's Own* with its vision of the great woman writer of the future, ends on an almost messianic note. While "the days of Victorian biography are over," we cannot yet "name the biographer whose art is subtle and bold enough to present that queer amalgamation of dream and reality, that perpetual marriage of granite and rainbow. His method still remains to be discovered" (155). Even as the word "marriage" enables the perplexed reader at last to link granite and rainbow distinctly to gender categories, the word "queer" dismantles those very categories. "Queer amalgamation" unsettles "perpetual marriage," suggesting sexual lawlessness, while the second phrase suggests a kind of unendingly fecund enactment of patriarchal, Victorian law. Chiasmically, the reader deduces a "queer marriage"— and just what does such a marriage look like? Perhaps like Harold Nicolson's. He and Vita Sackville-West had a highly unusual relationship, in which each accepted the other's affairs with a good many people of the same sex. (Like the Woolfs' marriage, it was unusual also in that the wife pursued her writing career unhindered—indeed, encouraged—by her husband.) But "queer marriage" might also—indeed logically would, except that the practice was illegal—indicate a legal union of members of the same sex. What, then, happens to the gender distinctions on which our sense of order rests? In what ways is that sense of order determined by preexisting legal and grammatical structures? How can these structures be unsettled when language is a constitutive part of their operation? Such questions, raised in recent decades by gender theorists, are adumbrated in the disarmingly creative play of Woolf's 1920s literary experiments.

The writer envisioned in the final paragraph of "The New Biography" is the counterpart of the androgynous poet whom Woolf invoked that same year in the lectures at Newnham and Girton which became *A Room of One's Own*. In that book, too, the creative combination of opposing elements is described as a figurative marriage of equals. Woolf presents her famous image of the man and woman getting into a taxi in a moment of perfect mathematical balance; declares that the male writer's phallic "I" must not obscure his woman character's subjectivity; and describes the ideal—actually, she calls it the "normal and comfortable"—state of mind as one in which male and female elements "live in harmony together, spiritually cooperating" (102). The difficulty with Virginia Woolf's attempts to prophesy a writing, as well as a writer, integrating male and female, granite and rainbow, is the difficulty of imagining something outside the bounds of vocabulary. "Androgynous" is the adjective Woolf uses in *A Room of One's Own*; contemporary pseudoscientific discourse provided the notion of a "third sex"—a phrase that appears in Radclyffe Hall's *The Well of Loneliness* and in Vita Sackville-West's private diary.[3]

The trouble with ideas of androgyny is reflected in *A Room of One's Own*, as in "The New Biography," by Virginia Woolf's fluctuation between different metaphors of conjunction. Woolf posits the "intercourse" between male and female parts of the brain as a "fusion [in which] the mind is fully fertilised and uses all its faculties" (102). Like the granite-and-rainbow compound in "The New Biography," however, the metaphor of "fusion" self-destructs. Woolf ultimately finds herself insisting upon the importance of difference instead of advocating a mixture that erases boundaries; the word "difference" recurs in her discussion, as when she maintains that "the nerves that feed the brain would seem to differ in men and women, and if you are going to make them work their best and hardest, you must find out what treatment suits them—what alternations of work and rest they need, interpreting rest not as doing nothing but as doing something but something that is different; and what should that difference be?" (81).[4] Ten pages later she asks, "[I]f two sexes are inadequate, considering the vastness and variety of the world, how should we manage with one only? Ought not education to bring out and fortify the differences rather than the similarities?" (91).[5]

If the "fortification" of difference is what Woolf desires, then the "marriage of opposites" in the mind of the writer decidedly cannot mean a fusion of two into one. "Fortification" implies a self-protective separateness, a barricading that would virtually disallow "intercourse." The central problem of Woolf's argument, the source of its various contradictions, is the

question: what *is* an androgyne? A being in whom male and female characteristics are juxtaposed—or amalgamated? Fascinated (as well as, briefly,
seduced)[6] in the late '20s by her friend Vita's bisexuality, Virginia Woolf
was trying to theorize the transcendence of gender. Yet she felt that the
sexes were differently constituted, and Vita's own case only confused matters. On the one hand, Vita classed herself as one of Krafft-Ebing's "inter-
mediate sex"; on the other hand, as her diary attests, she did not necessarily
think of herself as *at once* masculine and feminine but saw herself fluctuating
between phases—with each phase, rather than the fluctuations themselves,
representing the "truth" of the moment. *Challenge*, Vita's novel about the
prolonged "masculine" phase during which she carried on a tempestuous
affair with Violet Keppel Trefusis, inscribes a highly conservative view of
relations between the sexes. Her two protagonists, Julian and Eve, are stereotypically male and female: he all granite, she all rainbow. Their relationship collapses when the woman attempts to impose her values and desires
on the man, and the novel ends with her suicide. In Sackville-West's world,
there is no androgyny, no middle ground—not even understanding between the sexes and tolerance of difference. The irony, of course, is that the
prototypes of Eve and Julian were both women. Able to inhabit a "queer
marriage" with a man, Sackville-West could not imagine or enact a shape
shifting between two women.[7]

Given Vita's difficulty depicting a lesbian affair in anything but rigid
heterosexual terms, the challenge for Virginia Woolf, attempting to posit
a subversive reconfiguration of heterosexual identities, was that much
greater (as was, perhaps, the inclination, Woolf being in all realms other
than sexuality far more of an experimentalist than her aristocratically ad-
venturesome friend). This challenge is reflected in the paradoxical metaphors of *A Room of One's Own*: the very literalism, for instance, of the notion
that two parts of the mind must have "intercourse" with one another makes
it all too easy to conceive of Woolf's "androgynous mind" as a kind of
hermaphrodite; or else a copulating couple, a sort of beast with two backs.
The mind is not a fleshly thing, but it is hard not to speak of it that way:
"The mind is a very mysterious organ, I reflected"—and from there, Woolf
goes on to vacillate between two different visions of communication: one
in which male and female are discrete and decidedly different, yet nonetheless able to make themselves understood to one another; the other in which
male and female intermix to form a new being. Looking out her window
at the man and woman getting in a taxi together, she calls this meeting "a
natural fusion" that arises from "co-operat[ion]." But fusion and cooperation are different things; it takes two things to cooperate, whereas what is
fused has become one.

These two paradigms—one involving juxtaposition, the other amalgamation—correspond to the elements whose combination they describe. The

former privileges granite, the latter rainbow, since only fortified objects can be juxtaposed, while liquids and gases blend together. The word "amalgamation," moreover, denotes the incorporation of a solid metal such as gold or silver by liquid mercury. (Mercury's household name, quicksilver, recalls Virginia's description of her mind working in "flashes" and "silver mists.") Woolf's three major works of the late 1920s represent a transition in her thinking about writing and gender from the former to the latter paradigm. *To the Lighthouse* depicts the patriarchal, superficially cooperative, model of marriage—literal marriage, in this case—in order to reject it; *A Room of One's Own* is caught between opposing models; and *Orlando* represents androgyny as the triumph of an indeterminate feminine. Finally, in 1931, *The Waves* reveals Woolf trapped in a dilemma—a dilemma best encapsulated in the metaphor of failed translation—as the masculine voices of the "real world" impinge on the fantasy of perfect communion and liberating non-sense embodied by *Orlando*. As history made it less and less possible to imagine hard fact carried off in swirls of imagination, and Leonard's "muscular" intellection came to seem the only way of comprehending and opposing fascism, Virginia Woolf's quicksilver mode was threatened. *The Waves* makes that very threat its theme, with its characters forever on the edge of permanent loss, their voices unable to pass intact from one mind to the next.

DOUBLE CROSSINGS

A number of critics have written about difference and contradiction in *A Room of One's Own*. In "Androgynous Vision and Artistic Process in Virginia Woolf's *A Room of One's Own*," Ellen Carol Jones describes Woolf's method as mirroring her theme of androgyny in that "she creates . . . a form which is at once fragmented and unified, the product of an imagination that can be simultaneously creative and 'strict and logical' " (Beja, *Critical Essays* 229). For John Burt ("Irreconcilable Habits of Thought in *A Room of One's Own* and *To the Lighthouse*"), the book, rather than combining two rhetorical methods fruitfully, undermines its own argument by vacillating between conservative and subversive impulses. On the one hand advocating a new and egalitarian relation between the sexes, on the other, Woolf falls into a dangerous nostalgia for old-fashioned romance and marriage that Burt attributes to her horror at truths about human nature revealed by World War I (Bloom, *Modern Critical Views* 191–206). She intends to look forward but cannot help gazing back at an era that suddenly seems innocent—the Victorian age she represented in so many of her other works as stultifyingly, quintessentially patriarchal.

To the Lighthouse is the novel that both inscribes and exorcises this nostalgia. In "A Sketch of the Past," Woolf claimed that her mother had obsessed her from childhood until the writing of *To the Lighthouse*; laying Julia Stephen's specter to rest in that novel was an act analogous to killing the Angel in the House. Early in the book, the relationship between Mr. and Mrs. Ramsay is likened to "that solace which two different notes, one high, one low, struck together, seem to give each other as they combine" (61). A closer look, however, at their interaction—particularly their argument over whether the next day's weather will permit a journey to the lighthouse— reveals discord in the "music" of the Ramsays: Mr. Ramsay "stamps," he "slap[s] the covers of his book together," he "snap[s] out irascibly" (50) and curses; and Mrs. Ramsay silently bends "her head as if to let the pelt of jagged hail, the drench of dirty water, bespatter her unrebuked" (51). To harmonize is *her* work, and hard work it is: she must perpetually counter his bluster and his blunders with soft and soothing words, words whose truth she doubts. The myth that this is true harmony is a kind of double-crossing the novel reinscribes in the dynamic of Lily Briscoe and Mr. Ramsay in the final section.

Ironically, while her husband accepts Mrs. Ramsay's reassurances about the value of his books, it is precisely her habit of affirmation he excoriates in the early scene when she—to his mind, falsely—holds out hope to her son James about the lighthouse trip. Later, on their walk in the garden, he tells her, " 'You're teaching your daughters to exaggerate,' "—as though women learned lack of precision from one another, and men always spoke exact truth. His insistence on precision—on proportion, in fact—is the method whereby Mr. Ramsay dominates others in the book, and the one that has gained him fame. We know about his remarkable brain: "[I]f thought is like the keyboard of a piano, divided into so many notes, or like the alphabet is ranged in twenty-six letters all in order, then [Mr. Ramsay's] splendid mind had no sort of difficulty in running over those letters one by one, firmly and accurately, until it had reached, say, the letter Q" (33). Mr. Ramsay's failure is, of course, his inability to reach the letter "R"— which suggests, as Rachel Bowlby hints, a failure in *self*-knowledge.[8] Yet this failure never leads him to question his method; the criticism he might usefully turn inward gets projected onto others, in particular his wife, whose mind functions differently from his own.

In *A Room of One's Own*, Woolf puts herself as narrator in the place of Mrs. Ramsay, the woman whose thoughts are disorderly according to male standards, and creates a number of male foils with which to mock those very standards. Working in the British Museum, for instance, she observes "the reader next door, who was making the neatest abstracts, headed often with an A or a B or a C," and greatly exaggerates the difference in his and her respective research methods:

The student who has been trained in research at Oxbridge has no doubt some method of shepherding his question past all distractions till it runs into its answer as a sheep runs into its pen. The student by my side, for instance, who was copying assiduously from a scientific manual was, I felt sure, extracting pure nuggets of the essential ore every ten minutes or so. His little grunts of satisfaction indicated so much. But if, unfortunately, one has no training in a university, the question far from being shepherded to its pen flies like a frightened flock hither and thither, helterskelter, pursued by a whole pack of hounds. Professors, schoolmasters, sociologists, clergymen, novelists, essayists, journalists, men who had no qualification save that they were not women, chased my simple and single question—Why are women poor?—until it became fifty questions; until the fifty questions leapt frantically into mid-stream and were carried away. (28)

Woolf's method in this passage is so to emphasize the Oxbridge student's apparent access to answers, as against her own perplexity, that the values are reversed and the student is clearly a ninny. The object common to both the narrator and the student is "the question" that each pursues; though the subjects of their research are different, it is the treatment to which each figure subjects his or her "question" that Woolf examines. The word "pen," first of all, is punned upon. Both narrator and student are using pens, but the student's functions as a weapon, and the narrator's is useless for controlling information. The student uses his pen as a sort of prod with which to "shepherd" (the Christic image is belied by the violence of the act) his question into its proper "pen," while the narrator loses her question to a pack of male hunters likened to hounds. Her question multiplies, and its offspring commit suicide.

The passage ultimately identifies the student with his male cohorts, the professors, clergymen, and so on, and, through his "little grunts," with lower forms of animal life: the hounds who victimize the poor sheep, Woolf's question about women. It is the primeval contest of the rapacious male and the female seeking to protect herself: only here the contest is intellectual, and the man wins by the power of his outline. The student's outline—a reflection of men's classifications of women—is, of course, rendered absurd as soon as we read Woolf's list of these classifications: "*Condition in the Middle Ages of, Habits in the Fiji Islands of, Worshipped as goddesses by, Weaker in moral sense than,*" and so on (28). It is the classificatory impulse itself, however, that Woolf exposes as insidious. The compulsive student with his A, B, and C is a forerunner to the hideous figure that dominates *Three Guineas*: "a monstrous male, loud of voice, hard of fist, childishly intent upon scoring the floor of the earth with chalk marks, within whose mystic boundaries human beings are *penned*, rigidly, separately, artificially; . . . while we, 'his' women, are locked in the private house . . ." (105; italics mine). Here the word "pen" has acquired frighteningly literal associations: Hitler's concentration camps had, by this time, been operating for five years. And indeed, the figure of Professor von X, whom Woolf invokes just a few pages after that of the categorizing undergraduate in *A Room of One's Own*, represents the link between sophomoric classifying and full-fledged dictatorship: his name embodies both another point in the linear system of masculine thought and the impulse to censor or cancel whatever does not conform to this system. Professor von X, a Ramsay purged of humanity, is the censor who will be countered in *Orlando* through methods, not of reverse censorship, but of creative engulfment.

In *A Room of One's Own*, Woolf insistently draws attention to the link between Ramsayan precision—the stereotypically "granite" way of deducing "truth" by herding facts into categories—and sexual tyranny, in part through satirical use of the metaphor of measurement. The word "measure" occurs a number of times throughout the book, notably during the famous excursus on Judith Shakespeare when Woolf asks, "Who shall measure the heat and violence of the poet's heart when caught and tangled in a woman's body?" (50). Later, she claims, "There is no mark on the wall to measure the precise height of women. There are no yard measures, neatly divided into the fraction of an inch, that one can lay against the qualities of a good mother or the devotion of a daughter, or the fidelity of a sister, or the capacity of a housekeeper" (89). This is one of the text's radical moments, for Woolf is implicitly comparing the keeping of house and raising of children to Columbus's discovery of America and Newton's of "the laws of gravitation" and refusing to call one more important than the other. Thus she demonstrates her own rejection of categories, of the "mark of gender" that designates superiority and inferiority even as it might appear neutral.[9] Winding toward her peroration, Woolf encourages her audience of young women to free themselves of critical categories and ignore reviewers (whose remarks are implicitly analogous to the censorship imposed on writers like Radclyffe Hall):[10]

> No, delightful as the pastime of measuring may be, it is the most futile of all occupations, and to submit to the decrees of the measurers the most servile of attitudes. So long as you write what you wish to write, that is all that matters. . . . But to sacrifice a hair of the head of your vision, a shade of its colour, in deference to some Headmaster with a silver pot in his hand or to some professor with a measuring-rod up his sleeve, is the most abject treachery. . . . (*ROO* 110)

In Part I of *To the Lighthouse*, James Ramsay finds himself being measured for the sock his mother knits. His unease in this role measures the text's own ambivalences: its nostalgia, its fantasies of progress, its halfway stance between the affirmative signals of Mrs. Ramsay and the warning negations of her husband. In a sense, James replaces the lighthouse as the object of contentious speculation, the indeterminate signifier of both possibility and danger. He is the "cause" of the Ramsays' disagreement, both in spawning the question—will they, or won't they, make the desired crossing?—and as the spawn, literally and figuratively, of their combative intercourse. Born of an engagement both harmonious and embattled, he will come to represent both continuity and difference. He is the sign of an imagined, as-yet-unachieved future: again, literally, as Ramsay descendant; and figuratively, as a posited androgyne, a being who combines—who might yet successfully integrate—"object and subject" ("subject and object and the nature of reality" is the phrase Andrew Ramsay uses to describe to Lily Briscoe his father's philosophic inquiries). Already, James Ramsay is an unusual child: "[H]e belonged, even at the age of six, to that great clan which cannot keep this feeling separate from that, but must let future prospects, with their joys and sorrows, cloud what is actually at hand"—in short, a Woolfian modernist, one for whom rainbow envelops and resolves granite; and at the same time—at least in his mother's wishful, collusive vision—very much a boy in the Stephen/Ramsay tradition of patriarchal authority: "the image of stark and uncompromising severity, with his high forehead and his fierce blue eyes, impeccably candid and pure, frowning slightly at the sight of human frailty, so that his mother, watching him guide his scissors neatly round the refrigerator, imagined him all red and ermine on the Bench or directing a stern and momentous enterprise in some crisis of public affairs" (3–4).

But the cutter is still his mother's child, and a few scenes later will find him in a position similar to that of the childlike Peter Walsh parrying his pocketknife against Clarissa's needle. It is a scene that recapitulates in miniature the very critique that formed the central seam of *Mrs. Dalloway*:

> "And even if it isn't fine tomorrow," said Mrs. Ramsay, raising her eyes to glance at William Bankes and Lily Briscoe as they passed, "it will be another day. And now," she said, thinking that Lily's charm was her Chinese eyes, aslant in her white, puckered little face, but it would take a clever man to see it, "and now stand up, and let me measure your leg," for they might go to the Lighthouse after all, and she must see if the stocking did not need to be an inch or two longer in the leg.
>
> Smiling, for it was an admirable idea, that had flashed upon her this very second—William and Lily should marry—she took the heather-mixture stocking, with its criss-cross of steel needles at the mouth of it, and measured it against James's leg.
>
> "My dear, stand still," she said, for in his jealousy, not liking to serve as measuring block for the Lighthouse keeper's little boy, James fidgeted purposely, and if he did that, how could she see, was it too long, was it too short? she asked. (26)

Like Rezia in *Mrs. Dalloway*, Mrs. Ramsay is figured as a creator of wearable objects—an artist manquCe, whose very "failing" suggests criticism of a system that values mind work over handicraft and labels only the non-utilitarian as "art." Yet Mrs. Ramsay colludes in that system, for interwoven with her knitting (in the deft "knitting" of Woolf's own narrative) is another, cerebral, activity of measurement that calls into question the charity in her provision of a therapeutic garment for a working-class boy. The stocking is intended for the potentially tuberculous hip of the lighthouse keeper's son, and James, given the class system that rears him, as well as his jealous oedipal anxiety, understandably chafes at the "fitting." As with the metonymic devices of *Mrs. Dalloway*, the interchangeability suggested by the action—James as substitute for the other, unnamed little boy—is belied by the action itself: a healthy leg is used as measure *against* rather than *for* an undernourished limb. And mirroring this well-meaning yet questionable act of empathy is a simultaneous process of cogitation in which Mrs. Ramsay, again in pursuit of a felicitous "fit," embodies the very coerciveness of the "family system" that *To the Lighthouse* both celebrates and exorcises. Just as the creative knitting of the narrative brought about a shedding of her mother's ghost—a murder of the Angel in the House—those knitting needles, romantically evocative of maternal nurturance, also recall their opposite, the teeth of a machine Woolf describes in "A Sketch of the Past" in her excursus on George Duckworth:

> If father had graved on him certain large marks of the age . . . George filled in the large marks with a criss-cross, a spider's web, of the most minute details. . . . And so, while father preserved the framework of 1860, George filled in the framework with all kinds of minutely teethed saws; and the machine into which we were inserted in 1900 therefore held us tight; and brought innumerable teeth into play. (*MB* 131)

This almost Kafkaesque description of a paternal/fraternal torture machine uncannily recalls the knitting needles of Mrs. Ramsay; and it follows a scene with affinities to the sock fitting of James. The young Stephen women, under their half-brother's reign, were compelled to appear every evening in full Victorian dinner dress. Virginia, descending one night in a gown made of furniture cloth—this being affordable by a young woman without an income—is roundly scrutinized: "He looked me up and down as if [I] were a horse turned into the ring. . . .[11] 'Go and tear it up,' he said at last, in that curiously rasping and peevish voice which expressed his serious displeasure at this infringement of a code . . ." (*MB* 130). The violence of this condemnation, the "rasping" voice that combines petty emotion with something disturbingly mechanistic, of course bears links to George's late-night molestations. The brother's supposedly nurturing aim—to "fit" his half-sister with the right husband—is undercut by his own depredations.

The lawful production of proper wives is shadowed in this instance by the unlawfulness of incest, and this dark brotherhood illuminates the economics of a system functioning through exchange of women.

The measurement of James by his mother operates both as a demeaning feminization—James is literally measured even as Lily is assessed for her marriageability—and as a reminder of class privilege: he is not, nor will ever be, the lighthouse keeper's boy.[12] The knitting needles at the mouth of the stocking signify his mother's collusion in the machine of patriarchal values even as her nurturing would seem to contradict the violent negations produced by men. Her charity is not truly subversive, for it depends on and perpetuates a system that marginalizes compassion.[13] Thus Mrs. Ramsay's "Yes" *can* be seen as a kind of lie, the lie in service of harmony that Victorian wives were required to utter. The mother's optimism upholds the polarities of both gender and class in a society that works through differentiation and exclusion.

Yet it would be a mistake to "blame" Mrs. Ramsay, for her knitting metaphorically signals—although it cannot accomplish—a more fertile interchange. Even as she supports the traditional exchanges, the "giving" of women in marriage and the meager charities that supposedly compensate for larger economic inequity, she represents a dissolution of traditional polarities. The famous passage that figures her as a "wedge-shaped core of darkness" suggests a different kind of instrumentality, an undercutting of the entire social system.[14] Like *Mrs. Dalloway*, the novel is filled with metonymies of linkage offset by tools of violence. Where *Mrs. Dalloway* conflates these, *To the Lighthouse* seeks—nostalgically; hopefully—to make distinctions. The mother's "criss-crossing" needles adumbrate a crossing that does and does not occur late in the novel: a literal crossing to the lighthouse, but also a productive crossing of different points of view. Her binding, despite coercive undertones, is conditional; from the very start, her "Yes" to James is followed by an "if," and certainly her matchmaking schemes for Lily prove ineffectual. The needles, for all their sharpness, are still innocent—if only through relative frailty—compared to the "arid scimitar" of Mr. Ramsay. Indeed, it might be said that her *contingent* optimism is the novel's most fruitful stance, translating the husband's gloomy vassalage to hard facts into something more palatable. (But fruitfulness kills her finally; the mother's life-giving speech—elided with her womb in the image of the stocking's mouth—which leads always to further demands, in essence stabs her to death. Her very affirmations bring down the scimitar of condemnation.)

The very opening scene of the novel presents wife, son, and husband as a trinity of weapon-wielders that anticipates the trio in the boat—Cam, James, and Mr. Ramsay—in the book's final passages, as well as encapsulating the tripartite configuration that structures the novel: its division into

"The Window," "Time Passes," and "The Lighthouse," which is mirrored in Lily's creation of a balanced painting with a single line down the middle (even the weapons themselves, being pointed, are triangular in shape). As the bearer of scissors, James *is* that line: precisely transitional between the domestic act of knitting and the divisive speech of the father, his cutting suggests both the connectivity of women's piecework (or peacework) and the martial violence that germinates through Part I to be realized in the massive destruction of the Great War invoked in Part II. Sadly, the father— the only one of the three to be metaphorized *as* a weapon—elicits through his harshness an age-old oedipal response, one that produces repetition rather than change: "Had there been an axe handy, or a poker, any weapon that would have gashed a hole in his father's breast and killed him, there and then, James would have seized it. Such were the extremes of emotion that Mr. Ramsay excited in his children's breasts by his mere presence; standing now, lean as a knife, narrow as the blade of one, grinning sarcastically, not only with the pleasure of disillusioning his son and casting ridicule upon his wife . . . but also with some secret conceit at his own accuracy of judgment" (4). As for Mrs. Ramsay, she reacts with the underhanded violence of women, "making some little twist of the reddish-brown stocking she was knitting, impatiently" (4). Without the weapons of men, mothers, too, do violence to children, "twisting" their growth through sheer frustration.[15] The rhyme between "knife" and "wife" suggests both the ways in which she echoes him, and the echo's ineffectuality; once again, surface harmony is belied by deep inequity. She knits, he cuts: the knife severs the yarn. In the end, one instrument negates the other, so that the "crossing" of opposites is singular rather than reciprocal: like the great "I" that lies across the male novelist's page in *A Room of One's Own*, obscuring female subjectivity.

This false, or double, crossing is fully realized at the novel's end when the much-anticipated passage to the lighthouse finally occurs. Critics have traditionally focused on the harmonies of the book's final pages; Woolf herself recorded her desire to present the boat trip occurring *at the same time as* Lily's successful completion of her painting, so that the two acts are not just mutually dependent but appear as analogous formulations simultaneously uttered—the one a translation, as it were, of the other. Yet neither the act of writing nor the printed page permits such simultaneity; the reader will inevitably absorb the events sequentially, and only a concerted crosscutting can undermine this effect. Even as Woolf strives toward such crisscrossing, however, the burden of her tale is the triumph of sequence over simultaneity, teleology over exchange. The boat journey, for all that its depiction assays evenhandedly to present Mr. Ramsay's irresistibility, his gentle, playful side and his lovableness, culminates as an "I" laid across the water: Ramsay's "I," which corresponds to his cyclopian vision. If Lily, too, succeeds in affirming her subjectivity with the line down the center of her completed painting, this is not, as Gayatri Chakravorty Spivak has argued, through the fertilizing engagement of Mr. R. ("Unmaking and Making in *To the Lighthouse*"); hers is a vision achieved, the more admirably, alone. It is also a vision that depletes her, for in the passages leading up to this climax, she has done the work of two: her own, self-affirming work—in defiance of Mrs. Ramsay's promotion of marriage as woman's proper destiny—and the work of Mrs. Ramsay. Looking back at Lily from the vantage point of the late twentieth century, one might see her as an early victim of the double bind entangling so many supposedly liberated middle-class women today: she has her vocation, *and* she is enjoined to care for others (a double duty never unfamiliar to working-class women).

Lily's psychic replacement of Mrs. Ramsay is embodied metonymically in a scene that recalls the unfinished sock of Part I. If that sock represented efforts of empathy, as well as their failure—the charitable gift was never delivered; cataclysm struck in its place—its counterpart in Part III is the boots that unite Lily and Mr. Ramsay in a moment of good fellowship before the launch of their respective journeys. It is a wonderfully comic scene in which Lily, casting about under the pressure of his demand for sympathy, lights felicitously on Ramsay's boots. Exclaiming, " 'What beautiful boots!,' " she expects a wrathful response from this petulant man seeking balm for his soul rather than praise for his soles—but

> [i]nstead, Mr. Ramsay smiled. . . . Ah, yes, he said, holding his foot up for her to look at, they were first-rate boots. There was only one man in England who could make boots like that. Boots are among the chief curses of mankind, he said. "Bootmakers make it their business," he exclaimed, "to torture and cripple the human foot." They are also the most obstinate and perverse of mankind. It had taken him the best part of his youth to get boots made as they should be made. (153)

And it had taken Mrs. Ramsay's life to knit socks, if one reads her early death—following the signals of the text, and recalling Woolf's own conviction that Julia Stephen died at forty-nine from the demands of family life—as the outcome of so much giving, so many efforts to knit others together, even as she herself came unmoored.[16] Thus, while the passage does enshrine a moment of fine intimacy, the arrival at "a sunny island where peace dwelt, sanity reigned and the sun for ever shone, the blessed island of good boots," this intimacy is founded on lack of reciprocity: between boot-wearer and bootmaker, husband and wife, Mr. Ramsay and Lily, who takes the wife's place in giving solace. The scene ends, indeed, with Lily feeling cheated: "So they're gone, she thought, sighing with relief and disappointment. Her sympathy seemed to be cast back on her, like a bramble sprung across her face. She felt curiously divided, as if one part of her were drawn out there—it was a still day, hazy; the Lighthouse looked this morning at an immense distance; the other had fixed itself doggedly, solidly, here on the lawn" (156).

Unable to embark on painting, Lily walks to the end of the lawn to watch the Ramsay trio setting sail. Her watching is mixed with imagining, for she is uncertain which boat belongs to them; "[s]he decided that there in that very distant and entirely silent little boat Mr. Ramsay was sitting with Cam and James. Now they had got the sail up . . ." (162). It is as if the voyage were dependent on Lily's cogitation, almost on her conscious decision.[17] Meanwhile, Mr. Ramsay has no thought of her; he has found another young woman with whom to share his narcissistic vision (sharing his narcissism being just the sort of oxymoronic notion the stringently logical but self-deluded Ramsay allows himself):

> "See the little house," he said pointing, wishing Cam to look. She raised herself reluctantly and looked. But which was it? . . .
>
> . . . He had found the house and so seeing it, he had also seen himself there; he had seen himself walking on the terrace, alone. He was walking up and down between the urns; and he seemed to see himself very old and bowed. (165–66)

Looking back, Mr. Ramsay sees, not Lily, not the ghost of his wife Lily will see, but himself. As for the nearsighted Cam:

> But Cam could see nothing. She was thinking how all those paths and the lawn, thick and knotted with the lives they had lived there, were gone: were rubbed out; were past; were unreal, and now this was real. . . . [H]er father, seeing her gazing so vaguely, began to tease her. Didn't she know the points of the compass? he asked. Didn't she know the North from the South? . . . He wished she would try to be more accurate, he said: "Tell me—which is East, which is West?" he said, half laughing at her, half scolding her, for he could not understand the state of mind of any one, not absolutely imbecile, who did not know the points of the compass. Yet she did not know. And seeing her gazing, with her vague, now rather frightened, eyes fixed where no house was Mr. Ramsay . . . thought, women are always like that; the vagueness of their minds is hopeless; it was a thing he had never been able to understand; but so it was. It had been so with her—his wife. They could not keep anything clearly fixed in their minds. (166–67)

In failed dialogue, Mr. Ramsay here represents a spurious objectivity—his old insistence on the separateness of subject and object—even as, self-fixated, he casts his own image on the land; while Cam falls painfully into the pure subjectivity her mother had seemed to embody in life. (Does she fall, or is she pushed? Woolf suggests the familiar psychological mechanism whereby those accused of certain weaknesses, without recourse to an articulate or articulable self-defense, find themselves inhabiting the position of weakness.) In this reencapsulation of the novel's opening dialectic, James is again caught between two points of view, on a border representing the possibility of reconciliation—a true "knitting," a simultaneous translation—unrealizable as long as Mr. Ramsay is in the boat. The division in his consciousness not only encompasses the perspectives of his father and his sister but mirrors Lily Briscoe's dual awareness, her sense of being at once "drawn out there" and "fixed . . . here":

> James looked at the Lighthouse. He could see the white-washed rocks; the tower, stark and straight; he could see that it was barred with black and white; he could see windows in it; he could even see washing spread on the rocks to dry. So that was the Lighthouse, was it?
>
> No, the other was also the Lighthouse. For nothing was simply one thing. The other Lighthouse was true too. It was sometimes hardly to be seen across the bay. In the evening one looked up and saw the eye opening and shutting and the light seemed to reach them in that airy sunny garden where they sat. (186)

The irony of Mr. Ramsay's incapacity to reach "R"—his inability to know himself—is the unidirectionality of his mode of travel. As Cam might tell him, were she not as paralyzed in her myopia as he is caught in cyclopia, "R" might be reached from the other side of the alphabet. The setting-off of Cam's view against her father's recalls Mrs. Ramsay as wedge to her husband's weapon. The wedge, triangular, might resolve a frozen dialectic by getting *underneath* the simplistic antinomies of East and West, Q and S. In a sense, James is that wedge; the whole triangular family group is that wedge—if it could only communicate. But the potential remains inchoate, and James is alone in his capacity to see "R" from both both angles: the lighthouse up close, and the remembered, subjectively observed lighthouse. Longing for his mother—"She alone spoke the truth; to her alone could he speak it"—and intensely frustrated by Mr. Ramsay's dominance, his apparent surveillance even of his son's thoughts, James reverts to a childhood fantasy: "A rope seemed to bind him . . . and his father had knotted it and he could only escape by taking a knife and plunging it . . ." (187). The ellipsis that ends the sentence leaves a question open: "plunging it" into Mr. Ramsay's heart; or into the binding rope? It is this uncertainty that suggests a liberation, however compromised, at the end of *To the Lighthouse*; it suggests that James, choosing his target correctly, might escape the oedipal fate of simply reembodying his father, the father as murderous knife. A few pages earlier, James is privy to a realization that illuminates and melts the frozen dialectics of the novel up to this point. Though largely untouched by critics, it is perhaps the text's most powerful offering in terms of Woolf's vision of the future of gender paradigms:

He had always kept this old symbol of taking a knife and striking his father to the heart. Only now, as he grew older . . . it was not him, that old man reading, whom he wanted to kill, but it was the thing that descended on him—without his knowing it perhaps: that fierce sudden black-winged harpy, with its talons and its beak all cold and hard, that struck and struck at you (he could feel the beak on his bare legs, where it had struck when he was a child) and then made off, and there he was again, an old man, very sad, reading his book. That he would kill, that he would strike to the heart. Whatever he did—(and he might do anything, he felt, looking at the Lighthouse and the distant shore) whether he was in a business, in a bank, a barrister, a man at the head of some enterprise, that he would fight, that he would track down and stamp out—tyranny, despotism, he called it—making people do what they did not want to do, cutting off their right to speak. . . . Yes, thought James . . . there was a waste of snow and rock very lonely and austere; and there he had come to feel, quite often lately . . . there were two pairs of footprints only; his own and his father's. They alone knew each other. What then was this terror, this hatred? . . . [H]e sought an image to cool and detach and round off his feeling in a concrete shape. Suppose then that as a child sitting helpless in a perambulator . . . he had seen a waggon crush ignorantly and innocently, some one's foot? Suppose he had seen the foot first, in the grass, smooth, and whole; then the wheel; and the same foot, purple, crushed. But the wheel was innocent. So now, when his father came striding down the passage knocking them up early in the morning to go to the Lighthouse down it came over his foot, over Cam's foot, over anybody's foot. One sat and watched it. (185)

Trying to pinpoint the origin of this sensation, James recalls the argument that began the novel. The foot, of course, was his mother, mown down by the father's verbal brutality; and it was his own vulnerable psyche. James's detachment, his newfound capacity to "sit and watch" his own foot being crushed, is both hard-won and problematic.[18] In one sense, the oedipal identification that produces the heterosexual male is complete, as conveyed by the indeterminacy of the masculine pronouns in the second sentence; the son has joined his father on an eerie no-woman's-island where both men are disembodied, metonymized not as real feet but as their mere traces. Physicality is ascribed to the mother, who *is* the crushed foot, in the age-old projection that absolves men of corporeal susceptibility. Yet even as James's fantasy spiritualizes him and his father, he resolves to "fight," to "track down and stamp out" tyranny, in language that, like a wheel revolving, merely repeats—or adumbrates—the highly physical image he coins in the following sentences. He will use the methods of tyranny to destroy tyranny. With guilt objectified as an unidentifiable wheel crushing a non-specific foot, the father is freed from responsibility, and the son can follow in his footsteps.

With a difference, though, it seems to me. For James's absolution of his father is followed by his double vision of the lighthouse, suggesting that he can "follow" without merely repeating Mr. Ramsay's trajectory. While Cam's paralysis deprives her of a trajectory—she seems encased in subjectivity—James, sitting in the boat (unlike the helpless infant in the pram), is at the focal point of (at least) two possible narratives. He has a choice: will he stab the father's heart in an act that merely mimics; or cut the rope that binds the little family, against its will, in a tired oedipal configuration? Will James's revenge be the simplistic substitution of his "I" for his father's, or will it take the form of endorsing multiple "I"s? To cut the rope would mean to loosen each of the three persons from their fixed roles. James's story ends, of course, with the ending of *To the Lighthouse*—an ending that is not conclusive, as Randall Stevenson points out, but instead represents a kind of fading away: Lily Briscoe looks up from her canvas and finds the lighthouse nearly vanished from her field of vision (Stevenson 162). Woolf herself would later write, "I meant *nothing* by The Lighthouse. One has to have a central line down the middle of the book to hold the design together. . . . Whether its right or wrong I don't know but directly I'm told what a thing means, it becomes hateful to me" (*L* 3:385). The final words of the novel, Lily's "Yes . . . I have had my vision," though they would seem to complete a sentence begun in its first words, represent a tenuous finality. As the party in the boat have shown us, there is always more than one vision; and Woolf's choice of the lighthouse as her "central line down the middle" (her very firmness fading into redundancy) is a paradoxical use of symbol to designate the eschewal of symbolism. As a turning "eye," the lighthouse cannot be pegged by another's vision; it is essentially anticyclopian. The novel's argument must continue in another form, James's revenge be newly launched in another place and time. The double crossing Mr. Ramsay wreaks on "his" women, whereby he excoriates their subjective relation to the world while maintaining the absolute primacy of his own self, will be canceled through dually authored acts of translation.

RAINBOW AND GRANITE

In the "Roundtable on Translation" published among other colloquia in *The Ear of the Other*, Jacques Derrida retells the biblical story of the Tower of Babel, an edifice that signifies both a unitary Symbolic and a multiplication of tongues. This signification, in turn, is tripartite: first come the Shems, attempting to impose a single language on the world; then God, in punishment, imposes the proper name Babel, a singular enforcement of multiplicity:

> The Shems decide to raise a tower—not just in order to reach all the way to the heavens but also, it says in the text, to make a name for themselves. . . . [b]y imposing their tongue on the entire universe on the basis of this sublime edification. Tongue: actually the Hebrew word here is the word that signifies lip. . . . Thus, they want to impose their lip on the entire universe. (101)

The etymology Derrida refers to recalls the impositions of Mr. Ramsay. That father, whose first name is never divulged (nor is his wife's—the two together representing poles of propriety), bears a name that denotes the way he uses names: Ram-say. The speaking ram, whose speech is ramming . . .

> Had their enterprise succeeded, the universal tongue would have been a particular language imposed by violence. . . . [T]he master with the most force would have imposed this language on the world and, by virtue of this fact, it would have become the universal tongue. . . . God . . . interrupts the edification and in turn imposes his name on their tower (or his tower). . . . God says: Babel. . . . He imposes confusion on them at the same time as he imposes his proper name, the name he has chosen which means confusion. . . . (Derrida, *The Ear of the Other* 101)

God then "imposes a double bind"

> by forcing men, if you will, to translate his proper name with a common noun. In effect he says to them: Now you will not impose a single tongue; you will be condemned to the multiplicity of tongues; translate and, to begin with, translate my name. Translate my name, says he, but at the same time he says: You will not be able to translate my name because, first of all, it's a proper name and, secondly, my name . . . signifies ambiguity, confusion, et cetera. (102)

Et cetera: the very repetitiousness of Derrida's speech signifies the "double bind" of human beings both condemned to repetition—to carry on, as James Ramsay must, a patronymic—and enjoined to perpetual translation.[19] It is a bind embodied perfectly by *Orlando*, the book whose name designates its character, a book that *is* its name and its character, engaged in perpetual shapeshifting yet tangled in repetition. The name Orlando collapses into one both common and proper names, for the main character—unlike many others in the book, whose names are absurdly, fecundly long—is never known by any other. Beginning and ending with "O," the name suggests the book's own circularity, its inconclusiveness; yet "Orlando" is not a palindrome: its translation from one end to the other contains difference at the center. This is the principle of the novel—translation without transparency, translation that maintains the aural differences: translation as a form of mutation. This principle, as Rachel Bowlby has noted in *Feminist Destinations*, is embedded as "and/or" in the title (50); and it is embodied in Woolf's favorite mark of punctuation, used here more than in any other novel: the semicolon.

The definition of a semicolon contained in the *OED* itself makes use of the convenient mark: "1800, L. MURRAY, *Eng. Gram.* 227[:] The semi-colon is sometimes used, when the preceding member of the sentence does not of itself give a complete sense, but depends on the following clause; and sometimes when the sense of that member would be complete without the concluding one."

An ambivalent mark, which can signify opening and interdependence, or stand for a closed gate and mutual autonomy, the semicolon mirrors Woolf's own vacillating definitions of androgyny in *A Room of One's Own* and "The New Biography." It can be granitic, or it can mimic rainbow; as both-in-one, however, it is more the latter than the former, for granite inevitably signifies exclusion. In the novel's proliferating catalogs, both principles are represented. Sometimes differences are absolute, as when the narrator describes the Elizabethan age, using *both* "and" and "or" to signify division:

> Everything was different. The weather itself, the heat and cold of summer and winter, was, we may believe, of another temper altogether. The brilliant amorous day was divided as sheerly from the night as land from water. . . . The rain fell vehemently, or not at all. The sun blazed or there was darkness. . . . Violence was all. The flower bloomed and faded. The sun rose and sank. The lover loved and went. (27)

Or differences may function as a set of permutations, each arising, however incongruously, from the last:

> Images, metaphors of the most extreme and extravagant twined and twisted in his mind. [Orlando] called [Sasha] a melon, a pineapple, an olive tree, an emerald, and a fox in the snow all in the space of three seconds; he did not know whether he had heard her, tasted her, seen her, or all three together. (37)

The indeterminacy or endless translatability of Orlando's metaphors for his beloved goes hand-in-hand with his uncertainty about her gender, and, for that matter, about his own. This capacity of metaphor to mutate continually is literalized, at the center of the novel, in Orlando's own sex-change—a "literalization" that, because "literally" unbelievable, casts doubt on the very distinctions between the literal/bodily and the figurative/metaphysical. These distinctions are already called into question in the opening paragraph of the "biography" (itself a generic category destabilized by Woolf's text), a passage that echoes, in fabulous-historical terms, the family scenes of *To the Lighthouse*:

He—for there could be no doubt of his sex, though the fashion of the time did something to disguise it—was in the act of slicing at the head of a Moor which swung from the rafters. . . . Orlando's father, or perhaps his grandfather, had struck it from the shoulders of a vast Pagan who had started up under the moon in the barbarian fields of Africa; and now it swung, gently, perpetually, in the breeze which never ceased blowing through the attic rooms of the gigantic house of the lord who had slain him. (13)

This is an unsettling start, consonant with *Orlando*'s whole project of unsettling, or denaturalizing, the conventional trajectory of narrative; as in Orlando's name, beginnings and endings are elided in a refusal to come to conclusions. This refusal embraces history even as history is rejected; Orlando's act is a repetition of his fathers', but a repetition with a difference, for his phallic feint is essentially impotent. The Moor is long dead and the imperial battle would seem to have been won. There is nothing to slice at but a dis-bodied round, "the colour of an old football, and more or less the shape of one," so that what was once earnest is now mere boys' sport. "Mere" sport, however, is a notion undermined by the book's persistent elisions. The very words often used by critics to classify, and partially dismiss, *Orlando*—words like "escapade" and "interlude" (Lee, *Virginia Woolf* 612, 520)—encapsulate the book's intermingling of earnestness and play, its refusal to take genealogy seriously, *as* a serious, or at any rate subversive, political gesture. *Orlando*'s form acknowledges the impossibility of true escape—there is no outside-history—and raises "escapade," a seemingly harmless, carnivalesque performance within the temporal and spatial bounds of the sanctioned, to the level of an enormous question. Where did history begin, and what exactly is at issue in genealogies and myths of origin? By parrying sonorous beginnings—parodying the notion of a determinate original—*Orlando* suggests possibilities. Suppose, for instance, the blade missed the head and cut the bond instead?

The opening passage demands the closest of possible readings. As a start, it requires attention, since what follows will presumably follow *from* it (as was the case, for instance, in the last family scene of *To the Lighthouse*). Yet the novel has multiple beginnings, periods of activity in Orlando's life punctuated by mysterious phases of near-death torpor; long immersions in habit interrupted by abrupt epiphanies; and epiphanies undermined by contradiction. Periodically, Orlando's very body gives a start, as when, returning from Turkey in her new status as woman, she realizes "the penalties and the privileges of her position. But that start," we are told, "was not of the kind that might have been expected. . . . Orlando's start was of a very complicated kind, and not to be summed up in a trice" (153–54). Slowing the reader down, the narrator draws attention to the word "start," an etymological border case containing, or at least suggesting, opposite meanings (and a word, as the text also continually implies, can only suggest, can never *really* "mean"). To start is to be unsettled, to be displaced from a previous position or assumption—thus "start" is at least a second, not an originating, term. But it also originates new trains of thought, new assumptions. The dash that follows the first term of *Orlando* functions as such a start, undermining the preceding "He"—by implication also undermining the *very* first He: "In the beginning, God created. . . ." (The question as to whether "God" can precede a "beginning" that, syntactically, he follows, has itself been the subject of exegetical debate.) The assurance that follows this interruption is that much more forceful—and that much weakened—*for* the interruption; it is as if Woolf demonstrates the hard work culture must perform to keep its subjects rigidly defined. The excessive protest of "for there could be no doubt" is in any case undermined again by a qualifying "though," though the assertion that clothing merely covers sex does something to reassure the reader. But danger has already entered the text: as the narrator says later, describing one of Orlando's contemplative interludes, "Still he looked; still he paused. It is these pauses that are our undoing. It is then that sedition enters the fortress and our troops rise in insurrection" (80).

In these lines, as throughout the text, Woolf's writing draws attention to itself as, ultimately, its own subject. "These pauses," explicitly referring to the main character's activity in the previous sentence, seem also to refer to the sentence itself; again and again, the character Orlando is the text *Orlando*. Divided by a semicolon, the anaphoric halves of the sentence are both equivalent and distinct: they begin the same way and end differently, so that the structure of the sentence reflects the function of the semicolon, keeping things symmetrical even as it creates distinction. The semicolon *is* the pause, breaching as it fortifies, so that more and more words can proliferate on its far side; the words about troops are the troops themselves. (The word "fortress" recalls the "fortif[ication] of differences" that Woolf hopes, paradoxically, to see proliferate in *A Room of One's Own*.) *Orlando* is a text of verbal excess; to continue the metaphor of violent insurrection, it "blows up" the signifying function of language by using language with a vengeance.[20] Orlando's pause in fact leads to his reincarnation as a writer—and a writer of absurd and hilarious copiousness, whose description allows Woolf an unparalleled deployment of semicolons:

> Anyone moderately familiar with the rigours of composition will not need to be told the story in detail; how he wrote and it seemed good; read and it seemed vile; corrected and tore up; cut out; put in; was in ecstasy; in despair; had his good nights and bad mornings; snatched at ideas and lost them; saw his book plain before him and it vanished; acted his people's parts as he ate; mouthed them as he walked; now cried; now laughed; vacillated between this style and

that; now preferred the heroic and pompous; next the plain and simple; now the vales of Tempe; then the fields of Kent or Cornwall; *and* could not decide whether he was the divinest genius *or* the greatest fool in the world. (82; italics mine)

Just as "read and it seemed vile" revises the allusion to the God of Genesis in the previous clause, the final and/or of the sentence both explodes all possibility of a decisive conclusion and exposes *Orlando* as a text that brings down the "divine," raises up the "foolish," and finally intermixes categories of rank. Like Orlando's own class and ethnic background, *Orlando* is constitutionally confused—a grandmother, we are told, had been a milkmaid, and thus "some grains of the Kentish or Sussex earth were mixed with the thin, fine fluid which came to him from Normandy. He held that the mixture of brown earth and blue blood was a good one" (28). (Here the solid element is associated with a woman, the milkmaid, and the liquid in theory with Orlando's male ancestors—a reversal of the values of granite and rainbow, and an allusion, perhaps, to Sackville-West's overriding conservatism?) At other times, elements appear to be juxtaposed rather than intermixed, as when the narrator tells us that

> [n]ature, who has played so many queer tricks upon us, making us so unequally of clay and diamonds, of rainbow and granite, and stuffed them into a case, often of the most incongruous, for the poet has a butcher's face and the butcher a poet's; nature, who delights in muddle and mystery . . . has further complicated her task and added to our confusion by providing not only a perfect ragbag of odds and ends within us—a piece of policeman's trousers lying cheek by jowl with Queen Alexandra's wedding veil—but has contrived that the whole assortment shall be lightly stitched together by a single thread. (77–78)

The image of an "assortment" of "odds and ends" that is "lightly stitched together" would at first suggest an ensemble of discrete entities in imminent danger of disintegration. Like the famous taxi of *A Room of One's Own*, which is, of course, bound to stop, open its doors, and release both passengers, the "case" of the individual seems on the verge of losing its contents. But the very grammatical confusion into which Woolf is led by the task of detailing this congeries illustrates the impossibility of differentiation. And while the phrase "odds and ends" seems so clearly and even redundantly to designate the juxtaposition of incongruous solid objects, a few pages further on, even they are drawn into an amalgam. Attempting to solve such problems as "What is love? What friendship? What truth?" Orlando finds time and again that he can't get them straight, because "directly he came to think about them, his whole past, which seemed to him of extreme length and variety, rushed into the falling second, swelled it a dozen times its natural size, coloured it all the tints of the rainbow and filled it with all the odds and ends in the universe" (99)—quite like the text of *Orlando*.

Woolf figures her "marriage of granite and rainbow" as Orlando's androgyny; but marriage makes literal appearances in the text, as well. The author alludes to her husband in the preface. After a great many acknowledgments to a heterogeneous group—as if to suggest that the book, like Orlando's brain, is a case overstuffed with incongruous influences—he is the penultimate person she invokes:

> . . . I will conclude by thanking the officials of the British Museum and Record Office for their wonted courtesy; my niece Miss Angelica Bell, for a service which none but she could have rendered; and my husband for the patience with which he has invariably helped my researches and for the profound historical knowledge to which these pages owe whatever degree of accuracy they may attain. Finally, I would thank, had I not lost his name and address, a gentleman in America, who has generously and gratuitously corrected the punctuation, the botany, the entomology, the geography, and the chronology of previous works of mine and will, I hope, not spare his services on the present occasion. (ix)

Woolf's two and a half pages of acknowledgments are both a satire on an old academic habit and an attempt to turn an outworn form into something new and heterodox. The preface's final flourish represents the same double gesture. "Therefore I will conclude" quickly becomes absurd as Woolf goes on for several more lines, at once spoofing the pompousness of an endless academic peroration and enacting the same deliberate inconclusiveness that informs the whole book. Woolf's recurrent use of the phrase "odds and ends" suggests that like starts, endings can be endless, for what is "odd" stands out, evoking incongruity instead of resolution. The fact that the start of the novel is in fact preceded by a long start drawing attention to the book's own constructedness reminds us to question beginnings—as does the fact that the technical start of the tale (or tail?) is an act of slicing. The Moor's head is itself an odd end, a synecdochal leftover of an act now merely parodied by the androgyne Orlando.

Leaving aside for the moment censorious Americans and accurate husbands, we must consider the Moor and his significance. Jaimie Hovey has elucidated *Orlando*'s racial and imperialist discourses, emphasizing the novel's ambivalent reinscription of the values of white, upper-class masculinity and femininity. "Beginning with an image of a decapitated Moor," writes Hovey, "*Orlando* appropriates the exoticized subjects of colonial discourse to create for its protagonist a sexuality that is not bourgeois or heterosexual. However, *Orlando*'s playful but insistent production of white femininity allows the protagonist to pass as respectable and heterosexual by displacing her transgressive sexuality onto racial others. . . . The 'playful' exchange of racial others for sexual tolerance allows the novel both to interrogate and to affirm the national belonging of the queerly gendered Englishwoman, notwithstanding Woolf's well-known mistrust of the nation as a political affiliation for women" (" 'Kissing a Negress,' " 398). Despite the clear applicability of this critique especially for the passages that take place in Turkey, appropriating tropes of exoticism and gypsies as metaphor, neither the displacement nor the exchange is as textually clear-cut as Hovey implies. The narrative begins not with "an image of a decapitated Moor" but with the ancient head of a Moor, suggesting the very obsolescence of such appropriations. In short, decapitating Moors for the sake of reinvesting Caucasian heads with authority is a gesture *Orlando* eschews from the outset. It is a gesture already rejected implicitly by James's epiphany in the boat at the end of *To the Lighthouse*, in which his vengeful energies are redirected from his father's breast to the bondage that includes the father with the children. There is an *un*mooring at work here that plays against traditional oedipal tropes of unmanning, for the latter act—the decapitation—has already occurred, and Orlando's slicing is a tired imitation that can function as the first act of the profuse text that follows only by performing some radical turn.

That turn is embodied in the self-reflexive imagery and language of the passage. The "vast Pagan" who "start[s] up" in the third sentence is a figure who will "start up" again and again in the text—a figure whose potent energies are far from being simply appropriated or exchanged, as he stands for the text's own disruptive energies. With its instant refusal of a unitary "He," *Orlando* establishes its own identity and mode as "Pagan," polyvalent and polymorphous. Albeit the young Orlando, who seems mostly to miss the head in his feints, purposely cuts the cord in order to rehang it "so that his enemy grinned at him through shrunk, black lips triumphantly" (14)— sooner or later, this fruitless repetition must cease or somehow mutate, or there will be no direction for Orlando to go in, nothing, in this queer bildungsroman, for him to learn. At issue here is not so much Woolf's entanglement in racist tropes—of this there can be little question—as her appropriation of them for purposes of deconstructing polarity and hierarchy. Not many pages after this initial scene, Orlando will be given a start that shakes him loose from imperialist hubris. In short, the Moor's opponent will find himself unmoored from all previous assumptions—to the point where he himself enters the consciousness of a Moor.

That other Moor is one whose name echoes Orlando's: Othello, who also inhabits a text named for himself. The performance of *Othello* that Orlando witnesses is significantly situated in the midst of the most dramatic events of the Elizabethan part of Orlando's history: on a temporal cusp between the day on which Sasha seems to have committed an infidelity with a sailor whose description suggests a reincarnation of the vast Pagan—

a "hairy sea brute . . . huge . . . [a] tawny wide-cheeked monster"—and the night in which the frozen Thames breaks up and the unmoored Russian ship disappears, bearing Sasha off forever. Skating across the ice, his "suspicions melt[ing] in his breast, [Orlando] felt as if he had been hooked by a great fish through the nose and rushed through the waters unwillingly, yet with his own consent" (53). This strange and remarkable image foreshadows the strange and remarkable subsequent events, beginning with Orlando's powerful, empathic response to Shakespeare: "The frenzy of the Moor seemed to him his own frenzy, and when the Moor suffocated the woman in her bed it was Sasha he killed with his own hands" (57). As the play ends, Orlando enjoins Sasha to elope with him at midnight. Her failure to appear is synchronous with the dramatic change in weather—"It was as if the hard and consolidated sky poured itself forth in one profuse fountain . . . the river had gained its freedom in the night"—and functions as a lesson to Orlando. His mistake, like Othello's, was to harden and consolidate, to strangle Sasha—both in his efforts to find the final, perfect metaphor for her and in his desire to possess her exclusively. The cataclysmic fragmentation of the Thames, the "swirling waters" that carry away Orlando's misogynist epithets along with his beloved, "toss[ing] at his feet a broken pot and a little straw"—metonymies like the Moor's head at the start—end chapter 1, decisively unmooring the polarities of the first scene. And they illuminate the crossing between *To the Lighthouse* and *Orlando*: the answer to the father and his blade is flood; appropriating James's revenge, Woolf chooses a distinctly "feminine" tactic of engulfment to counteract the Ram-says and other censoring professors. *X*es will be opposed with *O*s, not further feints, and the metaphor of crossing will be freed of its dangers.

DADDIES *NOT* A PRIG

As in both *A Room of One's Own* and "The New Biography," images of marriage serve as literalizations of androgyny in *Orlando*. In the Victorian section of the novel, the relationship of Orlando and Marmaduke Bonthrop Shelmerdine flourishes as the amalgamative revision of the double-crossings enacted between Orlando and Sasha. No longer will one lover try to encompass the other—though a socially sanctioned union paradoxically serves to free the partners to indulge their fantasies and realize their ambitions (as in the case of the Woolfs), and to liberate "infidelity" of its fateful consequences (as in the case of Nicolson and Sackville-West). It is, in fact, a "queer" marriage, a truer realization of the bond but not the bondage promised by that strange sentence which leads Orlando and Sasha to the silken rope dividing commoners from nobles, where they watch *Othello* from the fringes and, shortly, all ropes and bonds are torn into a thousand shreds. I read that sentence as emblematic of *Orlando*'s escapade; again: "[H]e felt as if he had been hooked by a great fish through the nose and rushed through the waters unwillingly, yet with his own consent" (53). Used to describe the headiness and bondage of a great passion, this image of a monstrous role reversal reverses all traditional notions of subject and object. The sentence must either stop the reader short—giving us a start, not to be summed up in a trice—or at least subliminally affect the reader's subsequent sense of who does what to whom. It is one of many fishing images in Woolf's works, and one of at least three that designate marriage or engagement as a bondage: Mrs. Bradshaw in *Mrs. Dalloway* had "caught salmon freely" before succumbing to her husband's "oily dominion" (152), and Isa in *Between the Acts* meets her husband, Giles, when both are fishing, and is instantly ensnared. (The woman writer's lack of freedom to write frankly about her sexuality is described in "Professions for Women" as an interruption in her fishing.) In this instance, it is the man, not the woman, who is caught; nor is he simply overwhelmed by a large fish, as sometimes happens to a fisher—he is "hooked . . . through the nose" as if he *were* the fish. This confusion of trajectories effected by a startling switch from active to passive, the distressing ambivalence that traditionally characterizes falling-in-love, is changed, in the marriage of Orlando and Shelmerdine, into a perpetual linguistic back-and-forth in which language itself comes to signify differently. The lines between them—spoken and written lines—function less as binding ropes than as acts of simultaneous translation that free the speakers from the subject positions grammar conventionally enforces. Like the genre of *Orlando* and the gender of Orlando, their conversation is unclassifiable: an odd conjunction of "stupid, prosy things" that are, according to the narrator, "often the most poetic"—and therefore cannot be transcribed. When we do get a sample of the couple's words to one another, we find out that what they say is never exactly what they mean, and yet they are able to understand each other perfectly—which leads inevitably to the questions:

> "Are you positive you aren't a man?" he would ask anxiously, and she would echo,
> "Can it be possible you're not a woman?" and then they must put it to the proof without more ado. (258)

The very notion that Orlando and Shelmerdine can "put it to the proof"—presumably through sexual intercourse—suggests a shedding of gender our literal minds can't quite conceive. Neither of them "is" a transvestite or hermaphrodite; it is their *language* that perpetually mediates between male and female, and continually suggests that each member of the couple is the opposite of what s/he appears to be. Thus the "stupid" and "prosy" is in fact poetry, and when M.B.S. says, " 'Here's the north. . . .

There's the south,' " Orlando hears him as not referring to fixed categories but instead describing "the phosphorescence on the waves, the icicles clanking in the shrouds" (257): precisely the free-and-open dialogue that fails between Cam and Mr. Ramsay through the latter's insistence on the precise valences of "East" and "West." When Woolf describes Orlando "echoing" Marmaduke's question, she ignores the apparently essential difference in the two questions: "woman" does *not* precisely echo "man." Boundaries blur: words, which exist to differentiate, mean differently in different ears, and this, rather than separating the lovers (and at the same time binding them uncomfortably, as his wife and children are bound by Mr. Ramsay's words), allows a loose harmony between them.

Because Orlando and Marmaduke's marriage thrives on such understanding, it also thrives on absence. It is primarily a textual relationship. Physical contact and even proximity are thus unnecessary, as long as the telegraph system functions:

> It may be taken as a comment, adverse or favourable, as the reader chooses to consider it upon her relations with her husband (who was at the Horn), that whenever anything popped violently into her head, she went straight to the nearest telegraph office and wired to him. There was one, as it happened, close at hand. "My God Shel," she wired; "life literature Greene toady—" here she dropped into a cypher language which they had invented between them so that a whole spiritual state of the utmost complexity might be conveyed in a word or two without the telegraph clerk being any the wiser, and added the words "Rattigan Glumphoboo," which summed it up precisely. (282)

The narrator asks the reader to judge the marriage of Marmaduke and Orlando according to our opinion of this telegraphic habit. Our answer depends largely on our reading of those two queer words "Rattigan Glumphoboo." We are in the position of the telegraph clerk, who is, in turn, in the position of the "American gentleman" of the preface, able either to accept what he doesn't understand or to censor it. Woolf asks us to admit the possibility of a language that we can't comprehend—a kind of babble or Babel that, though it eludes all but its speakers, is preferable to an enforced universal tongue.

But since this little language of lovers (to borrow a phrase Woolf uses in *The Waves*) is incomprehensible to anyone outside the charmed circle, it is impracticable for public use—therefore, what good is it? The larger question, of course, concerns the escapade or interlude of *Orlando*. In earnest fun, the book puts forward a radical re-vision of gender and of every kind of power relationship: between men and women, rulers and serfs, humans and fish . . . But how does any of this translate to the "real world," which is structured through and through by hierarchies of power? How does an invented language actually function in the grid of marriage? If "the reader" of *Orlando* is hard put to interpret "Rattigan Glumphoboo," what might the reader of Virginia and Leonard Woolf's letters make of this exchange, from the week Virginia spent in France with Vita in 1928:

> I wonder . . . whether you have "gathered" as you would say, being such a little prig—no daddies *not* a prig—we adore dadanko do-do—we want to talk with him; and kiss the poos. Have they really begun to play the violin, daddie? Are you fonder of them than of the marmoteski?—Now stop mots; go under the table. I can't hear myself speak for their chatter. How they sobbed when there was no letter from Dinkay at Avallon! Shall you be glad to see us all again? . . . Lord! how I adore you! and you only think of me as a bagfull of itching monkeys, and ship me to the Indies with indifference!
>
> I think we shall have a very happy and exciting autumn, in spite of the complete failure of Orlando. (*L* 3:539)

Or of this?

> . . . [M]y dearest Mistress Mandril, . . . you do know what a happy year we've had together & what another happy year will begin for us next week. I believe, Great One, you do want to take on your mongoose in service for another year—& if you'll only let him grovel before you & kiss your toes, he'll be happy. Goodnight, beloved. (*LLW* 186–87)

Outside *Orlando*'s fictional world, lovers speak a version of baby talk that is often predicated on power and fear—using those very valences in much the way *Orlando*, in Hovey's reading, questions the polarities of "whiteness and beauty, militarism and masculinity" even as it "also depends on them" (" 'Kissing a Negress,' " 399). Such language reproduces the insularity of the relationship between infant and mother, the small world in which one person can rest secure in the sense of the other's absolute power and protectiveness. This feeling depends entirely on the other's response in kind; if the other speaks as an autonomous adult, the charm can be broken—the initial speaker left bereft, having to fend for him- or herself. By invoking a private language, we reassure ourselves that we are not alone in the world: there is at least one other—if *only* one other—who feels and sees things just as we do. The fantasy produces a sense of organic sameness between two people, of the melding of consciousnesses. It is a linguistic soup in which differences are dissolved. Thus lovers often call each other by the same name, or by names denoting a generic relationship. Virginia and Leonard were, respectively, Mandril and Mongoose, but they were also both Marmots. Their contemporaries Rebecca West and H. G. Wells called each other Panther and Jaguar.[21] Vita Sackville-West and Harold Nicolson both called one another "Mar," a word denoting child in the Sackville-West family lingo, and punned upon by Woolf when Orlando shortens Marmaduke's name to "Mar."

The main purpose of the little language is reassurance; it constructs the love relationship as something apart from all other human connections, inviolable. Because the Marmots—or, for that matter, the Woolves—are a species unto themselves, no other animal can answer to their particular needs. Describing the relationship of Wells and West, Gordon Ray writes that

> Panther and Jaguar were far more than mere affectionate nicknames. They stood for the whole attitude towards life evolved by Rebecca and Wells, who continued to use these names as long as their love lasted. They emphasized the ruthless withdrawal from society that the relationship entailed, the fact that Rebecca and Wells were not part of the pack and did not acknowledge its law. Instead they were "carnivores" living apart in their hidden "lair," going forth to "catch food," and meeting "at the trodden place in the jungle." Wells' [married] life . . . became a mere "showcase for weekends," from which he escaped to be "loose in London." (*H. G. Wells and Rebecca West* 36)

For Wells and West, the little language was a way of dividing private from public, preventing the "pack" from impinging upon their sacred and illicit territory. Wells's publicly sanctioned relationship to his wife could be defused as a threat when cast as part of the superficial world of tame beasts. But the very intensity of the private language is linked to the power of that threat; the fact that the story of Panther and Jaguar ended with the end of their love suggests that that love was tenuous to begin with. The story of two carnivores who can derive nourishment only when they are together is created to feed the relationship; yet the fantasy narrative and the real one are so interdependent that it is hard to tell which expires first.

Virginia Woolf depicts precisely such a problematic relationship between the fantasy life and the actual marriage of a couple in her short story "Lappin and Lapinova." The story was written around the same time that Woolf was working on *Night and Day*, and revised for publication in late 1938. Susan Dick posits that "Lappin and Lapinova" is the work alluded to when Woolf wrote to Vanessa Bell on October 24, 1938 that "marriage, as I suddenly for the first time realised walking in the Square, reduces one to damnable servility. Cant be helped. Im going to write a comedy about it" (*CSF* 303).[22] The story is about a young wife, Rosalind Thorburn, who attempts to mitigate the dreariness of her marriage by engaging her husband in an elaborate narrative about two rabbits. Rosalind's Shakespearean name links her to Orlando; but "Lappin and Lapinova" is, in fact, a kind of reverse *Orlando*, in which the marriage of two utterly dissimilar people depends entirely on the painstaking creation of a "little language" that inevitably collapses. In the case of Orlando and Marmaduke, the language arises naturally from a "queer" kinship; in the Thorburn marriage, it is forced into being by an unhappy wife seeking, from the very start, to escape a relationship that squelches her. If "Lappin and Lapinova" is a comedy, it is a very dark one, ending in dissolution rather than union.

Like other lovers' animal stories, the Thorburns' depends upon a vision of themselves as set apart from the rest of the world. They are small wild animals in league against landowners and poachers, always running from the guns and traps of their persecutors. The story ends when Ernest himself—whose Victorian name, bourgeois background, and "ramrod" straightness have rendered him suspect all along—becomes one of the hunters simply by virtue of dropping out of the fantasy narrative. As the story progresses, it is painfully clear that the fantasy is Rosalind's only way of staving off the panic which comes with recognizing her husband's true identity as one of "them." The day that Ernest dismisses the fantasy as "rubbish" is the penultimate day of their marriage; the final blow comes when he returns from the office the next day to find Rosalind sitting in the dark:

> There was the crack of a gun. . . . She started as if she had been shot. It was only Ernest, turning his key in the door. She waited, trembling. . . .
>
> "It's Lapinova . . ." she faltered, glancing wildly at him out of her great startled eyes. "She's gone, Ernest. I've lost her!"
>
> Ernest frowned. He pressed his lips tight together. "Oh, that's what's up, is it?" he said, smiling rather grimly at his wife. For ten seconds he stood there, silent; and she waited, feeling hands tightening at the back of her neck.
>
> "Yes," he said at length. "Poor Lapinova . . ." He straightened his tie at the looking-glass over the mantlepiece.
>
> "Caught in a trap," he said, "killed," and sat down and read the newspaper.
>
> So that was the end of that marriage. (*CSF* 262)

Insofar as it is not only the end of the Thorburn marriage but also the end of a certain *type* of marriage that is described in "Lappin and Lapinova," the story is, perhaps, a comedy. For Rosalind, the ending is good: Lapinova has been trapped, but Lapinova was never a true identity, only one created to disguise the loss of Rosalind herself. Woolf's reference to the "damnable servility" of marriage recalls her warning, in *A Room of One's Own*, that "to submit to the decrees of the measurers [is] the most servile of attitudes." And Ernest's own transformation from a petty bureaucrat with infinitesimal charm to a hunter in league with all the other hunters echoes the scene in which the student making outlines in the British Museum joins the "pack" of pedagogues hounding the woman's question into a "pen." The dissolution of the Thorburn marriage thus represents Rosalind's own liberation from servility and, by extension, a feminist refusal of an oppressive model of marriage.

But what distinguishes the Thorburns from Orlando and Marmaduke, and why does their rabbit story fail while *Orlando* ends in an ecstatic reunion facilitated by nonsensical telegrams? More important here is the question implicit at the beginning of this chapter: to which paradigm does the Woolf marriage belong? What are the implications of their two different ways of assimilating information, narrating experience? Were Mandril, Mongoose, dadanko do-do and company merely gurgles covering an essential rift and preventing the union, linguistically at least, from disintegrating into its component parts? Or does the babble represent a simultaneous translation of the granitic element into the ethereal and vice versa—thus a marriage in which roles are flexible and differences are dissolved by understanding? How exactly does the husband thanked in the preface of *Orlando*—assuming that neither he nor "the author" is purely a fiction—differ from the pedantic American gentleman and his counterparts Professor von X, Mr. A (author of the masculinist story of Alan and Phoebe), and others? *Is* Daddie a prig, like all those other daddies? Or is he, at day's end, a "brother" or equal, like the "private brother" of *Three Guineas* before his mutation into a public male (and unlike the predatory half-brother, George Duckworth)?

The answer is probably both. Certainly Leonard could be stubborn and petty. But this had its causes. The challenges Leonard faced as Virginia's caretaker may have amplified his own sense of tenuous selfhood in the social stratum she represented. Virginia was not the only vulnerable or self-conscious Woolf. In *Beginning Again*, Leonard wrote:

> If I am to tell the truth, the whole truth, and nothing but the truth, I must admit that . . . I have always felt psychologically insecure. I am afraid of making a fool of myself, of my first day at school, of going out to dinner, or of a weekend at Garsington with the Morrells. What shall I say to Mr. Jones, or to Lady Ottoline Morrell, or Aldous Huxley? My hand trembles at the thought of it, and so do my soul, heart, and stomach. Of course, I have learnt to conceal everything except the trembling hand. . . . (*BA* 91)

Leonard ends the paragraph by explaining, somewhat incoherently, that money is the one thing he doesn't worry over: "I have had to be extremely careful about money for long periods in my life, but I have never worried about it, probably because I learnt by experience as a child and a youth to be insecure and comparatively poor and not to worry about it." He begins the next paragraph by maintaining that "Virginia's experience had been very different and had had a very different effect upon her."

This seeming non sequitur says a great deal. Why, if he doesn't worry over money, *does* Leonard worry about what he will talk about at Garsington—and what is the connection between these things? Because, unlike Virginia, Leonard is a penniless Jew. Beginning with his years in public school, he had moved among privileged Gentiles; he had always felt out of place. At Cambridge, he was the only Jew ever to be an Apostle. In confessing his insecurity, Leonard makes an extraordinary autobiographical gesture, dismantling his persona even as he creates it. Again and again in the course of his narrative he returns to one theme: the "carapace" that he constructed in boyhood and has maintained to this day. It is a defense people like Virginia don't need, because of either their background or their genius, or some felicitous combination of both. In describing the development of this carapace, Leonard adds light to the picture of boys' public schools and all-male universities that Virginia had described in *A Room of One's Own* with a mixture of envy and contempt. What Leonard explains is that even a male can suffer from exclusion and mockery at these institutions and is ultimately forced to create a mask for himself. He also reveals his own envy of the genius wife who was never pushed to such dissimulations (in part, perhaps, because Leonard acted as her buffer against the world):

> I have never known anyone who had no carapace or facade at all, but I have known people who seemed wonderfully direct, simple, spiritually unveiled. They may be highly intelligent and intellectual, but this nakedness of the soul gives them always a streak of the simpleton. They are, indeed, the simpletons—Kot. [the Russian friend with whom Virginia collaborated on translations] used to translate the Russian word as "sillies"— . . . whom Tolstoy thought were the best people in the world. There was something of the "silly" in Virginia. . . .
>
> I am afraid that there was never a touch of the "silly" in me. . . . At any rate, I certainly began to grow my shell at St. Paul's about the age of fourteen, and, being naturally of an introspective nature, I was always half-conscious of doing so. . . . I believe the male carapace is usually grown to conceal cowardice. Certainly . . . the character which I invented to face the world with originated, to a very large extent, in . . . the fear of ridicule or disapproval if one revealed one's real thoughts or feelings. . . . (*S* 71–72)

Leonard's depiction of the tender soul—what he calls "the gentle, eager, inquisitive, generous, vulnerable guest and companion of our bodies which seemed to have little or no connection with that other tough guest and comrade of the same body"—corresponds, in psychologically intrasubjective terms, to Virginia's vision of the self as composed of male and female elements, granite and rainbow. But Leonard deplores the predominance of the male part and envies people like Virginia, who need not hide their tender and fantastical side, whose genius derives precisely from their complete abandonment to that part of themselves.

Of course, Leonard points to a number of factors that forced him to create his own facade; his backhanded compliment to Virginia in calling her a "silly" only emphasizes the extent of his envy of the wife who possessed more power in the relationship than is often supposed. It was she, after all, who was considered the "great" writer; she whose books sold in large numbers compared to his; she who referred to him in company as "the Jew" and wrote in her diary that he was sometimes harsh with the servants because he was "not a gentleman" (D 4:326). And it was she who wrote, after a quarrel with Leonard and her own refusal to go to lunch with him and other friends, "The Virginia who refuses is a very instinctive & therefore powerful person" (D 3:81).

Leonard did not suppress Virginia's instincts, but he did help her to channel them creatively. When he put her to bed during a headache or a nervous spell, he was helping her to lie back and observe her own "gyrations" without being overwhelmed by them. He seems to have felt, and regretted, the suppression of his own instincts acutely at times. But to see Leonard as a self-sacrificing angel is a mistake as well. His life was not given over to Virginia; he was amazingly productive as a writer, editor, and political activist. Perhaps the best metaphor for the Woolf marriage is, after all, the taxicab of A Room of One's Own. They sat apart, each looking out the window: she at the sky, he at the municipal bricks. They spoke to one another in their respective languages, describing sky, describing bricks—describing bricks in an ethereal vocabulary and sky in an earthly one; and sometimes they moved closer and babbled in a private tongue that pretended away their differences. Their capacity to fluctuate between polar difference and mutual recognition functioned like a vehicle between the pure fantasy of Orlando-Marmaduke and the tragicomedy of the Thorburns. Unlike either of these fictional marriages, theirs produced a series of translations, neither perfect and perpetual, nor forced and doomed to final breakdown.

MISSED TRANSLATIONS

The division of *The Waves*, which has elicited much admiring commentary, does not seem successful to me, although from a certain point of view it could be hailed as a technical feat. The book's title indicates its structure in a wholly readable way. But that is just the problem: the procedure is too systematic, with the text artificially divided into waves, as though by some machine that had lost the sense of rhythm and no longer knew how to breathe. It resembles a dCcor made of pasteboard waves activated by a cold mechanism and pretending to go up and down. The title makes do with miming what is not there in the text: the supple, living rhythm of the wave which animates other novels does not manage to spread itself across the surface of this text. (Defromont, "Mirrors and Fragments" 76)

The Waves is a novel filled with impasses; impasse might even be deemed its subject matter. Just as *Orlando* is a text of plenitude, whose *copia verborum* enacts an ideal of endless translation, *The Waves* is a text of depletion, its structure embodying the constant threat of failed translation—between one subjectivity and another, and between subjectivities within the mind. Each of the novel's six characters ruminates throughout on the existential problems of intersubjectivity; the fact that a questionable hero like their adored friend Percival, a ruler of empire who falls from his horse, is needed to hold them all together suggests a sad return to the "real world" of power and hierarchy after the exuberant intermission of *Orlando*. (The relation between the interlude and the world of war and pain becomes the theme of *Between the Acts* a few years later.) Though Françoise Defromont over-states the case, she identifies the ethos of encasement that makes *The Waves*, despite its soaring beauties, a disturbingly hard-edged read. Within the novel, the waves themselves are described more often as solid, almost petri-fied, than as fluid and supple, a surprising turn given Woolf's use of waves as *the* trope—often explicit, always implicit—of constant change in all her other works ("Change was incessant, and change perhaps would never cease" [*Orlando* 176]). Perhaps *The Waves* serves to illumine the very illuso-riness of the interlude—it, too, is bounded—by recasting the liberating moment as an impasse. The threat always already inhabited the very struc-ture of "O": "Above and around this brilliant circle like a bowl of darkness pressed the deep black of a winter's night" (*Orlando* 55)—in short, beyond the seemingly liberatory roundness structuring the fantasy of an escape from hierarchical division is yet another round that signifies enclosure. The ideal of amalgamation—a fluid encompassing, and thereby fragmenting, rigidities—is exposed as a prisoning fiction: when Orlando's "mind . . . be-come[s] a fluid that flowed round things and enclosed them completely" (314), it, too, participates in an economy of appropriation, with its inevita-ble exclusions.

My interest is not to end this chapter with a critique of *The Waves*, nor to reduce its complex vision of intersubjectivity to a pessimistic assertion. Only, I want to return, O-like, to the fundamentally political problem of intersubjectivity embodied in Woolf's 1924 diary entry, in which she uses "the International situation"—reparations to Germany, "how money is paid"—to illuminate the differences between her thinking and Leonard's. Even as *The Waves* expounds on the fallaciousness of labeling a character, it suggests the often unbridgeable differences between two characters that can arise from circumstances of history (in the case of the Australian Louis, for instance) or chemistry (in that of the suicidal Rhoda, whose mind from the beginning functions in series of bipolar unsettlings). The very fact that these two fellow outsiders cannot join in a productive union like that of

Orlando and Marmaduke suggests that the problem of separate consciousnesses is never truly solved (or dissolved). And, as both history and the
Woolfs' subsequent works will show, it is a problem with international implications. When translation fails, the would-be translator resorts to force.
Louis, for instance—whose crippling complexes about his colonial origin
are sublimated into a rigidity and efficiency reminiscent of Leonard
Woolf's "carapace"—dreams of achieving "some gigantic amalgamation
between the two discrepancies so hideously apparent to me. Out of my
suffering I will do it. I will knock. I will enter" (53). His very frustration in
this existential enterprise—the "two discrepancies" are never specifically
labeled—leads him from the image of a polite mutual consensus ("I will
knock. I will enter") to a desire for bondage and, finally, a confused vision
of separate hardnesses:

> What the dead poet said, you have forgotten. And I cannot translate it to you
> so that its binding power ropes you in, and makes it clear to you that you are
> aimless. . . . To translate that poem so that it is easily read is to be my endeavor.
> I, the companion of Plato, of Virgil, will knock at the grained oak door. I
> oppose to what is passing this ramrod of beaten steel. (95)

Louis's frustration suggests an inevitable return, not of Mr. Ramsay himself, but of the Ram-sayan stance. When words fail, they turn to ramrods;
out of barren intercourse, swords are beaten. (Nor does the Gaia-like fertility of earthy Susan seem an adequate alternative; like Mrs. Ramsay—and
unlike Lily Briscoe—she chooses a life of acquiescence to the "natural"
order synonymous with quiescence toward the social order.) Even Bernard
the fiction writer, who succeeds more than his five friends in permeating
other minds, inhabiting alternative selves, is reduced again and again to
beating at a barrier; his leitmotif in this six-voice opera is a childishly comic
echo of Louis's door smashing—he bangs his spoon on the table. And it is
Bernard who sees that, "though the screens are in the excess," *both* separateness and amalgamation can be exploited for violence: "We exist not only
separately but in undifferentiated blobs of matter. With one scoop a whole
brakeful of boys is swept up and goes cricketing, footballing. An army
marches across Europe. We assemble in parks and halls and sedulously
oppose any renegade (Neville, Louis, Rhoda) who sets up a separate existence" (247).

The vision vouchsafed to Bernard is a dark one, and even his eternal
optimism, his unquenchable life force, expresses itself in the book's final
lines as immutably martial:

> "What enemy do we now perceive advancing against us, you whom I ride now,
> as we stand pawing this stretch of pavement? It is death. Death is the enemy.
> It is death against whom I ride with my spear couched and my hair flying back

like a young man's, like Percival's, when he galloped in India. I strike spurs into my horse. Against you I will fling myself, unvanquished and unyielding, O Death!"

The waves broke on the shore (297)

Granted, the book ends without a period—the waves' movement is eternal; yet the final images don't reassure. They are filled with collision and shattering. Dreams of intersubjective amalgamation don't define this novel; instead, the book led Woolf to the same doubts about her language that periodically stop Bernard short, as when, leaning on a garden gate, he loses the imaginary second self that has given his phrases meaning, and summarizes his life's work thus: "A shadow, I had been sedulous to take note of shadows" (285). Responding to a friend's praise of *The Waves*, Woolf wrote: "I'm annoyed to be told that I am nothing but a stringer together of words and words and words. I begin to doubt beautiful words. How one longs sometimes to have done something in the world" (*L* 4:397–98). Yet the rejection of words in favor of deeds is spurious, given that deeds so often translate as violence. In 1937, Julian Bell renounced the intellectual and artistic ethos of his parents and their friends; he went to Spain to fight fascism and was killed by a shell one month later. Writing about her nephew, Woolf "defend[ed] her pacifism as a form of action" (Lee, *Virginia Woolf* 685): "Still my natural reaction is to fight intellectually: if I were any use, I should write against it: I should evolve some plan for fighting English tyranny. The moment force is used, it becomes meaningless & unreal to me . . ." (qtd. in Lee, *Virginia Woolf* 685). Woolf's words echo her refusal of symbolism in *To the Lighthouse*: "Directly I'm told what a thing means, it becomes hateful to me." The equation is a clear one: words used to a purpose are equivalent to force. The politically committed writer is an oxymoron. Yet Woolf's own work thrived on such crossings; its fertility arose from ever unlikelier oppositions and, in the face of virtual impossibility, grew ever more resourceful—until it could grow no longer.

CHAPTER V.

Monstrous Conjugations

Every rational and civilized man is aware that not very
far below the surface of his mind there lurks a
savage, primitive instinct of self-glorification. One's
own family, house, village, county, nation, school,
university are all *felt* to be in some way superior to
those of other people. Reason, if it be used,
teaches us that the feeling must be a delusion and a
superstition. Even the most patriotic can hardly
believe that every family is superior to every other
family and every tribe or nation superior to every
other tribe or nation. . . .
(*Leonard Woolf*, Quack, Quack!)

"*We?*" said Giles. "*We?*" He looked, once, at William. . . .
It was a bit of luck—that he could despise him,
not himself.
The good man contemplated the idiot benignly. His
faith had room, he indicated, for him too. He too,
Mr. Streatfield appeared to be saying, is part of ourselves.
But not a part we like to recognize, Mrs. Springett
added silently. . . .
(*Virginia Woolf*, Between the Acts)

OLD WORDS

In her description of a decidedly nonandrogynous novel in *A Room of One's Own*, Virginia Woolf complains of the barred and barring shadow cast over its pages by the recurrent pronoun "I." The ego of the writer looms so large that all interest and all variety are obscured. There is no perspective apart from those of the author and his male protagonist—which are one and the same. The book is finally dull and unreadable.

In the 1930s, a similar shadow loomed over all Europe. It was the shadow of the authoritarian proclaiming his will, his desire, his intention. He had taken over and was dictating the narrative of European history. Other voices and other perspectives were squelched by his insistent "I," which could only evoke an echo: the cry of misery Woolf transcribes in *Three Guineas* as "Ay, ay, ay, ay" (141). "It is not a new cry," she writes, "it is a very old cry."

History was repeating itself, and repetition became a theme in both Woolfs' writings of the late thirties. To disrupt the litanies of the patriarchs, reactionaries, and dictators became their necessary aim as writers. One tactic was derisive mimicry: Virginia Woolf describes the status quo of male dominion and capitalist greed as "the old tune which human nature, like a gramophone whose needle has stuck, is now grinding out with such disastrous unanimity . . . . 'Here we go round the mulberry tree, the mulberry tree, the mulberry tree. Give it all to me, all to me, all to me. Three hundred millions spent upon war' " (*TG* 59).

Elsewhere in the same book, Woolf describes the female response to the word "society," which "sets tolling in memory the dismal bells of a harsh music: shall not, shall not, shall not" (105). Leonard Woolf gives his 1935 analysis of fascist rhetoric, *Quack, Quack!*, a title that encompasses both repetition and nonsense and uses such repetitive nonsense words as "juju," "abracadabra" and "mumbo-jumbo" throughout to debunk Hitlerian incantation.

On the heels of this satirical mimicry, however, the Woolfs' writings of the late thirties indicate their concern with finding an alternative to fascistic discourse. As Hitler's territorial ambitions grew and his persecutions became more monstrous, satire must have seemed less and less efficacious. Satire is, after all, still an echo of the thing satirized. Some new narrative, some entirely different perspective, must be inserted between the dictator's "I" and the resultant universal wail of "Ay, ay, ay, ay." The authoritarian's solipsism must be disrupted by some new form of writing. Authorship needed to be reinvented along democratic lines; a new, more egalitarian relationship between author and audience had—once again, it seems, some fifteen years after "Mr. Bennett and Mrs. Brown"—to be discovered. Virginia Woolf's last long work, the generically hybrid *Between the Acts*, represents such an attempt; as does Leonard Woolf's antirealist political tract, *The War for Peace*, published in 1940. This chapter will briefly examine the two satirical works, *Three Guineas* and *Quack, Quack!*, before focusing on both Woolfs' attempts to recover language from the dictator's grasp and posit a new historical narrative in *Between the Acts* and *The War for Peace*.

WORDS WITHOUT MEANING

In the fourth volume of his autobiography, *Downhill All the Way*, Leonard Woolf begins his recollections of the 1930s by saying, "I have reached the point . . . in which our lives and the lives of everyone [became] penetrated, dominated by politics" (*DAW* 27). Politics had occupied Leonard professionally and intellectually since his return from Ceylon in 1911, but his words here denote the inescapability of political issues in the 1930s. Virginia Woolf's letters and diaries of the period are dotted with the complaint that the public life has permeated the private. This was due in part to her own fame, which had greatly expanded her circle of acquaintance. This very circle, however, included young writers whose approach to their work—generally in poetry rather than prose—was a challenge to her own method and attitudes. These were the leftist, explicitly political writers whom she addresses in the person of John Lehmann in her "Letter to a Young Poet" of 1932 and criticizes, not without a tinge of admiration, in the 1940 lecture to the Workers' Educational Association of Brighton, which became her essay "The Leaning Tower."

Virginia's reluctance to engage in discussions and activities that seemed to her not only peripheral to her real vocation but often futile as well emerges in her many complaints about committees on which she refuses to sit and organizations she would rather not join.[1] She pities the refugees she meets but has little to offer them; after meeting one of the most famous of them in January 1939, she described the encounter thus:

> Difficult talk. . . . When we left he took up the stand What are *you* going to do? The English—war.
>
> . . . Freud said It would have been worse if you had *not* won the war. I said we often felt guilty—if we had failed, perhaps Hitler would not have been. No, he said, with great emphasis; he would have been infinitely worse. . . . A certain strain: all refugees are like gulls with their beaks out for possible crumbs. . . . The strain on us too of being benefactors. (*D* 5:202)

While the Freuds, cared for by the psychoanalyst's protégée Princess Marie Bonaparte, would hardly have put "their beaks out" when Virginia and Leonard visited, Virginia clearly felt her sympathies being enlisted in a manner she was inclined to resist.[2] She uses the word "strain" twice to describe the aura of the visit, as if to indicate a conflict of wills: the beaks demanding, the hand witholding. Her use of pronouns in the above passages is telling. By emphasizing the word "you" in Freud's question, she stresses the responsibility he places on the shoulders of his adoptive country, and, by implication, the power relations between Freuds and Woolfs: the latter voting citizens of a powerful nation that can go to war, the former a family in flight, deprived of the rights of citizenship. Thus Virginia is drawn into a declaration of national allegiance she would probably have denied in another situation: "we often felt guilty," she maintains, that "we" had not lost the previous war. But what had *she* to do with the previous war when, as she so vehemently stated in her 1938 polemic *Three Guineas*, women neither make nor fight wars, nor do they possess nationality? It is Freud's own interpellation—"What are *you* going to do?"—that forces the pronoun "we" into her response before she has time to think about it.[3]

Virginia Woolf's eschewal of the pronoun "I" in favor of solidarity with the homeless and the disenfranchised—" 'I' rejected: 'We' substituted . . . 'We' . . . all waifs & strays" (*D* 5:135)—is often cited as the stance that dominates her work of the thirties. But her "we" makes a shift when, for instance, she is reminded that from the perspective of the truly powerless, she belongs to a "you" who wield power. In *Three Guineas*, she easily identifies herself as an outsider, excluded from the society men have constructed, while she circles uneasily around her other identity, that of potential benefactress, witholding her guineas though the beaks clamor. The photographs her male correspondent has sent—photographs of dead children and ruined houses—confront her with a responsibility, implying the complicitousness of inaction. In October 1935, she wrote in her diary, "Happily, uneducated & voteless, I am not responsible for the state of society" (*D* 4:346); this observation was the basis of her famous distinction in *Three Guineas* between patriarchal society, which excludes, and the Society of Outsiders, which should consist of the excluded. The excluded are not responsible for the actions of the patriarchs. Yet they are complicit if they remain silent, and this recognition compelled Virginia Woolf in the end to "fight . . . for freedom without arms; [to] fight with the mind" (*DM* 244).

To fight with the mind meant, of course, to fight with words. The "strain" between Woolf's continuing reluctance to engage and her sense of responsibility to "fight . . . on the side of the English" (243) is linked to her misgivings about the use of words as weapons and permeates her writing of the thirties. She begins *Three Guineas* by admitting that she has dragged her feet for more than three years, hoping that her correspondent's letter "would answer itself, or that other people would answer it for me," and ends by stating that "this letter would never have been written had you not asked for an answer to your own" (*TG* 3, 144). The fictional letter from a gentleman thus plays the same role as Freud's interpellation: it demands an answer to the question, "What are *you* going to do?"[4] While doing, for Virginia Woolf, could only mean writing, she had moral hesitations even about using words for political ends. Rhetoric and propaganda were the method of the enemy, of Hitler and Mussolini, and this awareness continually complicates not only her own writing of the thirties but her husband's too.

The difference in the Woolfs' literary styles continued to inform their writing in the face of fascism. Carolyn Higginson writes that Leonard "tells us what we are to think. . . . [H]e uses this informative approach almost exclusively in his persuasive political writing." In Virginia's writing, on the other hand, "Speech falters as it does in real life. . . . Repetitions, pauses, unanswered questions . . . these are Virginia's substitutes for Leonard's clear-cut verdicts. Leonard, who agreed with Virginia that there was too much ego in her cosmos, seldom escapes from his own egotistic certainties" ("The Concept of Civilisation" 30–31). Higginson goes on to link the difference to the fact that "Leonard was a man and by instinct an administrator and law-giver, while Virginia was a woman and temperamentally an individualist" (57). Yet the couple's works of the thirties blur these apparently fundamental differences. Both *Quack, Quack!* (1935), Leonard's impassioned denunciation of fascist political and intellectual rhetoric, and *The War for Peace* (1940), whose main theme is an interrogation of "realist" politics, display an acute consciousness of the abuses to which "egotistic certainties" can subject language. In these books, Leonard argues for language as a communicative tool and against its use as an instrument of power; if he is less delicate than Virginia, who continually dismantles her own rhetoric, his aim is the same. Their common enemy was authoritarianism.

The primary question for both Woolfs was how to clear the slate of history, to begin again. For Virginia, who had no chance of fighting the Germans with arms even had she wanted to, the question was primarily literary. In *Between the Acts*, she links it to Genesis and posits (without enacting) a redemptive rewriting of the heterosexual ur-plot. Isa and Giles, at the end of the novel, become the new Adam and Eve whose first words constitute the start of the playwright Miss La Trobe's next composition. Leonard, too, uses a textual analogy with biblical resonances in his discussion of how to effect political change. In *The War for Peace* he writes, "In history and all human affairs it is never possible to turn over a page and begin writing on an absolutely clean sheet of paper. Every page is blotted with the sins and stupidities of the fathers which are visited upon the children for generation after generation" (180).

Both Woolfs were pursuing the recovery of an innocent language, a language that might connect instead of dividing. The odds, they knew, were immense. Their own small texts were up against the urtexts of oppression, which, in the literary conception of history that informs both *Between the Acts* and *The War for Peace*, begin with the Bible and culminate in the founding texts and speeches of Nazism. The former, with its male God, jealousy, violence, and scapegoating of women, provided the West with a sanction for war and oppression that can be undone only by an act of total deconstruction: in effect the founding of a *new* urtext. But finally, there was the nature of language itself to be dealt with, and the question of its efficacy for acts of union. Language defines and differentiates; the moment of access to language is the moment when self and other, "I" and "you," are distinguished. It is this very distinction that tyrants and warmongers employ so effectively in their rhetorical constructions of the enemy.

To find a language that might link people instead of dividing them re-quired the elimination of countless old phrases and the creation of new ones; simultaneously it required a change in what Leonard called "communal psychology." Both Woolfs were familiar with the theories of Freud. Virginia was reading *Civilization and Its Discontents* as well as *Group Psychology and the Analysis of the Ego* at the end of 1939. In *Civilization*, Freud maintained that "[i]t is always possible to bind together a considerable number of people in love, so long as there are other people left over to receive the manifestations of their aggressiveness" (72). Both Woolfs knew that the instinct to take sides, along with the desire to dominate, is ancient, primitive, and ingrained. In *Three Guineas*, Virginia calls it the "infantile fixation" of the fathers. In *Quack, Quack!* and elsewhere, Leonard defines fascism as a recurrence of savagery, a return to superstition and shamanism. In *Between the Acts*, a novel filled with Darwinian allusions, the warmongering mentality is embodied by Giles, who can control his aggressions only by projecting them onto scapegoats:

> This dry summer the path was hard as brick across the fields. This dry sum-mer the path was strewn with stones. He kicked—a flinty yellow stone, a sharp stone, edged as if cut by a savage for an arrow. A barbaric stone; a pre-historic. Stone-kicking was a child's game. He remembered the rules. . . . The gate was a goal; to be reached in ten. The first kick was Manresa (lust). The second, Dodge (perversion). The third, himself (coward). And the fourth and the fifth and all the others were the same. (98–99)

The linear, masculine mode of thinking that Virginia had criticized in *A Room of One's Own* is here shown at its worst extreme. Giles's progress to the gate mimics an army's march across the map; the "path strewn with stones" recalls battlefields strewn with corpses. The academic outline has become a chart of destruction. The observation that Giles's aggression springs largely from self-hatred is a Freudian insight that occurs also in *Quack, Quack!*, where Leonard attributes the grandiose rantings of *Mein Kampf* to Hitler's "inferiority complex."

Yet Giles Oliver, who in ways epitomizes the brutal patriarch, is never altogether unsympathetic. In her depiction of him, Woolf follows the ex-ample of Sophocles, whom she admires in *Three Guineas* for his character-ization of the tyrant Creon as a human being corrupted by power and fearful of ridicule. Giles, like his wife, is a victim of the patriarchal system. Because society decreed that he must support his family, "he was not given his choice" and became a stockbroker instead of a farmer (47). One phrase above all serves to characterize Giles: "He had no command of metaphor" (53). The closest he can come is a reverse form of metonymy whereby a concrete object—the stone he kicks—comes to stand for what he despises.[5] This corresponds to the primitive form of thinking, which embodies emotions in natural objects and effigies, that Leonard describes in *Quack, Quack!*; his scapegoating, though directed at an inanimate thing, links him to the Continental savages who project their fears and aggressions onto groups of human beings.

While Virginia Woolf's project, in *Three Guineas* especially, is to mobilize the daughters of educated men, to rescue the Isas from their isolation and powerlessness, ultimately she wishes to convert the world's Gileses. Planning her essay, "Thoughts on Peace in an Air Raid," to be published in the *New Republic*, she writes to her friend Shena, Lady Simon:

> What the Americans want of me is views on peace. Well, these spring from views on war. . . . [D]o cast your mind further that way: about sharing life after the war: about pooling men's and women's work: about the possibility, if disarmament comes, of removing men's disabilities. Can one change sex characteristics? How far is the women's movement a remarkable experiment in that transformation? Mustn't our next task be the emancipation of men? How can we alter the crest and spur of the fighting cock? Thats the one hope in this war: his soberer hues, and the unreality, (so I feel and I think he feels) of glory. . . . So it looks as if sexes can adapt themselves: and here (thats our work) we can, or the young women can, bring immense influence to bear. (*L* 6:379–80)

Woolf emphasizes through repetition both the difficulty and the importance of changing men's minds: it is "our next task" and "our work" to discover effective methods of persuasion. How does one bring over the Gileses of the world? One of Woolf's answers appears to be "by using his weapons against him"—or for him, since it is his enlightenment one ultimately seeks. Thus, in a tone that fluctuates constantly between irony and earnestness, Woolf barrages her reader in *Three Guineas* with facts and citations, lists and deductions—using all the paraphernalia of masculine intellectual discourse to justify a feminist claim.

Three Guineas becomes a rhetorical proving ground in the battle against the patriarchs. Woolf debunks old phrases and creates neologisms. She exposes the contradictions and intellectual weaknesses in the texts of men. At times she appears to become entangled by contradictory devices and to employ the methods of the enemy with no irony, as in that mystifying passage, which has troubled so many readers, in which she proposes to burn the word "feminism." In Germany, too, books were being burned, neologisms created, old words eradicated. According to Chancellor Von Papen, "Germany, on January 30th, 1933, struck out the word pacifism from its vocabulary" (qtd. in Russell, *Which Way to Peace?* 166). Woolf complicates her proposition by maintaining that we must also burn the words Tyrant and Dictator. But this statement suggests a surprising literalism, like that of Giles imagining he can eradicate lust by kicking a stone. It makes words into symbols, while elsewhere in the book Woolf rejects symbols as the devices the tyrant uses to emphasize his stature and enforce his rule.

In a text that employs so many rhetorical devices to refute rhetoric, certain pitfalls are inevitable. Perhaps the most obvious is a special pleading that tends to reify the very concepts it attempts to debunk. While polemics differ in their method, and *Three Guineas* is distinguished by great irony and dexterity, the form could not ultimately satisfy a writer who was constantly searching for a wholly new genre. She returned to fiction in the late thirties out of the desire to find an associative, asymbolic way of communicating; *Between the Acts* performs her quest for a language beyond representation—for words that might free instead of ensnaring as symbols do.

In *Quack, Quack!*, Leonard links the human susceptibility to symbols to the deep fears that make primitive people turn to medicine men for protection and help, and gave rise to the notion of divine kingship. In England today, he says, this manifests itself in "the emotional attitude which the ordinary man is encouraged and expected to adopt towards the king and royal family, the ruling classes and 'the flag' " (*QQ* 20). In Germany, he perceives it in the hysteria with which the masses acclaim the Führer's apparition. The very word Führer is invested with symbolic significance by Nazi rhetoric; literally translated, it merely means leader, a fairly vague designation, but for Hitler's worshipers, it had transcendent meaning. If he was their leader, then they were naturally followers, and the fixed categories were not to be questioned. Virginia Woolf, it is worth noting, unfixes them through a deliberate mistranslation at the culmination of her description of the dictator:

> [A]s this letter has gone on, adding fact to fact, another picture has imposed itself upon the foreground. It is the figure of a man; some say, others deny, that he is Man himself, the quintessence of virility, the perfect type of which all the others are imperfect adumbrations. He is a man certainly. His eyes are glazed; his eyes glare. His body, which is braced in an unnatural position, is tightly cased in a uniform. Upon the breast of that uniform are sewn several medals and other mystic symbols. His hand is upon a sword. He is called in German and Italian Fuehrer or Duce; in our own language Tyrant or Dictator. (*TG* 142)

Woolf's description is a portrait of a portrait, its gist, that "Hitler" is no more than his own effigy. The "glaze" and "glare" of his eyes suggest a polished, unreceptive surface; his body, "cased" and "braced," is statuesque. The sentence "His hand is upon a sword," lacking an active verb, seems to reflect the work of some canny creator of propaganda images, rather than the Führer's own volition. Woolf will go on, however, to insist that behind the image is a human being, and "that we cannot dissociate ourselves from that figure but are ourselves that figure" (*TG* 142). In similar fashion, Leonard ends his comparison of Hitler's photograph with the mask of a Hawaiian war god (both reproduced in plates at the center of the book)[6] by implying a connection between him and us:

> The significant point is the psychological effect which the facial appearance is clearly meant to produce. The savage effigies admirably depict the superhuman sternness of the god and the terror which he instils. They are the faces not of individual human beings, but of generalized emotions of the savage. Somehow or other the fascist leaders have contrived to get their faces into the same mould. . . . [T]he most remarkable resemblance is to be noted between the photograph of Hitler and the first of the two Hawaiian effigies. The savage's effigy is obviously intended to represent the inspiration of terror by the god. But the curious thing is that the effigy itself is a vivid representation, not only of a terror-producing being, but of a terrified human being. Look at the eyes. And the photograph of Herr Hitler shows the same odd combination. It is an official photograph of the terror-producing Fuehrer, but it is also the photograph of a man who is himself terribly afraid. Look at the eyes. (*QQ* 47–48)

Leonard here invokes Freud's theories of the power of leaders over crowds. In *Group Psychology and the Analysis of the Ego*, Freud maintains that the leader represents the group members' ego ideal. The followers see themselves magnified in the larger-than-life image of their head, through whom they achieve vicarious satisfaction. What Leonard stresses is the weakness common to both Führer and followers, which creates a Hegelian interdependence. He shows how unstable is the tyrant's actual power, resting as it does on oversimplifying symbols. Like Virginia, Leonard focuses on the tyrant's physical self-representation in order to emphasize the artificiality and emptiness of his charisma. Leonard's aim is to shatter the mirror between the tyrant and his audience by questioning his use of regalia, the delusion he fosters that his stare, his medals, his raised hand, and his uniform possess magical powers. He begins with the tyrant's visual rhetoric in order finally to debunk his verbal rhetoric, to disconnect the symbol from what it is supposed to signify. Like Virginia, he purposely mistranslates: power, he explains, is nothing but exploited fear, just as the "Fuehrer" is not a benevolent leader but a "Tyrant," one who dictates.

It is the link between political and verbal dictation that characterizes fascism for both Woolfs. The dictator deprives his interlocutors of the ability to respond, except through echo. If he is the leader, then they must follow: there cannot be two leaders. This means that the followers have no language apart from that imposed upon them. Words' meanings are decided over their heads; there is no communication but only a sort of infernal catechism. "The clamour," Woolf writes in *Three Guineas*, "the uproar

. . . is such that we can hardly hear ourselves speak; it takes the words out of our mouths; it makes us say what we have not said" (141). The dictator uses language not only to silence dissent but also to mystify and obfuscate. What seems clear is in fact sheer nonsense: this is Leonard's thesis in *Quack, Quack!*, whose title is a pun on quackery—the charlatan's offer of a panacea—and the inarticulate noises of barnyard fowl. To expose both sorts of quack is, again, to unlink the symbol from its supposed signified: the tonic won't cure; the noise is merely noise.

But the crowd also hears what it wants to believe, and it is the crowd's willingness to be led into chaos and carnage that the dictator cunningly exploits. "The quack, quack of Herr Hitler's Aryanism or Herr Kube's hero-worship is the quack-quack of a goose," writes Leonard, "but in the quack, quack of the scapegoat hunters you can hear the sound change to the yapping of the pack that wants to taste blood" (105). Harold Nicolson, in a small volume entitled *Why Britain is at War*, published in 1939, quotes Hitler's own words on propaganda in *Mein Kampf*:

> "If once . . . the propagandist allows even the slightest glimmer of right to be seen upon the other side, he is raising doubt in the mind of the masses. . . . There must be no gradations, only positive and negative; love and hate; right and wrong; truth and lie; never half and half." Above all, logical or intellectual considerations must be avoided; they only confuse the herd mind. "The great revolutions of the world," he writes, "were not brought about by intelligence or knowledge, but by some form of fanaticism which was able to inspire the masses and drive them forwards in a hysterical trance." "The masses," he writes again, "will fall victims to a big lie more readily than to a small one, for they themselves tell only small lies, being ashamed to tell big ones. Untruthfulness on a large scale does not occur to them, and they do not believe in the possibility of such amazing impudence, such scandalous falsification, on the part of others." (35–36)[7]

Here we see the full insidiousness of the dictator. He is no fool; his quacking is quite deliberate. His words are not, in fact, without meaning: their real meaning is simply other than that which his listeners understand it to be. Two ingredients make up the dictator's recipe: lies and categorical statements. He appeals to his audience's cowardice and desire for certainty rather than to their ability to comprehend subtleties. He is, Virginia Woolf might say, the consummate craftsman. Without referring explicitly to politics, Woolf debunked fascistic language in a BBC lecture on April 20, 1937, entitled "Craftsmanship." The writer as craftsman, she maintains, is doubly a contradiction in terms:

> The English dictionary, to which we always turn in moments of dilemma, confirms us in our doubts. It says that the word "craft" has two meanings; it means in the first place making useful objects out of solid matter—for example,

a pot, a chair, a table. In the second place, the word "craft" means cajolery, cunning, deceit. Now we know little that is certain about words, but this we do know—words never make anything that is useful; and words are the only things that tell the truth and nothing but the truth. Therefore, to talk of craft in connection with words is to bring together two incongruous ideas, which if they mate can only give birth to some monster fit for a glass case in a museum. (*DM* 198)

From a woman who continually revised every one of her own works, often even after publication, an argument against craftsmanship must be at least partly disingenuous. But the essay is directed against the use of language as a means to an end. Woolf's aim is to unfix words, to insist on limits to the writer's or the speaker's control over them. Thus she even demotes the dictionary from its position of absolute authority to a text that "confirms . . . doubts." The very fact that it gives us at least two definitions for the word in question shows that no word can be pinned down. Words, Woolf goes on to say, cannot be used purposefully: first, because they are suggestive and protean instead of solid and fixed; then, because they speak for themselves—"*they* tell the truth and nothing but the truth" (italics mine). To deny their autonomy is to produce a monster. It is a specific monster, too, the very same one that Woolf had described ten years before in *A Room of One's Own* when she wrote: "Poetry ought to have a mother as well as a father. The Fascist poem, one may fear, will be a horrid little abortion" (107).

In "Craftsmanship," Woolf is writing not just against a use of language she would call fascist, but against language used in the service of any cause. To write without craft, as Woolf advocates doing, is to write from the un-conscious, and only later to reshape what one has written. Indicting the leftist poets of the Auden generation in "The Leaning Tower," she insists that they write too consciously. Their work, she maintains, is "oratory, not poetry. It is necessary, in order to feel the emotion of [its] lines, that other people should be listening too. We are in a group, in a class-room as we listen" (*M* 146). No matter that Day-Lewis, Spender, Auden, and friends are politically at odds with fascism: their method is the same. It preaches instead of engaging its audience. The writer is making a point of himself, making a point of his point—he is attempting to convert. His product, too, is an abortion, though Woolf does not use the metaphor in this essay. But like the other literary abortions she discusses, it is the result of a travestied relationship: in this case, between writer and audience.

What all literary travesties have in common is the writer's denial of a vital factor in the creative process: the autonomy of words themselves. Like the fascist who denies the feminine and gives birth parthenogenetically,[8] the leaning tower poets block the presence of their readers. Invoking the sexual metaphor once again, one might say that they commit a rape rather than engaging in intercourse.[9]

What solution, then, does Woolf propose to writers whose social conscience prevents them from ignoring politics, at a time when politics affect the entire English population? She herself, after all, had felt compelled to write polemically—and had sometimes become trapped in her own rhetoric—in *Three Guineas*. The answer, she suggests, lies in the leaning tower poets' one virtue, the frankness they have learned "with help from Dr. Freud," what she calls their "unconsciousness." The distinction she makes is implicitly a distinction between private and public self-exposure (thus, for instance, she recommends in her "Letter" to John Lehmann that poets not publish until they have turned thirty). Her own decision was to turn away from the more public form of the essay and back to fiction, a genre whose independence of the need to impress permitted greater experimental freedom. While she knew and acknowledged that this was an escape from what was happening around her, she felt also that "reality" had itself become fantastical. Fiction was a way to rectify the obscenity of "the ravings, the strangled hysterical sobbing swearing ranting of Hitler," to counteract the radio's din of lies. "Theres no getting at truth now all the loud speakers are contradicting each other," she wrote in November 1939. "[I]ts all bombast, this war," she wrote the following May. "One old lady pinning on her cap has more reality" (*D* 5:245, 285).

Thus Woolf returned to the old lady whom she had invoked so many times before. Mrs. Brown and the old woman across from Clarissa Dalloway's window become Mrs. Swithin in *Between the Acts*. But there is a feebleness about Mrs. Swithin that suggests a change in Woolf's attitude toward her own project. Maria DiBattista describes her as "the incorrigible, perhaps anachronistic monist indigenous to Woolf's fictional world, a reminder of the effortless epiphanies—and certitudes—of the past" ("*Between the Acts*" 143). A potentially redemptive figure who falls short, she suggests the insufficiency of Woolf's traditional literary goal—a goal she still espoused in 1932 when she recommended to John Lehmann as his "task . . . to find the relation between things that seem incompatible yet have a mysterious affinity, to absorb every experience that comes your way fearlessly and saturate it completely so that your poem is a whole, not a fragment" ("Letter to a Young Poet" 230). *Between the Acts* is a work that insists on its own fragmentedness, its disruptions and disjunctions as well as its moments of harmony. Thus Mrs. Swithin's "one-making" is her limitation. La Trobe, the real seer of the novel, fails in the project of uniting her audience, while Swithin's visions of unity are too easily achieved.[10]

What makes Swithin ultimately questionable is her inability to resist authority in the form of the patriarchal God. She wears a cross around her neck in a novel that invokes rings, nooses, and yokes as images of enslavement by convention, and whose subtext is biblical revision. "How could she weight herself down by that sleek symbol?" William Dodge wonders. "How stamp herself, so volatile, so vagrant, with that image? As he looked at it, they were truants no more" (73). Lucy Swithin is a figure possessed by symbols, seduced by propaganda. In rejecting the fiction of harmony Swithin represents, compromised as it is by her adherence to old gospels, Woolf paradoxically embraces an even purer fiction—a fiction, that is, defined by constant flux rather than by a unifying principle. Isa Oliver articulates Woolf's desire for such a redemptive writing when she wishes for "a new plot," even as Miss La Trobe begins to conceive her next work in "words without meaning—wonderful words." The language Woolf imagines, and La Trobe engenders, lacks verisimilitude: there are no objects behind its words. It is language used entirely without craft, or the intention of impressing, and in it lies the only hope of a new plot for the world.

This idea of language is a consummately political conception, much as Woolf may have thought she was insulating herself from politics by returning to fiction. In casting La Trobe as the rewriter of Genesis, she was propounding a reconception of human—and international—relations. Her project is mirrored in more explicitly political terms in Leonard Woolf's book *The War for Peace*, published in 1940. The book is an argument against the realpolitik that conceives of relations between people and states in terms of power rather than cooperation. Over and over Leonard attacks the terms used by the promoters of power politics, insisting that such words as "realist" and "utopian" have no fixed meaning. He refutes the notion that war is inevitable and cooperation between nations, as between people, unimaginable. He, too, argues for a new plot. To undermine the rhetoric of history-making politicians, he employs a number of rhetorical devices of his own. One is continually to place certain central terms in quotation marks, to question their accepted meanings:

> "Realists" deride the view that there can be a harmony of interest among all nations in peace. But the whole history of Europe since 1815 makes it probable that the view is correct. It is true that at any particular moment, if the international system is based upon conflict and the psychology of the majority of Europeans is nationalist, it may be to the immediate interest of a particular nation not to keep the peace. But for the realist to say that would be to beg the question. For by changing the system and psychology the interest of that nation might have been served far better by peace than war. That people, looking round Europe to-day, can refuse to change the word "might" in the last sentence into "would" reduces one to amazed despair. (*WFP* 200–201)

Leonard's emphasis, like Virginia's, is on vocabulary as the molder of plot. History can be reshaped only when words are newly deployed. Although Leonard does not go so far as to imagine a language without meaning, he echoes Virginia's insistence in "Craftsmanship" on the protean character of words. A "realist" means one thing to one person, another to the next. A change of verbal auxiliary could change the world order. And such change, Leonard insists, can and must be made by ordinary people: individuals must reclaim the historical narrative from the irresponsible leaders who impose upon the public a false notion of their "interests." Both Leonard's argument and his method are fundamentally antidictatorial. He attempts to engage his audience through a fiction, a fantasy about the future that, he claims, only they can make fact. Like the invisible author at the end of *Between the Acts*, who recedes into blank space just as the "new plot" begins, he leaves the narrative to his readers. Since it is to be a narrative of cooperation rather than coercion, this is only logical.

THE THREE EMOTIONS

It would be a mistake to obfuscate the differences in method and medium between Virginia's last novel and Leonard's political treatise. Some of these will be discussed below. What I here emphasize is the goal and vision common to the two books. Both debunk old verities and promote a new historical narrative. Both base history and politics in language, and both are concerned to counteract the abuse of language by dictators and other self-interested politicians and to resurrect it as a medium of communication. Finally, both books are caught between the "realistic" recognition that the page can never be made blank, and a mythifying nostalgia for prelapsarian innocence. The Garden is never far from either Woolf's mind.[11] The equivalent in Leonard's book of Virginia's "old lady" who possesses "more reality" than dictatorship and war is a simple cultivator: "[T]here is more reality," Leonard writes in *The War for Peace*, "more utility, and more glory in the occupation of a man sowing a threepenny packet of cabbage seed in his back garden than in that of a man winning the great battle at Austerlitz" (27). The homely garden scene, however, is inevitably countered later in the book by the story of an eerie jungle incident. The garden is always already a jungle, a site of primal sin. The beginning is never a real beginning, as Virginia acknowledges in one of her last and most nostalgic texts, the unfinished sketch entitled "Anon.," where she admits that even in the days of King Arthur,

> save that self consciousness had not yet raised its mirror, the men and women are ourselves, seen out of perspective; elongated, foreshortened, but very old, with a knowledge of all good and all evil. They are already corrupt in this fresh world. They have evil dreams. Arthur is doomed; the Queens are lustful. There never was, it seems, a time when men and women were without memory;

There never was a young world. Behind the English lay ages of toil and love. That is the world beneath our consciousness; the anonymous world to which we can return. (385)

The passage is an admission that Woolf's proposal to the leaning tower poets, to reject "conscious" writing and delve into "unconsciousness," may not be a solution in troubled times. Woolf draws a Freudian equation between the unconscious and the childhood of humankind, and exposes both as impure. Freud, whose theories underlie much of both Woolfs' thinking about war and fascism in the thirties, finds aggressive and erotic instincts warring beneath the consciousnesses of all human beings. It is that war Woolf represents in *Between the Acts*, a book that dreams of a space between the two instincts, a lull in the battle.

The deadlock of love and hate, and the impossibility of finding a solution that doesn't merely reverse the terms and restart the cycle, are dramatized in *Between the Acts* by an episode critics inevitably fix upon. No single interpretation ever seems sufficient to comprehend the scene when Giles, at the end of his stone-kicking game, stumbles on a disturbing sight:

> There, couched in the grass, curled in an olive-green ring, was a snake. Dead? No, choked with a toad in its mouth. The snake was unable to swallow; the toad was unable to die. A spasm made the ribs contract; blood oozed. It was birth the wrong way round—a monstrous inversion. So, raising his foot, he stamped on them. The mass crushed and slithered. The white canvas on his tennis shoes was bloodstained and sticky. But it was action. Action relieved him. He strode to the Barn, with blood on his shoes. (99)

This strange image seems vastly overdetermined. In her diary entry of September 4, 1935, Woolf describes its original and, without explanation, the profound, seemingly disproportionate psychological impact the sight had upon her:

> Oh how it pours! I used my umbrella . . . to cross the garden. Cant write today. I suppose after yesterday. Nessa in London. We saw a snake eating a toad: it had half the toad in, half out; gave a suck now & then. The toad slowly disappearing. L. poked its tail; the snake was sick of the crushed toad, & I dreamt of men committing suicide & cd. see the body shooting through the water. (D 4:338)

Virginia was often elliptical in her diary and is especially so here. The links between events are unclear: what happened "yesterday" to keep her from writing "today"? When and where did she see the snake and the toad? If yesterday, then her dream must have occurred that night. Or, by "dream," did she mean "fantasize"? Evidently, her vision of drowning men is connected both to the snake regurgitating the crushed toad and to the pouring rain in the garden. But there is a political backdrop, too, which surely plays into the psychological impression made by the snake and the toad. The diary entry begins with a brief description of the political atmosphere of the previous two days: "The most critical day since Aug 4th 1914. So the papers say. In London yesterday. Writings chalked up all over the walls. 'Dont fight for foreigners. Briton should mind her own business.' Then a circle with a symbol in it. Fascist propaganda, L. said" (*D* 4:337).

The day was critical because the Council at Geneva was trying to find means to stop Mussolini from using force in Abyssinia. The question of isolationism or intervention was an acute one; Virginia at this time still tended to favor the former, along with such friends as Clive Bell, who insisted as late as 1938, in his pamphlet *Warmongers*, that even a German invasion would be preferable to another world war. The dilemma was terrible, and images of a small entity being devoured by a larger might be applied to both its sides. On the one hand, there was Mussolini attempting to swallow up Abyssinia, and the necessity of going to war to stop such acts of engulfment. On the other, there was the threat that England itself might be sucked into another maelstrom, in which thousands of civilians as well as young men of military age might lose their lives. Hence, perhaps, the image of young men drowning. That Woolf's sense of her own impotence in the face of these questions might prevent her from writing for a day is entirely believable.

The image of a satanic creature devouring a smaller animal only became more relevant as the thirties wore on and Hitler's territorial ambitions seemed illimitable. England felt less and less like a safe island; Shakespeare's "demi-paradise . . . built by Nature . . . against infection and the hand of war" was suddenly isolated and vulnerable. Vita Sackville-West, ensconced at Sissinghurst while Harold Nicolson shuttled back and forth to Parliament and the Ministry of Information, wrote her "Country Notes in Wartime" for the *New Statesman and Nation*. In the spirit of Voltaire rather than Genesis, she described the pleasures of cultivation as a stronghold. But even the garden at Sissinghurst was not immune from the surrounding corruption. "In these days," writes Vita,

> one readily interprets the happenings of nature into symbolism. It is, I suppose, a psychological effect of war strain. One clings to the permanence and recurrence of nature. It is a calming and reassuring thought. Nature goes on in spite of the mess mankind makes of mankind.
>
> Yet nature is a nasty cruel thing. I had an example of it when I watched a small, horrifying sight: a young frog panting and injured on the garden path. As I came up to him . . . I observed an evil head shooting out of a hole in the wall, an adder, a beautiful snake full of venom, that drew the frog towards him, terrified and fascinated by the superior power. The frog, instead of turning

towards me, who would have rescued him from danger, limped towards the wall, tried to clamber up it and remained clinging onto the bricks by his fore-feet while the pointed head of the adder shot out at intervals. . . . I watched. The frog remained frozen . . . his body flattened in terror against the wall. The snake put out his dangerous, his fanged head. He did not dare send out the length of his lithe body because of my presence there. (*Country Notes in War-time* 77)

The same "psychological effect of war strain" that made Woolf dream of drowning men impels Vita Sackville-West to allegorize the incident in her own garden. In her first sentence about interpretation, she seems to refer to the peacefulness of nature as providing a sense of security. While she knows that this security is a fiction, it is founded on an evident fact: nature *does* remain serene in the face of human chaos. Then we discover that her first sentence actually refers to the incident recounted in the next paragraph. The disjunction between the two paragraphs emphasizes the sense of "unreality" that Virginia kept describing in her diary: nothing is what it seems to be. No sooner have we created a story with a moral than that moral changes. In an era of broken promises, no text is stable. Leonard Woolf ironically entitles the first chapter of *Downhill All the Way* "Peace in Our Time, O Lord!"[12] Neville Chamberlain's words and the piece of paper in his hand proved meaningless. With so many words broken, the status of language itself must have seemed doubtful to writers in the thirties.

Both Vita Sackville-West and Leonard Woolf were gardeners, and both turned to their gardening as therapy. Leonard concludes *Downhill All the Way* with his own garden allegory:

I will end . . . with a little scene which took place in the last months of peace. They were the most terrible months of my life, for, helplessly and hopelessly, one watched the inevitable approach of war. One of the most horrible things at that time was to listen on the wireless to the speeches of Hitler, the savage and insane ravings of a vindictive underdog who suddenly saw himself to be all-powerful. We were in Rodmell during the late summer of 1939, and I used to listen to those ranting, raving speeches. One afternoon I was planting in the orchard under an apple tree iris reticulata, those lovely flowers. . . . Suddenly I heard Virginia's voice calling to me from the sitting-room window: "Hitler is making a speech." I shouted back: "I shan't come. I'm planting iris and they will be flowering long after he is dead." Last March, 21 years after Hitler committed suicide in his bunker, a few of those violet flowers still flower. . . . (*DAW* 254)

If in retrospect Leonard seems somewhat facile about the survival of his irises long after the death of Hitler (not to mention the millions of other deaths Hitler left in his wake), in 1939 his gardening provided a small relief from tension. Gardening had always been an outlet to Leonard, a hobby to offset his other work. For Virginia, writing was most of life; *cultiver son jardin* meant, to her, to compose fiction. But the stress of watching "helplessly and hopelessly" the rise of fascism and the approach of war resulted for her in doubts about the efficacy of her own words. In her diary, she often describes her sense of the tininess of her enterprise in animal images echoing that of the toad and the snake. "[I]ts odd," she writes on March 13, 1936, "how near the guns have got to our private life again. I can quite distinctly see them & hear a roar, even though I go on, like a doomed mouse, nibbling at my daily page" (*D* 5:17).[13] On May 24, 1938, she speculates that *Three Guineas* "may be like a moth dancing over a bonfire—consumed in less than one second" (*D* 5:142). And on August 19 she describes the experience of looking up at a German warplane, "like a minnow at a roaring shark" (*D* 5:312).

What appalled Virginia Woolf and so many of her contemporaries was the fact that the "insane rantings" of one man could cast the world into a second great war. Vita Sackville-West's parable of the snake and the frog emphasizes the utterly incomprehensible, hypnotic effect of the one over the other. "Hypnosis" was a word commonly used to describe Hitler's effect on his mass audiences; Freud also uses it, along with "paralysis," throughout *Group Psychology and the Analysis of the Ego*. Trying to puzzle out the extreme suggestibility of groups, he likens it to "the hypnosis of fright which occurs in animals" (60). This hypnosis is easily produced by rhetoric: "A group . . . is subject to the truly magical power of words; they can evoke the most formidable tempests in the group mind, and are also capable of stilling them" (16).

The question of how to rescue the hypnotized toad occupied Virginia Woolf on two levels. There was, on the one hand, her own position as a writer. Words themselves were being devoured and disgorged by the fascist serpent; how did one restore their innocence and protean versatility? How did one find a language to appeal not to passion, not to fear, but to the simple, rational desire for peace? ("Peace was the third emotion," thinks Isa. "Love. Hate. Peace. Three emotions made the ply of human life.") Leonard Woolf attempts to find such an antirhetorical rhetoric in *The War for Peace* when he assaults the common conception that power politics are "real" while the politics of cooperation are a mere "utopian" fantasy. But the question, increasingly and heartbreakingly, became also a practical one. "Civilization," that conception so treasured by Virginia and Leonard and all their Bloomsbury friends, was itself being destroyed. Words could do nothing, because words were part of what was being destroyed. England had to abandon her isolationist stance, and even Virginia Woolf had to concede, as she does in "Thoughts on Peace in an Air Raid," that peace must be fought for.

The proposition is, of course, a tormenting paradox. The complexity of the scene in which Giles destroys the snake and toad derives in part from its being an illustration of this very paradox. Giles, coming upon the awful sight, is confronted by the quandary that occupied all England: to intervene, or to stand aside and watch? Either way, lives are lost. It is difficult to see the value of intervention when this means a mimicry of the enemy's own violence. But Giles, in June 1939, decides as England decided a few months later. Woolf indicts Giles's self-satisfaction at the end of the paragraph, when he strides off, relieved by action, with blood on his shoes. Giles is crass and aggressive, and his action is in part a mere extension of his stone kicking: the toad and snake simply replace the stones as convenient scapegoats for his anger. But Giles is also frustrated: frustrated by the failure of his ambitions, frustrated by the ineffectuality of the talk he hears around him, and frustrated by his own impotence in the face of the bristling guns across the Channel. Frustration is the feeling he shares with his wife, and it is in portraying this feeling that Woolf humanizes him.[14]

If the snake-toad scene can be read as an articulation of Woolf's ambivalent feelings toward a national quandary in the late 1930s, it can also be seen as a response to her husband's less ambivalent stance. In *The War for Peace*, Leonard expresses his "sympathy with the pacifist view." "If you are on the side of civilization," he writes, "you must be against the use of force. But that unfortunately does not settle the matter. In human affairs the choice is rarely between what is good and what is bad; it is usually between what is bad and what is worse" (216). He goes on to cite an incident that proves the inefficacy of pacifism in certain situations:

> There is not the slightest evidence . . . that unilateral pacifism would be successful in the actual world of the twentieth century. When I hear the pacifist arguing in this way, I am often reminded of something which I once saw in a Ceylon jungle. . . . I was traveling on foot in thick jungle. . . . Suddenly I saw upon a tree rather higher than the rest a group of monkeys. Their behaviour was so strange that I stopped . . . to watch them. They jumped up and down, up and down, up and down, always in the same place, raising their thin arms to heaven. And then . . . I heard a strange noise—click, click, click. The tracker behind me whispered: "leopard." . . . I was witnessing an incident of jungle life which I had been told of. . . . When a leopard sees monkeys on a tall tree, he lies down under it and clicks his teeth together. The monkeys, fascinated or hypnotized by the sound, begin to leap up and down with their arms raised to heaven above him until sooner or later one of them misses his footing and falls to the ground. He is eaten by the leopard. All my sympathies were, and are, with my collateral ancestor, the grey monkey, the pacifist, silhouetted against the sky with his thin arms raised, as it seemed to me, imploringly to heaven and protesting by non-resistance against the violence of jungle life. I crept

round . . . and fired with a .303 British army rifle at the aggressor. It was a bad shot; there was a flash of yellow fur and the leopard had disappeared into the shadow. But it was force used against force and power against power, and the pacifists on the branch above my head scuttled away in safety. If they had been left to themselves . . . one at least of them would have died a violent death. (*WFP* 217–19)

The moral of this story, Leonard concludes, is that "in so far as [the monkey's] near relation man has escaped from the life of the jungle, it has been by resisting force, not by the anarchic individualism of the lion or the tiger, but by establishing a communal law which forbids the use of force and controls the use of the individual's power and then places communal force behind the law" (219). Well aware of the inherent absurdity of a war for peace, Leonard was also conscious that in certain situations, only violence can bring a new beginning. To this extent, he is himself a political realist. He argues for the use of force at the present moment so that the ideal of international cooperation, whose supposed "utopianism" he ardently denies, can be realized when the enemy has been defeated. As a Jew and a socialist, he could hardly concur with Clive Bell that even a Nazi invasion would be preferable to war.[15] As a political thinker, he advocated a reinstatement of the League of Nations along more efficacious lines. This organization would be loose enough to allow differences among nations but would also act as a kind of police presence to prevent or punish aggression by one nation against another.

Leonard goes on to make a distinction between "confederations" and "federations." The League of the future is to be a confederation consisting, in theory, of smaller federations of nations. Federations, he writes, would be much tighter alliances and would be unnatural among nations run along entirely different principles. He uses a sexual metaphor to describe the impossibility of certain types of federation:

> It is . . . inconceivable that a dictatorship could be married successfully with a democracy in a federation; the marriage service might be read over them in a conference and treaty, just as you might read the marriage service over a dog and a cat, but in neither case would the union be real, permanent, or fertile. . . . It is a delusion to think that you could produce such political monstrosities as a federation of the Persia of Xerxes with the Athens of Themistocles or of the Spain of General Franco with the democracy of Switzerland and make them live. They would merely remain specimens in the museum of history. (*WFP* 205)

Here, again, is Virginia's image of the monster in a glass case. Leonard's monster, however, is not the fascist's spawn but the sexual alliance itself, in which two become one—but, as the old adage about marriage has it, "Which one?" His fascist-democratic marriage bears a striking resemblance to the "olive-green ring" of snake and toad in *Between the Acts*. Inevitably, the dictatorship would incorporate the democracy by force, like the tiger clicking its teeth until the monkey falls into its maw. Such obscene conjugations, Leonard suggests, must themselves be prevented. Failing prevention—and it is the fact that Hitler's gluttony might have been foreseen *and* prevented that Leonard continually bemoans—they need to be destroyed.

For Virginia, the question remained morally problematic, and *Between the Acts* dramatizes her incertitude. While readings casting Giles as a villain oversimplify, it is impossible to read him as a hero. His snake stamping, like his stone kicking, is instinctive and childish. Not unlike the toad, he has been sucked into a cycle of violence—even as this violence angers him. He is, in a sense, one of the drowning young men in Virginia's dream: unable to stop the maelstrom, he flings himself in. He is the victim of a society that is short on alternative plots, and of his own failure to command metaphor; like the dictator's, his visions tend to harden into symbols, rather than staying open to revision. Could he metaphorize, he might find constructive ways to reject the patriarchal plot that has made him a stockbroker in the city, alienated from the land and the wife he yearns for. He seems aware, however dimly, that the old methods are no longer good. There is a spark of potential in Giles; he represents the young man Virginia Woolf pities and wants to nurture in "Thoughts on Peace in an Air Raid," when she writes: "We must help the young Englishmen to root out from themselves the love of medals and decorations. We must create more honourable activities for those who try to conquer in themselves their fighting instinct, their subconscious Hitlerism. We must compensate the man for the loss of his gun" (247).

To rescue her audience from their subconscious Hitlerism is Miss La Trobe's quest in *Between the Acts*. In assuming the task Virginia prescribed to young women in her letter to Lady Simon, La Trobe is confronted with the difficulty of persuading without dictating. In her effort to unite her audience in a common vision, she inevitably winds up mimicking the dictator's methods. The continual collapse of unity into dispersal amongst the audience, which to La Trobe feels like failure, is in fact a redemptive movement.[16] Too much unity, as Woolf has already demonstrated in her image of the snake-toad, is dangerous. It leads to intolerance and persecution.

The audience's sudden swings from harmony to disjunction mirror the playwright's own alternating stances. At moments La Trobe epitomizes the sort of tyranny Woolf despises in men, as when she is likened to "a commander pacing his deck." At others she is the democratic Miss Whatsername, anonymous and egoless, who refuses to come out from the bushes and take credit for her production. It is the midpoint between these attitudes toward which Woolf gestures in portraying the extremes. The ideal society—the ideal group—would be one in which solidarity is achieved without the compromise of individuality. As Freud writes in *Group Psychology*, "The problem consists in how to procure for the group precisely those features which were characteristic for the individual and which are extinguished in him by the formation of the group" (25).

For Woolf, once again, the problem concerns rhetoric: how to invoke a "we" still capable of discriminating—without discriminating *against* a "they"? Two metaphors in Woolf's work embody the dangerous extremes. One, which she links to orality—the snake's mouth, the dictator's tongue—is the trope of incorporation I have already discussed. This vision of oratory made her wary of all discourse intended for an audience: hence her condemnation of the leaning tower poets for their supposed preaching. But the written word is equally suspect and associated not with incorporation but with incarceration. Throughout *Three Guineas* Woolf attacks the patriarchal texts that have confined women to the private house; she calls for a college in which books won't be chained to library tables. In "Craftsmanship" she describes the dictionary as a kind of word-prison (albeit a prison that paradoxically confirms its inmates' freedom). Words, she says "are the wildest, freest, most unteachable of all things. Of course, you can catch them and sort them and place them in alphabetical order in dictionaries. But words do not live in dictionaries; they live in the mind" (*DM* 204).

Dictatorial language, then, occurs in writing as well as in speech. What the dictator does to words—prisoning them, pinning them down—is also what he does to people with words. Woolf condemns the dictator's oratory as well as his inscriptions in *Three Guineas* when she insists on women's status as outsiders. "Inevitably," she writes,

> we look upon society, so kind to you, so harsh to us, as an ill-fitting form that distorts the truth; deforms the mind; fetters the will. Inevitably we look upon societies as conspiracies that sink the private brother . . . and inflate in his stead a monstrous male, loud of voice, hard of fist, childishly intent on scoring the floor of the earth with chalk marks, within whose mystic boundaries human beings are penned, rigidly, separately, artificially; where, daubed red and gold, decorated like a savage with feathers he goes through mystic rites and enjoys the dubious pleasures of power and dominion while we, "his" women, are locked in the private house without share in the many societies of which his society is composed. (105)

In his final apotheosis, the dictator is satanic scribe and satanic orator in one. In a loud voice, he marshals his society; with chalk and pens, he labels and incarcerates the excluded. The patriarch of this passage is connected, two pages earlier, to the tyrant whose victims are Jews as well as women, and a repeated pun establishes the link between his words and his concentration camps:

He is interfering now with your liberty; he is dictating how you should live; he is making distinctions not merely between the sexes but between the races. You are feeling in your own persons what your mothers felt when they were *shut out*, when they were *shut up*, because they were women. Now you are being *shut out*, you are being *shut up*, because you are Jews, because you are democrats, because of race, because of religion. (102–3; italics mine)

The dictator uses language to distinguish between "us" and "them." His neat distinctions silence those who have been labeled, and their silencing is synonymous with their imprisonment. The writer who opposes fascism, then, must tread delicately so as to avoid both oral seduction and prisoning inscription. *Between the Acts* is Woolf's enactment of the effort to locate the border between these dangers. La Trobe is the preacher-*cum*-playwright who seems to succeed (even as she feels herself a failure) in assembling the sort of group Freud imagines—a group in which the characteristics of the individual are not lost. Because La Trobe keeps her audience disagreeing, her play's power is subversive rather than authoritarian.

Both Virginia and Leonard Woolf were ardent individualists. Only by maintaining the distinction between "I" and "you" could human beings, in their view, truly communicate. Empathy, so easily disposed of when self is distinguished from other, paradoxically also depends upon that boundary. Only when one can respect the other's differences does one wish to prevent the other's suffering. Groups too readily exclude the unassimilable and make them into scapegoats. The dialectic of "us" and "them" differs from that of "I" and "you" in its indirectness, its rejection of the essential link between first person and second. The third person is denied a face like our own and becomes the repository of damning fictions. In *The Journey Not the Arrival Matters*, Leonard Woolf explains the connection between individualism and empathy in a discussion of Montaigne's essay on cruelty:

The combination in Montaigne of intense hatred of cruelty and intense awareness of individuality is not fortuitous. . . . It is only if you feel that every he or she has an "I" like your own "I," only if everyone is to you an individual, that you can feel as Montaigne did about cruelty. It is the acute consciousness of my own individuality which makes me realize that I am I, and what pain, persecution, and death means for this "I." . . . What is so difficult to understand and feel is that all other human beings, even the chicken, the pig, and the dew bedabled hare [pursued by hunters in Montaigne's essay], each and all have a precisely similar "I" with the same feelings of personal pleasure and pain, the same fearful consciousness of death that destroyer of this unique "I." (19)

Virginia Woolf's last novel is dominated by this vision of solidarity founded upon individualism. Her stated intention to "reject 'I,' substitute 'we'" does not mean an erasure of individuality. Instead, it denotes an authorial stance intended to be antiauthoritarian and communicative. This stance is embodied by Reverend Streatfield, who falters in his speech at the end of the pageant and refuses to proffer a definitive interpretation. La Trobe, while more talented than Streatfield, is also more ambivalent: at times she wishes to dictate, at others to withdraw. It is this very ambivalence, however, that defines her achievement—an achievement dependent not solely on herself but also on the cooperation of the audience and even of nature, as in this moment at the pageant's center: "The view repeated in its own way what the tune was saying. The sun was sinking; the colours were merging; and the view was saying how after toil men rest from their labours; how coolness comes; reason prevails; and having unharnessed the team from the plow, neighbors dig in cottage gardens and lean over cottage gates" (134).

The synesthesia that this description of peace and harmony initially suggests is belied by its emphasis on difference and boundaries. The view says what the tune says, but in its own language. Colors merge, but neighbors do not: their communication is defined by the gate. Unlike the national boundaries that were being so fiercely drawn and so fiercely threatened as Woolf was writing, the gate can be opened or closed, according to the neighbors' need for privacy. Open *or* closed, it still admits dialogue. This was Virginia and Leonard Woolf's vision of international as well as interpersonal politics.

THE FIRST WORDS

Between the Acts ends with the possibility of renewed recognition between an "I" and a "you" that may, in turn, renew the world. Marriage is posited as a microcosm whose repair can be cosmically redemptive. Miss La Trobe, indeed, becomes a kind of Creatrix in the final pages of *Between the Acts*. Sitting in her pub after the pageant, she imagines a new man and a new woman fashioned from primeval mud: "The mud became fertile. Words rose. . . . Words without meaning—wonderful words" (212).[17] These words of La Trobe's become, in the book's last sentence, the deferred words of reconciliation between the protagonists. If Giles and Isa can begin again, their story will displace Genesis and perhaps even Darwin. But not until the war has been fought will the slate be wiped clean: "Before they slept, they must fight; after they had fought, they would embrace. From that embrace another life might be born. But first they must fight, as the dog fox fights with the vixen, in the heart of darkness, in the fields of night" (219).

This is Woolf's concession that the war had to be, that only force could destroy force. It is also a statement of hope in the face of horror. Men and women, she says, have the capacity to speak like neighbors across the garden gate, to engage in an intercourse defined by respect for difference. Marriage need not be an olive-green coil in which one ego incorporates the other, choking in the process. And if marriages between individuals are capable of redefinition, so are marriages—or, to use Leonard's term, federations—between nations. If the sexes, so different in their upbringing and thus in their perspectives on the world, can communicate, civilization can yet be saved—or better, re-created.

Virginia and Leonard Woolf differed not only in their gender but in their ethnic heritage as well. Their marriage mediated, not always successfully, multiple disjunctions. If Leonard belonged to the privileged sex, he was also a member of a monstrously persecuted group. Virginia's empathy was imperfect at best. While she pays lip service to the plight of the Jews in both *Three Guineas* and *Between the Acts*, her diaries and letters are dotted with disparaging remarks about individual Jews. She could not meet a Jew, it seemed, without labeling him. Often the word "Jew" in her diary is accompanied by a disparaging adjective such as "underbred." To Ethel Smyth in 1930 she wrote, "How I hated marrying a Jew!" (*L* 4:195) And although we are told that Mrs. Manresa's husband in *Between the Acts* is Jewish, he does not enter the narrative as a character.[18]

A passage in *Three Guineas*, partially quoted earlier in this chapter, while it does not explain away her prejudices, illuminates Woolf's attitude toward Jews in the 1930s. Her use of pronouns, once again, is particularly striking:

[The dictator] is making distinctions not merely between the sexes, but between the races. You are feeling in your own persons what your mothers felt when they were shut out, when they were shut up, because they were women. Now you are being shut out, you are being shut up, because you are Jews, because you are democrats, because of race, because of religion. . . . The whole iniquity of dictatorship, whether in Oxford or Cambridge, in Whitehall or Downing Street, against Jews or against women, in England, or in Germany, or in Spain is now apparent to you. But now we are fighting together. The daughters and sons of educated men are fighting side by side. (103)

The "you" Virginia addresses in this passage might be Leonard Woolf, the Jewish son of an educated man who now "feels in [his] own person" what all mothers have felt from time immemorial. Curiously, Virginia leaves herself out of the equation, referring to persecuted women as "they" and men as "you." But she is very much present in the accusing voice, the voice that trembles with anger and resentment toward men, who have never suffered as women have, even as it rises toward a note of celebration.

The "we" of the penultimate sentence denotes a solidarity achieved through the empathy of men for women's suffering, and not vice versa. Men, even Jews, are only now in a position to understand what women have always experienced.

The flaw of *Three Guineas* lies, in part, in this fallacy of the age-old oppression of women versus the more recent persecution of groups such as Jews. (Woolf does not mention doubly persecuted female Jews or immigrants, adumbrated in the figure of Rezia Warren Smith but never, perhaps, truly or deeply considered in her work.) Woolf's resentment toward the men of such groups seems misdirected. Certainly she is justified in her complaint of being "shut out, . . . shut up," by even the most liberal of males. Even Leonard's political tracts—and this, perhaps, represents his own failure of empathy—are rhetorically directed toward men. In her essay on the Woolfs' antifascist writings, "The War between the Woolfs," Laura Moss Gottlieb maintains that Virginia and Leonard "wrote for different audiences," citing as an example a book Leonard edited in 1933, entitled *The Intelligent Man's Way to Prevent War*. All the essays are by well-known male thinkers, and the title clearly asserts both male authorship and male readership. Indeed, throughout his books of the thirties, as in the epigraph to this chapter, Leonard appeals to "the rational and civilized *man*."

But to glean from this, as Gottlieb does, a fundamental conservatism on Leonard's part as well as a difference in his and Virginia's aims in their work is a mistake. Gottlieb claims that

> Although Leonard recognises that "ultimately . . . a world order to prevent war requires a different psychology," the general thrust of his book is toward envisioning new "structures, organisations [and] systems . . . for peace" (*Intelligent Man's Way*, p. 16). It is Virginia who uses her "psychological insight . . . to decide what kind of qualities in human nature are likely to lead to war" (*TG*, p. 58). It is a difference in emphasis which leads to a radical difference in conclusion. For Virginia argues that war is an exclusive male activity and that the same social conditions which encourage war are those which permit men to dominate women economically, sexually, and intellectually. So, while Leonard argues for the League of Nations (one *more* patriarchal institution) as a means of arbitrating international disputes, Virginia advocates the elimination of the patriarchal system altogether as a way of altering human psychology and of abolishing war. (246–47)

Leonard hardly ignores "human nature" in favor of impersonal organizations; instead, he insists over and over in his political writings that world politics imitate interpersonal relations and must be organized in order to bring out the best in human nature. While Leonard seldom likens international power politics to the oppression of women by men, it is not an equation he rejects; indeed, implicit in his insistence that power politics simply means the oppression of one group of individuals by another group of individuals is the notion that only when equal rights and recognition are granted to all human beings can the world be newly ordered. Leonard's individualism is no less radical than Virginia's vision of the overthrow of patriarchy. In advocating a renewed League of Nations he simply recognizes that the removal of existing tyrannies can happen only by stages and with the help of an official authority. But like Virginia, he reconceives authority by reconceiving authorship. He rejects the "realistic" historical narrative according to which cooperation is a chimera and power is essential, even as he maintains a limited realism with regard to method. The reformed League of Nations that he espouses, far from being "one more patriarchal institution," is a significant step away from authority in the form of dictators and kings and toward a cooperative ideal.

Virginia, on the other hand, is in some ways less "radical" than Gottlieb claims and her own late writings superficially suggest. While *Between the Acts* edges toward the postmodern in its continual self-undoing, the attention it draws to its own fragmentariness, the novel also paradoxically gestures backward to a literary style Woolf had earlier rejected. If Mrs. Swithin, who conceives grand fictions of unity while soldiers rape women in Whitehall and Jews are rounded up in Germany, demonstrates the inadequacy of earlier Woolfian epiphanies, she also represents a revision of Mrs. Brown. In her 1924 essay, Woolf had indicted Arnold Bennett's literary realism for its preoccupation with material detail and advocated a delineation of character that would encompass the universal elements of the individual soul. Mrs. Brown, she said, must be depicted as "an old lady of unlimited capacity and infinite variety; capable of appearing in any place; wearing any dress; saying anything and doing heaven knows what. But the things she says and the things she does and her eyes and her nose and her speech and her silence have an overwhelming fascination, for she is, of course, the spirit we live by, life itself" (*CDB* 119).

This is a grandiose vision, and perhaps somewhat facile, too. The individual character as archetype appealed less to Woolf in the late 1930s: fascist discourse, after all, dealt ad nauseam in archetypes. Curiously, in October 1940 Woolf describes the story she would like to write about the life of her former servant Mabel as "something like an Arnold Bennett novel" (*D* 5:328). Woolf's vision of the old lady in the railway carriage had depended upon empathy: the woman was clearly suffering at the hands of a man Woolf refers to as Mr. Smith, and Woolf wished in some way to rescue her from exploitation by presenting all the richness of her character without miring it in "realistic" detail. Galsworthy, Wells, and Bennett resemble the masculinist writer Woolf describes in *A Room of One's Own*, whose ego overshadows the entire novel. They thus resemble Mr. Smith, as well, in their power to dwarf Mrs. Brown and obscure her perspective. Paradoxically, however, Woolf reconstrues literary empathy toward the end of her life in terms of the very realism she had earlier rejected. Thus she and her husband meet one another halfway; he rejecting "realist" politics up to a practicable point, she turning toward realism again even as she embraces a new experimentality in her last novel.

The link between empathy and literary realism suggested by Woolf's wish to write an Arnold Bennett novel about the suffering Mabel is implicit already in a diary entry of March 1936, in which she describes a disturbing incident, concluding with the inadequacy of her own response:

> [D]own I go to the Press . . . & theres a tap on my window. I thought it was a little dressmakers apprentice come with my dress. But it was oh dear—a girl, fainting. Can I have a drop of water? She was hardly able to walk. Then I took her in: got L.: hotted soup. But it was a horrible thing. Shed been walking all day to get work, had neuritis—cdnt sew, had had a cup of tea for breakfast, lived in one room alone in Bethnal Green. At first she cd hardly speak—"I'm hungry" she said. . . . Said You look like brother & sister, both have long noses. I'm a Jewess—a curious stress on the word as if a confession. So's he I said. Then she perked up a little. But my God—no one to help her, she said. . . . Never saw unhappiness, poverty so tangible. And felt its our fault. . . . And what could we do. . . .
>
> Now its raining, & I suppose . . [*sic*] well, whats the use of thinking? As usual what was so vivid I saw it all the evening becomes stylized when I write. (*D* 5:19)

The entry anticipates the description, quoted early in this chapter, of another encounter with a wandering Jew. Like Freud, the young "Jewess" confronts Woolf with a sense of her own responsibility. In this case her responsibility is not only social but literary as well. The inclusion of realistic details in the fashion of Bennett—the cup of tea, the one room in Bethnal Green—is followed by an admission of literary failure. Woolf indicts her writing for *lack* of realism, for her inevitable aestheticization of what she observes. No sooner does the incident begin to fade than Woolf can capture it only through a recomposition that cannot be true to life. The cup of tea and the single room, however, suggest her straining toward a new/old literary ideal, a realism that might repair social inequities.

Yet again, Woolf's use of pronouns is striking. The passage represents a vignette: a triangle in which a third person simultaneously unites and polarizes two others. The young woman, literally an outsider, enters the conjugal space and demands acknowledgment as a person both like and unlike her hosts. The two Woolfs are united in the act of nourishing her. The Jewess, moreover, imposes upon Leonard and Virginia a kinship that transcends the marital: "You look like brother & sister." In confessing her ethnic identity, however, she links herself to her host and not her hostess: "So's he," Virginia answers. This may be the only time Virginia ever drew attention to her husband's Jewishness to set herself, rather than him, apart.

But the Jewess is a woman, too, and this connects her to Virginia. While both Woolfs possess privileges to balance their social disadvantages, the Jewess is doubly disadvantaged. Momentarily, she unsettles the Woolfs in order to align them with one another. In a moment of empathy toward a third party, they appear as equals who cannot feel either superiority or pity toward one another. They are, suddenly, innocent: not "man and wife," not Gentile and Jew, but simply siblings, caught at that moment before the "private brother" has become a "monstrous male," before the sister has become a snob. No olive-green ring theirs, but the recognition of an I and a you. In that moment of recognition, a new world appears faintly possible. But the first words must still be spoken.

Introduction

1. These figures from *To the Lighthouse* meet their ends both at the center of a tripartite structure and in a parenthetical space. Their deaths are at once vital and trivial. The same is true of Jacob Flanders in *Jacob's Room* and of Percival in *The Waves*: cogs in the wheel of overweening political forces, they die offstage, yet their loss irrevocably affects the characters who remain.

2. In the past several years, many if not most of the MLA convention panels dealing expressly with modernism have focused on such questions. Anthologies such as Bonnie Kime Scott's *The Gender of Modernism* and her more recent, two-volume study *Refiguring Modernism* have initiated a reconsideration of the movement and period as a network of intersections among artists and writers of varied class, national, racial, and ethnic background, as well as infused with ideologies of gender. Continuing studies of T. S. Eliot's ideological and especially antisemitic leanings have broadened into recent considerations of the figure of "the Jew," especially in conjunction with ideas about sex and character, in modern British literature. See, for example, Andrea Freud Loewenstein, *Loathsome Jews and Engulfing Women: Metaphors of Projection in the Works of Wyndham Lewis, Charles Williams, and Graham Greene*, and Bryan Cheyette, *Constructions of "the Jew" in Modern English Literature and Society: Racial Representations, 1875-1945*.

A fascinating study elucidating the way the definers of literary high modernism—in particular, Hugh Kenner—have privileged exile over national rootedness as the condition for membership in the canon (and thus excluded Virginia Woolf) is Michael Gluzman's "Modernism and Exile: A View from the Margins" in Biale, Galchinsky, and Heschel, *Insider/Outsider: American Jews and Multiculturalism*.

3. Michael Tratner's book *Modernism and Mass Politics: Joyce, Woolf, Eliot, Yeats* is the first to extensively discuss her politics in conjunction with these other figures'; it also argues convincingly for modernism as a movement composed of splinters and antithetical currents.

4. Thomas C. Caramagno, *The Flight of the Mind: Virginia Woolf's Art and Manic-Depressive Illness*. My conviction derives from Caramagno's detailed research into Leonard's care of Virginia and attitude toward her illness, but also from notations in Virginia Woolf's own diaries and Leonard Woolf's descriptions in his autobiography of his painful efforts to help Virginia understand her "phases" as somatic episodes rather than symptoms of moral weakness—the latter being an all-too-common explanation of mental illness, especially in women, in those early post-Victorian times.

5. See the second chapter in Tratner's *Modernism and Mass Politics* for an in-depth analysis of the relation between sections of the novel and sectors of society within the novel. The work of postcolonial theorists, such as Edward Said in *Culture and Imperialism*, discusses the simultaneously buttressing and unsettling presence of the colonies even in texts whose main locus is the metropole.

6. This corresponds to Randall Stevenson's analysis of modernists' use of Bergson's "time in the mind" against "time on the clock," which "enables readers to recognise *any* ordering of temporality as a construct, an artifice and not an absolute" (Stevenson, *Modernist Fiction* 136, 221). Continually privileging mind-time, Woolf draws attention to the inherently political tyrannies of clock-time.

7. In *The Daughter's Seduction: Feminism and Psychoanalysis*, Jane Gallop encapsulates this same awareness: "I hold the Lacanian view that any identity will necessarily be alien and constraining. I do not believe in some 'new identity' which would be adequate and authentic. But I do not seek some sort of liberation from identity. That would lead only to another form of paralysis—the oceanic passivity of undifferentiation" (xii).

8. I borrow this phrase from Alex Zwerdling, whose *Virginia Woolf and the Real World* was the first study to focus from beginning to end on Woolf's engagement with sociopolitical facts. (In the coming chapters, I use the phrase again with conscious indebtedness.)

9. The emphasis on "unity" in the central works of high modernism receives a closer examination in Kevin J. H. Dettmar, ed., *Rereading the New*, whose introduction points out that unifying schemas were often imposed on these works by the New Critics, whereas the first wave of critics and reviewers were—albeit often disapprovingly—alert to the formal splinterings and outrages committed by modernist writers. Thomas McLaughlin makes the same point in the introduction to Lentricchia and McLaughlin, *Critical Terms for Literary Study*.

10. The novel received positive reviews in the Sinhalese press at the time of its appearance; when Woolf returned to Ceylon for a visit in 1960, he was warmly welcomed, he writes, for several reasons: "Chief among them was *The Village in the Jungle . . .*" (*JNAM* 199). In *Running in the Family*, his 1982 memoir of a return to Sri Lanka, Michael Ondaatje refers to Leonard Woolf as one of the only Europeans to have understood Ceylon, as evinced by *The Village in the Jungle* (83).

11. In *James Joyce and the Problem of Justice*, Joseph Valente points out that "justice" is a system ratified by its own terms; in my reading of the metonymic operations of *Mrs. Dalloway*, Woolf makes an analogous point about such apparently neutral and objective notions as "proportion," which cannot be unlinked from their proponents' sense of property.

12. First presented at a conference in France in 1974, Inglis's essay is published in English in Bowlby's 1992 volume, 46–59.

13. A number of recent critics have also called into question postmodernism's claims of an awareness apparently not possessed by the more blinkered modern(ist)s. In *Sexual Dissidence*, Jonathan Dollimore points out that

> [t]heories of the post-modern are typically premissed on either a simplified construction of the modern, or a suspect retrospective reconstruction of it. The more adequate the history of the diverse modernisms, the less plausible is the representation of the postmodern as a break into the radically new or different. Relatedly, the concept of the postmodern also runs the risk of overvaluing the contemporary and investing it with a significance it does not possess: the imagined radical break is in fact a development more or less compatible with, or at least predictable from, what has gone before. (22)

In her essay "Naming and Difference: Reflections on 'Modernism *versus* Postmodernism' in Literature," Susan Suleiman ruminates on the often contradictory distinctions brought to bear on the two categories, finally suggesting that we view "modern writing as a single category . . . [with] types and strands and brands and various lineages . . . —but not Modernists *versus* Postmodernists" (266).

14. See Gluzman, "Modernism and Exile," for the case of a Hebrew poet, Leah Goldberg, whose work was built on the contradiction of feeling at home in the land that expelled her, yet considering herself an exile in the Jewish "homeland."

Chapter I
Strange Crossings

1. *La Cousine Bette* is one of the books Rachel Vinrace borrows from her aunt and uncle's library in South America. Certain events and symbols in *The Voyage Out* recall Balzac's novel. The irresistible bourgeoise courtesan, Mme. de Marneffe, dies of a tropical illness that has been deliberately transmitted to her by a jealous South American lover. She turns from a beauty into a hag almost instantly, and dies an agonizing death. It is her own sexuality, by implication, that has killed her—whereas Rachel Vinrace seems to be killed by *men's* sexuality. The title character's name is a pun—la cousine bête—suggesting that beastliness is the kin of even the most high-minded, that the mind cannot deny the body. Indulgence in mindless bodily passion, however, leads to degradation.

2. Among biographers, Lyndall Gordon and, most recently, Hermione Lee, revise the common view of the Woolf marriage as altogether sexless. Both emphasize Virginia and Leonard's affection for one another, and invoke one or two of Virginia's diary entries alluding to some sexual activity. These entries are themselves exceptional; but enough to suggest that Virginia Woolf's sexuality was not simply repressed *or* directed only toward women—common interpretations in the past. I agree with recent writers, among them Lee and Gillian Beer, who see Woolf's writing as saturated by a sensual relationship to the object-world that belies her supposed frigidity and suggests that such categorizations oversimplify sexuality. As for the Woolfs' marriage bed, I have chosen not to touch that—to refrain from either speculation or judgment.

3. Or, initially, two works in one volume: the first book published by the Hogarth Press was the pamphlet *Two Stories*, containing Leonard's "Three Jews" and Virginia's "The Mark on the Wall," two seemingly disparate fictions to be discussed in the next chapter.

4. I have borrowed the term "ambiance" from Abdul R. JanMohamed's Introduction to his *Manichean Aesthetics*. It is a subtle and flexible word for capturing the hegemony of colonialism, suggesting the largeness, worldliness, and diffuseness of that hegemony.

5. Garnett seems to have had a habit of such phrasings-for-effect: the back cover of *Growing* quotes his comment on the book: "It may seem surprising that the arrival of a stiff-necked Jewish intellectual from Cambridge should have been wel-

comed in the outposts of empire, but actually he was an immediate success. . . ." This is more to the point than his Arabian fantasia.

6. From a letter to Edward Garnett, June 12, 1915, excerpted in Majumdar and McLaurin, *The Critical Heritage* 61–62.

7. The exact nature of his gropings remains uncertain, as Virginia never described them in detail; they have been discussed by numerous biographers and critics, among whom the most sensationalistic is Louise DeSalvo, the most sensitive, Hermione Lee.

8. DeSalvo's pronomial confusion exemplifies the identification between Rachel and Virginia that she sees as fundamental to the novel, and suggests a certain forcing of the issue.

9. Ashis Nandy, many of whose ideas have informed my readings in this chapter, remarks in one of his discussions of the way colonialism defined resistance, forcing the desire for autonomy to formulate itself in the vocabulary and values of the oppressors: "In a moment of terrible defeatism Vivekananda had said that the salvation of the Hindus lay in three Bs: beef, biceps, and Bhagvad-Gita" (*The Intimate Enemy* 47).

10. F. R. Leavis, quoted by Chinua Achebe in "An Image of Africa: Racism in Conrad's *Heart of Darkness*" 253.

11. As well, perhaps, as for his "desire to copulate with a bronze bottom without copulating with a bronze face"? Hirst's homosexuality is merely implied, but his prototype Strachey wrote this in a letter in early 1905, responding to Leonard Woolf's anecdotes of open homosexuality in Ceylon: "The reign of Sodomy pleases me. How romantic! But then—black!" (*LLW* 76).

12. Lewis Wurgaft, in *The Imperial Imagination: Magic and Myth in Kipling's India*, writes about the myth of India as a fetid, seducing female as it appears in Kipling's stories as well as other literature of colonialism.

13. De Silva's phrase is from his preface to the *Diaries in Ceylon*.

14. Though an exact equation, as the work of recent anthropologists and historians suggests, would be oversimple. See Hyam, *Empire and Sexuality*; Cooper and Stoler, *Tensions of Empire*; and White, *The Comforts of Home*, on the complexities of concubinary arrangements in the colonies, the advantages such arrangements often held for the female concubines, and the linkage of an ever more martial and rigid ethic of imperialism to the outlawing of sexual relations between European men and colonial women.

15. For a discussion of the first and second phases of British colonial incursion, see, among others, Nandy, *The Intimate Enemy*; Hyam, *Empire and Sexuality*; and Cooper and Stoler, *Tensions of Empire*.

16. Historically, Jews were sometimes lumped together with, sometimes distinguished from, Catholics as dissenters from Anglicanism. See Israel Finestein, *Jewish Society in Victorian England*, for detailed discussions of the relation between Jews and Catholics in the emancipation debate of the nineteenth century.

17. See Spotts, in *LLW* 470, on the antisemitism of Leonard's friends. See also Lytton's correspondence with Dora Carrington, where he continually refers to the painter Mark Gertler as "the Jew" or "the jewboy"—and she responds in the same vein, although Gertler was for many years her close friend and lover. On the ques-

tionable notion of "parlour" antisemitism, see chapter 2 of Loewenstein, *Loathsome Jews and Engulfing Women*, "The Jews of Britain," which debunks the notion that British attitudes toward Jews were largely tolerant.

18. To Europeans, the Jew in their midst represented a form of multiplicity-in-unity—an amphibian—that was, like Ashis Nandy's definition of synthesis as that which destroys the thesis through incorporation (*The Intimate Enemy* 99), profoundly threatening to binary structures:

> The fact was that the Jew who was to Dr Arnold the rightless "lodger," to Sir Robert Inglis the unassimilable "stranger," to Stanley a mystery in his survival and ultimate purpose, and to the young Arnold a unique leaven in the composition of society—all such were one and the same Jew. The Jews were seen to be, and were, multifaceted, contradictory, belonging and not belonging. At one and the same time they inspired caution, suspicion, perhaps animosity, and yet respect, wonder and perhaps awe. This newly-admitted group in the European polity became the chameleon of the modern world, inward-looking and yet possessed of the most far-reaching humanistic aims; particularist and yet genuinely professing a proven universalism. They exhibited a highly developed and self-acknowledged international kinship in which the religious and the national features of Judaism appeared to mingle inextricably. (Finestein, *Jewish Society in Victorian England* 137–38)

19. In *The Comforts of Home*, her study of prostitution in colonial Nairobi, Luise White seeks to revise both the analytical paradigms and the metaphoric language used to describe prostitutes and their work: they are neither necessarily exploited by pimps, husbands, or johns, nor are they containers of dirt that is transmitted to others: "Filth, degradation, depravity . . . these were the clichés of nineteenth-century outrage and control; they have no specificity. . . . They have naturalized prostitutes in the language of biological processes, explaining women's labor in an idiom of inevitability, corruption, and decay. In such scholarship, actions by and attitudes toward prostitutes are not the result of specific interactions . . . but biological and cultural absolutes" (7).

20. "In order to truly live, the inviolable core of Indianness seems to affirm, it might be sometimes better to be dead in somebody else's eyes, so as to be alive for one's own self" (Nandy, *The Intimate Enemy* 111)—again, a viable proposition for Sinnatamby, perhaps, but not for the doubly oppressed female subaltern.

Chapter II
Incongruities; or, The Politics of Character

1. "I've been writing about you all the morning," Virginia told Vanessa on April 22, 1918, "and have made you wear a blue dress; you've got to be immensely mysterious and romantic. . . ." In the preceding paragraph, she has just described a shop in Holborn where she encountered an "enormous Jewess in black satin issuing solemnly from a wardrobe" (*L* 2:232). The contrast between the two figures is striking: Katharine Hilbery elegant and dignified in celestial blue, the black-clad "Jewess" grotesque in her attempts at both fashion and "solemnity." Celestinahami may be worth recalling in both connections.

2. As he emphasizes in *Sowing*, Leonard grew up in haute bourgeois circumstances until the age of eleven, when his father died suddenly and the family underwent a "complete break . . . from considerable affluence to the menace of extreme poverty," as a result of which "we became almost in a night economically serious and mature" (35, 37–38). What this meant practically was that the family moved from a sprawling house in Lexham Gardens with numerous servants to a "much smaller house in Putney, into which [my mother] packed her nine children, a cook, a parlourmaid, and a housemaid," and that most of the sons could not have gotten through to rewarding careers without the scholarships they received to public school and university.

3. This, as numerous biographers and Virginia's own letters and diaries attest, was more than a little disingenuous.

4. The Leonard-Thoby connection is one that Virginia reiterates elsewhere; in another letter to Violet Dickinson, who has met Leonard in the meantime, she writes that "[t]here is something very like Thoby about him, not only in his face" (*L* 1:505). It is only with some effort, in my opinion, that one can construe a facial resemblance between the two men.

5. In his chapter entitled "Anger and Conciliation in *A Room of One's Own* and *Three Guineas*," Alex Zwerdling notes Virginia Woolf's habit of getting her anger out privately so as to be more delicate in her published writings. He quotes a diary entry in which she says, "Yes, these flares up are very good for my book: for they simmer & become transparent: & I see how I can transmute them into beautiful clear reasonable ironic prose" (*D* 4:297–98; Zwerdling, *Virginia Woolf and the Real World* 244).

6. Many years later, Leonard also received a furious letter from his brother Edgar, accusing him of meanness and betrayal. "You showed what a cad you were, when you published the Wise Virgins—after solemnly promising not to!" He goes on to make a scathing remark: "Having always been the lickspittle of greater intellects, you suffer from the deformity of the little man, who thinks it makes him greater to cry out 'See how I have risen above my degraded beginnings!' " (Edgar Woolf to Leonard Woolf, November 27, 1953, Sussex MS 13 IIB5.) Curiously, Edgar makes no specific reference to Leonard's denigration of his own Jewishness.

In *Downhill All the Way*, without giving specific evidence, Leonard claims that he was always his mother's least favorite child.

7. It is perhaps somewhat surprising that Leonard would liken Virginia to the lover of Pericles. Presumably he has in mind not so much Aspasia's sexuality as her extraordinary intellectual independence, her refusal to be confined in a traditional female—and wifely—role, and her status as the hostess of an Athenian salon.

8. Israel Finestein quotes Elie Halévy to the effect that the English Jews' "insatiable appetite for work" endowed them, in the eyes of English Gentiles, with a threatening potency (*Jewish Society in Victorian England* 189).

9. See endnote 1.

10. This phrase, which has become a catchword in discussions of the Stephen family, was coined by Virginia's cousin, J. K. Stephen. See Jane Marcus, chapter 4, *Virginia Woolf and the Languages of Patriarchy*.

11. Just as Harry is not wholly self-hating, the misogyny implied by his stereotypical portraits of the women in the book is also ambivalent. At one point Harry

expresses his wish that he were able to bear children, at another he advocates women's suffrage, and in the Lawrence circle, it is the women's intellects he primarily admires. He believes that women as well as men should be free to choose their way of life.

12. On the other hand, Virginia begins *Night and Day* with a paragraph indicating that Katharine Hilbery is not at all unique but only one among many upper-crust young women performing the same function at the same moment day in and day out. It is the stranger, Ralph Denham, who provides relief and the possibility of escape from this stultified existence. He, however, sees Katharine much as Harry sees Camilla: at one point he feels "as though he were addressing the summit of a poplar in a high gale of wind" (94); at others he thinks of her as a kind of rare object that he wants more than anything to possess.

13. Camilla seems to be alluding directly to Leonard's "Aspasia" sketch, in which he writes: "When I think of Aspasia I think of hills, standing very clear but distant against a cold blue sky; there is snow upon them which no sun has ever melted & no man has ever trodden."

14. Unbeknownst to Harry, apparently, and perhaps to Leonard as well, he is paraphrasing a daily Jewish prayer in which men thank the Lord for not creating them female.

15. Hermione Lee remarks on Vanessa's involvement in the progress of Leonard's courtship, suggesting that Vanessa may have put some pressure on Virginia, while witholding information about Virginia's earlier breakdowns from Leonard, in order to transfer guardianship of Virginia's well-being from herself to Leonard (*Virginia Woolf* 302).

16. Strachey's homoerotic imagery is also conspicuous.

17. See especially Virginia Blain, "Narrative Voice and the Female Perspective in Virginia Woolf's Early Novels," in Clements and Grundy, *Virginia Woolf: New Critical Essays*, and Janis M. Paul, "*Night and Day*," in *The Victorian Heritage*. Blain writes that "part of the comparative failure of *Night and Day* as against *The Voyage Out* . . . springs from the imposition of a comic-romantic ending upon a story which has placed so much stress on the tragic impossibilities in life" (129).

18. It is curious that in both Leonard's and Virginia's novels, the mother, in enforcing marriage, becomes the final arbiter of the rules of patriarchy. In *Night and Day*, Mrs. Hilbery is also the representative of England's literary forefathers.

19. For a discussion of the phrase "the family system," see Alex Zwerdling's chapter "The Bonds of Family Life" in *Virginia Woolf and the Real World* (147). Zwerdling quotes Samuel Butler in *The Way of All Flesh*: "[T]he question of the day now is marriage and the family system." Leonard Woolf read *The Way of All Flesh* at Cambridge and greatly admired it; the marriage of Harry Davis and Gwen Garland in *The Wise Virgins* and the ensuing train ride of the newlyweds are reminiscent of the wedding and carriage ride in Butler's novel.

20. See Bill Williams, " 'East and West': Class and Community in Manchester Jewry, 1850–1914," in Cesarani, *The Making of Modern Anglo-Jewry.*

21. The lack of a real Anglo-Jewish literary tradition has often been remarked, especially in contrast to America, which boasts a Jewish literature both distinct from and contributing to the twentieth-century canon. Finestein lists several prominent

Jewish writers who migrated from England to America, where they found a climate more conducive to their creativity (*Jewish Society in Victorian England* 198).

22. On the relations between "East" and "West" (Eastern and Western Europe, but also East End and West End) in Anglo-British Jewry, see Cesarani, *The Making of Modern Anglo-Jewry*. Bill Williams's essay " 'East and West': Class and Community in Manchester Jewry, 1850–1914," revises the commonly invoked polarity by describing a third group, the "alrightniks" (after Irving Howe in his history of American Jewry)—immigrant businessmen who mediated between the newly arrived poor and the more acculturated, well-to-do families. Several of the essays in Cesarani discuss the rhetoric used by the latter to describe their mission toward the immigrants; Finestein also offers acute discussions of the subject:

> [T]he assimilation of the Eastern European Jewish immigrants around the closing decades of the century into English and Anglo-Jewish life was of prime importance. Upon the success of that operation was thought to depend the success of Anglo-Jewry and much else besides. Anglicization thus became a moral imperative. Anglo-Jewish communal policy was dominated by considerations of public image. (*Jewish Society in Victorian England* 162)

Hermann Adler, Chief Rabbi from 1891 to 1911, "did not quite live down his language about the immigrants in a much publicized Succot sermon in 1887 at the New West End Synagogue. It was necessary, he said, 'to anglicise, humanise and civilize' them" (Finestein 177). The language is redolent of British colonialist rhetoric, with the vital exception of "anglicise." "The Very Reverend Herman [*sic*] Adler," according to Cooper and Morrison, "became known as the 'West End goy' " (Cooper and Morrison, *A Sense of Belonging* 73).

23. Paul Morrison, director of a BBC series on Anglo-Jewry, remarks:

> I looked at my own back catalogue of documentaries made over twenty years. It is an honourable list. I had dealt with many important social issues—racism, unemployment, education. I had explored many themes of identity and empowerment. . . . There was much that could be said to be Jewish in my identification with the underdog, in my focus on the psychological scars of marginalisation. . . . But not one of the films I had made was *explicitly* Jewish in theme or subject-matter. I wore my Jewishness in my films invisibly, as I had learned to do in my life. (Qtd. in Cooper and Morrison, *A Sense of Belonging* 5.)

24. "For Woolf," Caramagno writes, "manic-depressive illness periodically destroyed control . . . and so permitted her to return to the creative process unencumbered by the illusion that meaning lay in order alone" (*The Flight of the Mind* 80).

25. Virginia began referring to herself and Leonard as "the Woolves" during this period; the elegant head of a rather ferocious wolf, designed by Vanessa Bell, was the symbol of the Hogarth Press, appearing on the title page of all publications.

26. The terms belong to Jessica Benjamin.

27. In later published versions, the story ends with an additional piece of dialogue, in which the seemingly-male voice expresses a sense of impotence in the face of real-world events, along with a—compensatory?—certainty about the mark on the wall:

"Though it's no good buying newspapers. . . . Nothing ever happens. Curse this war; God damn this war! . . . All the same, I don't see why we should have a snail on our wall."

Ah, the mark on the wall! It was a snail. (*CSF* 83; ellipses in original)

28. According to Bowlby, the carriage is third-class; Woolf never makes the distinction explicit, but her statement that "I . . . jumped into the first carriage I came to," coming, as it were, from on high (along with her reference, also remarked by Bowlby, to "the character of one's cook"), suggests that this is a leap across class borders.

29. Bowlby's introductory chapter in *Feminist Destinations* elucidates the many implications of the train setting from the point of view of a critic familiar with British rail travel, both past and present. "The compartment," she remarks, "does have some of the qualities of the domestic sitting room [favored of Edwardian writers], but this only adds to its curiously ambivalent suspension half-way between two states. . . . This is a public space superficially identical to a private one, so that the anonymity of the limited number of passengers is all the more significant from its contrast to the scene of intimacy it resembles" (4).

30. In his essay on ethnicity, Werner Sollors questions "[t]he discussion of literature in tribal isolation": "The ethnic approach to writing . . . is often in danger of making one generalization (the writer is an X, meaning not a Y) the central, if not the sole, avenue to a text; yet making this Xness central may be circular and tautological (X writes like an X, not like a Y) since it reveals first and foremost this very Xness, a quality which cumulatively achieves the status of a somewhat mystical, ahistorical, and even quasi-eternal essence" (Sollors, "Ethnicity," in Lentricchia and McLaughlin, *Critical Terms for Literary Study* 290).

Chapter III
Links into Fences

1. Caramagno (*The Flight of the Mind*) deals with text and subtext in *Mrs. Dalloway* in terms of bipolar disorder; Elizabeth Abel (*Virginia Woolf and the Fictions of Psychoanalysis*) describes the novel as a Freudian palimpsest, in whose interstices the buried narrative of female sexuality pushes to the surface. Alex Zwerdling, in *Virginia Woolf and the Real World*, is the first critic to focus his analysis of *Mrs. Dalloway* primarily on Woolf's representation of class.

2. I am indebted to Deborah Guth, whose excellent essay " 'What a Lark! What a Plunge!' " culminates in a close reading of this famous early passage which reveals that Clarissa "plunged" from the French windows only in a reverie that took place within the house. Guth's reading of the novel is confluent with mine in exposing the fictionality of Clarissa's empathy; I, however, am inclined more than she is to believe that Woolf deliberately confuses connection and disjunction in her famous "web."

3. Zwerdling, *Virginia Woolf and the Real World*, goes on to say:

The passage is bound to give offense to anyone with strong egalitarian sympathies. Its detached hauteur is unmistakable and marks it as the perspective of someone whose better opportunities permit her to look down even on the motor car and house at Purley, the upper limit of Septimus's possibilities. There is neither anger nor warmth here, but there is a sense of the waste of a system that restricts the range of individual human achievement by raising the insurmountable barrier of class. (90–91)

A propos Septimus's reading: The later sections of *Life as We Have Known It* contain brief lists and commentaries by working women on the books, mostly borrowed from public libraries, they managed to read in the few spare moments in their arduous lives. With few exceptions, these women had no "evening after the day's work"; their work never ended; indeed, it generally cut short their sleeping hours. (Some of the women—among them Miss Harriet Kidd—cut these even shorter by reading late into the night.)

4. Rachel Bowlby's introductory chapter to *Feminist Destinations* contains this incisive remark on Woolf's "treatment" by critics and biographers:

> Childhood seduction, madness, confinement, frigidity, anorexia, lesbianism, suicide: in the very extremity of its outlines, the tale can become either a demonstration of common female oppression—the norm revealed at its outer edges—or proof of her exceptional status. In her oddness or in her representativeness, Virginia Woolf is always treated as a "case." (13)

That the character of Bradshaw was intended as a scathing portrait of Woolf's own psychiatric doctor Sir George Savage is generally assumed.

5. Yet "[f]or him, *integration is equivalent to self-destruction*, because it would require identifying with elements of self he can no longer recognize or understand" (Caramagno, *The Flight of the Mind* 219).

6. "Whereas Septimus Smith is the extreme 'case' of someone who has lost all contact with the external, common orders of daily life and daily time, Clarissa is questionably situated like St. Margaret's, neither within nor without, somewhere between utter differing and absolute conformity" (Bowlby, *Feminist Destinations* 12). "She occupies an object-relational space between Peter's defensiveness against chaos and Septimus's helpless surrender to it" (Caramagno, *The Flight of the Mind* 230).

7. Clarissa's maiden name, Parry, suggests a link between her virginity and a tricky defensive thrusting—as well as the armor that parriers wear.

8. "[Woolf's] independent income made it possible for her to devote her primary energy to the writing of fiction without constantly worrying about public taste and the pressures of the marketplace. It allowed her to write painstakingly rather than fluently, to invent alternatives to traditional narrative forms rather than follow the literary fashions" (Zwerdling, *Virginia Woolf and the Real World* 106). The *seeming* fluency of Woolf's writing, then, is a final surface based upon lengthy reworkings; women who had to write for their living could not afford to write other than fluently.

9. To do Woolf justice, it should be noted that Margaret Llewelyn Davies herself, in her memoir entitled "A Guild Office Clerk," represents Harriet Kidd as admirable but also bellicose, stubborn, even somewhat tyrannical: "How angry she was with what she felt was sham or self-seeking or pretentious in individuals, and

how resentful that the workers did not share in all the advantages of the rich! With so uncompromising and independent a nature, combined with a hard and difficult life, she was not an easy person to live or work with. She was jealous of anyone who might come between herself and her friends or work, and an imagined slight of any kind would fill the atmosphere with an overpowering gloom and silence" (*LAWHKI* 73). Shades of Doris Kilman and her bitterness?

10. It is no coincidence, I think, that Isa in *Between the Acts* cannot shake off the memory of a rape described in the morning paper, for war and rape are analogous. (That the rape is committed by soldiers only serves to reinforce the point.)

11. The development of the introduction as a piece mingling fact and fantasy was also complicated by the fact that in the United States, the *Yale Review* asked to publish a fictionalized version "to be read as literature simply" (*L* 4:191). The essay thus evolved from straightforward account to pseudo–short story and back again, with losses and embellishments along the way. The process is chronicled in Woolf's letters to Margaret Llewellyn Davies in volume 4 of the *Letters*; Jane Marcus briefly tracks and discusses the changes in *Art and Anger* 117–19.

12. Slick garish colors are always, to elitists, the emblem of the nouveaux riches. In *Between the Acts*, Mrs. Manresa, that compelling ambiguous character, married to a Jew, friendly with the lower orders, is distinguished by her garish dress—and her bold habit of putting on lipstick in public.

13. David Dowling reads Elizabeth's moment of democratic elation as a thoughtless merging with the crowd, ultimately supportive of the status quo. Dowling's comments on Elizabeth might lead to a very different reading of these passages, whereby the interval becomes a dangerous vacuum in which unthinking groups can be sucked into dangerous movements—as they will be before long, in Italy and Germany. But the imagery of dispersal-in-unity, which becomes the dominant motif in *Between the Acts*, is, in my opinion, always Woolf's way of representing an as-yet-unrealized social system in which individualism and community would coexist in perfect balance. (See Dowling, *Mapping Streams of Consciousness* 108–9.)

14. "The future . . . lay in the hands of young men like that" (50).

15. Kilman deserves more attention than the latitude of this chapter permits. She bears a crude resemblance to Miss Kidd and seems a product of Woolf's stance at the outset of the Newcastle congress. Like Clarissa's poor cousin Ellie Henderson, to whom the narrator is nearly as unkind as is Clarissa herself, she is shut out from sympathy in the novel. Her failing, of course, is orthodoxy, both religious and social; in this she is allied with the novel's villainous doctors, who seek to convert rather than cure. Her prototype in the "Prime Minister" notes is, however, the far more sympathetic, speechifying but generous socialist Mrs. Lewis. Why the change? Typically, perhaps, Woolf draws her lines in cruder fashion to render her "message" more complex: not everyone who takes the side of workers is admirable or truly well-disposed; a cause may be "good" without being perfect.

16. It is a trope of some *Mrs. Dalloway* criticism that Clarissa is an artist, and her parties are works of art. That claim strikes me as wishful. While, as Geoffrey Hartmann maintains, the parties are analogous to Woolf's own assemblage (the novel itself), their orchestration, quite unlike Woolf's experimentation, is based on staid, outdated principles, and their dynamic is dependent far more on servants,

guests, and circumstances than on anything Clarissa alone accomplishes (though note that that dependency does have its analogue in Woolf's admitted dependence on others to carry out menial tasks so that she may write). See Hartmann, "Virginia's Web," in Homans, *Virginia Woolf: A Collection of Critical Essays* 35–45.

17. In her preface to the American edition of the novel, Woolf explains that she originally intended Clarissa to commit suicide, before creating Septimus to do it for her.

18. Clarissa's sewing, however, supports the status quo figuratively as well as literally. She is mending the dress for her party; she can also be seen as repairing a small tear in the social grid, stitching it even tighter than before. Mrs. Scott's memoir, full of humor and acute intelligence, includes this description of hatmaking in the company of women of very different principles from her own:

> I had loved working at Christie's because of the workroom [where it was possible to conduct discussions], but the hats were very hard. If your wrist was not very strong you could not push the needle through or pull it out. Then, in the room I was in, there were several who worked for "honour," priding themselves in never putting a crooked stitch in their work. When they were put on to look over our work it was terrible. Just think of the binding on men's hat brims; if they were a quarter of an inch or even less crooked, back they came, and you had to take them off and do them over again. And the fine leathers—a crooked stitch in those, and you had to take them out. One of the old trimmers was terrible with me; she said it was for my good she wanted to make a perfect trimmer of me, but I could not see it. (89)

19. Engaging with Fredric Jameson's arguments about modernism in *The Political Unconscious*, Randall Stevenson writes that "[m]odernism may not have done much directly . . . to reshape the modern world or alter its politics. . . . More reasonably, [art] can be asked to shape and facilitate imagination of how the world might be ordered differently, a demand which, in some ways, modernism fulfills" (*Modernist Fiction* 221).

20. Unpublished MS, Berg Collection, New York Public Library.

21. One of the most important projects of the Women's Co-operative Guild was to educate women about birth control, health during pregnancy, and the proper hygiene for labor. (Another was divorce reform, to prevent women from being treated as their husbands' property.) A prior volume of working women's personal histories, also edited by Margaret Llewellyn Davies, and published in 1915, is entitled *Maternity* and chronicles the awful consequences of working women's ignorance about these issues.

Chapter IV
Translations

1. Garnett goes on to demonstrate a particular sympathy for Leonard's granitic character, thereby self-consciously differing from the general Bloomsbury attitude; her appreciation may, perhaps, have something to do with her youthful innocence of antisemitism. Cowed, on the one hand, by his rigidity, she writes that while "he seemed to be the father figure who was missing in my life . . . had [he] been my

father I would have resembled one of his dogs, never beaten but always intimidated by the force of his personality." On the other hand, she devotes an eloquent paragraph to her respect for this unusual personality:

> For my birthday one year he gave me a splendid Victorian copy of *Pilgrim's Progress*, filled with pictures of Christian marching onwards in stiffly engraved wooden drapery. For some reason this book meant a great deal to me, and my eyes met those of Leonard across the festive tea-table in a moment of intense understanding I seldom experienced. For once I felt limpid and transparent, purged by emotion of all the dross of puerile secrecy and prevarication that usually submerged me. I had unwittingly come into contact with the passion in Leonard's character, which was both convinced and inflexible, contrasting with Vanessa's tendency to compound and procrastinate in favour of those she loved, and Duncan's ability to laugh away and ignore things he didn't like. They were conscious of a moral force in Leonard which they repudiated as narrow, philistine and puritanical. Both he and Vanessa were natural judges and both were full of prejudice, but whereas she avoided morality, Leonard clung to it, always remaining something of the administrator of the Hambantota District in Ceylon. In Bloomsbury, vowed to amorality, this may have seemed a little heavy-handed and irritating, but with it went a refreshing purity which in later years I fully appreciated. (108–9)

It is striking that Vanessa's daughter here recapitulates some of the very terms of difference that characterize Leonard's description of Harry Davis and of Camilla Lawrence's set in *The Wise Virgins*, as well as those that represent Katharine Hilbery's attraction to Ralph Denham in *Night and Day*.

2. Leonard adopted the phrase as the title for one of her posthumous collections of essays.

3. See Barbara Fassler's "Theories of Homosexuality." In her chapter on *A Room of One's Own*, Jane Marcus points out allusions to the trial of Radclyffe Hall in Woolf's lectures (*Virginia Woolf and the Language of Patriarchy*). Vita Sackville-West's diary is printed in *Portrait of a Marriage*.

4. Here Virginia seems to be justifying her own frequent bouts of illness against the ceaseless activity of her husband, to be saying, as Lytton Strachey says in *Elizabeth and Essex* (a book that, like *Orlando*, plays with gender definitions, though less imaginatively—perhaps because of "biography" 's demand for "truth"), that "passivity, too, may be a form of action—may, in fact, at moments prove more full of consequence than action itself" (225). In her diary entry of February 16, 1930, she expresses a sense of inadequacy vis-à-vis Leonard, then retracts it: "I would like to lie down & sleep, but feel ashamed. Leonard brushed off his influenza in one day & went about his business feeling ill. Here I am still loafing, undressed. . . . But as I was saying my mind works in idleness. To do nothing is often my most profitable way" (*D* 3:287).

5. Contemporary gender theory comes some fifty-five years behind Woolf—though fortified by footnotes to recent anthropology—in observing that "even if the sexes appear to be unproblematically binary in their morphology and constitution . . . , there is no reason to assume that genders ought also to remain as two" (Butler, *Gender Trouble* 6).

6. Many critics and biographers have speculated about the nature of the affair between Virginia Woolf and Vita. Evidence in the diaries and letters points to at

least one late-night conversation that became a seduction; yet Woolf refuses to pin down her feelings. They were certainly, for a time, passionate.

7. Vita and Harold discussed the subject of marriage on a BBC radio broadcast of June 17, 1929. Harold said:

> Of course, I do not envisage the relations between the sexes in terms of superiority or inferiority. I envisage them merely in terms of difference. It is not latitude which separates them, so to speak, but longitude: one is not above or below the other; they are on the same level but wide apart. I believe profoundly in the essential *difference* between man and woman. I believe that the most virile woman is infinitely more feminine than the most effeminate man. . . . I contend that Heliogabolus, let us say, was temperamentally more virile than, let us say, George Sand: that the temperamental contrast between man and woman is so sharp and wide, that it is only superficially affected by forms of sexual aberration. It is upon the realization of this fundamental difference that any success in marriage must be based.

8. Bowlby writes that "Woolf is able to get maximum comic mileage out of the fact that P and Q really are the letters conventionally used in propositional logic, while Mr. Ramsay's name begins with the 'next' letter, R" (*Feminist Destinations* 64).

9. The "mark of gender" is Judith Butler's phrase (*Gender Trouble* 21). It is striking that Woolf uses the phrase which is the title of her 1917 short story. While here it suggests the marks made on house walls to measure the growth of children, in the story it was a metaphor for the very impossibility of reducing memories, impressions, and feelings to single and differentiated facts. And even the marks of measurement change as children grow—and would change further, if one persisted, as adults shrank.

10. Although Woolf herself thought *The Well of Loneliness* inferior as literature, her greater outrage at its legal censorship is inscribed in *A Room of One's Own* when she invokes the name of the judge in Hall's obscenity trial. See Marcus, *Virginia Woolf and the Languages of Patriarchy*, as well as Lee.

11. See Leonard Woolf's comparison of the Stephen sisters in their voluminous white garb to horses chafing at the bridle, as discussed in chapter 2.

12. It is perhaps worth comparing Mrs. Ramsay's "fitting" to the harmonizing efforts of Woolf in constructing her novel so carefully to contain opposites. In "Virginia Woolf and Postmodernism: Returning to the Lighthouse," Pamela Caughie remarks that Woolf's method inevitably entails exclusions, e.g., the dehumanization of the housekeeper Mrs. McNab in "Time Passes": Woolf's "narrative may tell a different story, eliding historical events and focusing instead on the daily existence of women and the upheavals of family life. Yet as long as Woolf's narrative, like Mrs. Ramsay's dinner, desires to bring all into harmony with a dominant theme, as Woolf describes her narrative method in her diaries of this time, it will necessarily produce its own exclusions even as it attempts to narrate what has been excluded from our monumental histories" (Dettmar, *Rereading the New* 315). My own argument is that Woolf's narrative exposes the dissonance beneath forced harmonies; Caughie reads in "Time Passes" "the acknowledgment on the part of Woolf's narrative of what it does not know," ascribing more consciousness to the text than to Woolf herself.

For a different take on Mrs. McNab, see Michael Tratner, *Modernism and Mass Politics*.

13. Compare, in recent years, "a thousand points of light."

14. Patricia Waugh's reading of this image in *Feminine Fictions* is opposite to mine:

> [Mrs. Ramsay] is the portrait of a woman whose constitution as "feminine" entirely within the terms of the patriarchal system threatens not only her own sense of existence but also that of others. The passage containing her sinking into the "wedge-shaped core of darkness" . . . *can* be interpreted as a celebration of her artistic negative capability, the capacity to become the things she sees. It seems to me, however[,] . . . that the description is less one of liberation of the transcendent artistic imagination than one of a suicidal impulse. (105)

Waugh's either/or paradigm seems insufficiently engaged with the psychosocial terms of the novel; her reading ignores the pattern of metonymies to which the "wedge" belongs even as it stands apart as an image of undermining rather than instrumental participation.

15. "Domination . . . is a twisting of the bonds of love" (Benjamin, *The Bonds of Love* 219). In *No Man's Land*, Gilbert and Gubar deal with the historical irony that women, liberated by the Great War to act in the public arena and perform jobs normally reserved by men, thus found it in their interest to support the war— and did so, regardless of political sentiments, among other ways through work in munitions factories.

It is perhaps telling that Lily Briscoe, thinking of Mrs. Ramsay as a glove, wonders what "the essential thing" is "by which . . . you would have known it, from its twisted finger, hers indisputably" (49). The image contains a disturbing suggestion that Mrs. Ramsay's "essence" is one constructed through torture—or perhaps it reflects merely the clear-sighted recognition that no "nature" precedes the work of culture.

16. A conclusion that lends some support to Waugh's reading of the "wedge-shaped core of darkness," though I still maintain the radical implications of the metonymy as an object that can get beneath the implanted order.

17. Again, the inverse of Spivak's Freudian reading: Mr. Ramsay needs *Lily* to "get [it] up," not vice versa. Or, following Judith Butler's elucidation of Lacan, Lily must "be" the phallus so Mr. Ramsay can "have" one.

18. It resembles, in this way, the English victory in World War I, which exacted both literal and psychic dismemberment from millions of young men—and killed Andrew Ramsay (his "death, mercifully, was instantaneous").

19. The conclusion of Butler's *Gender Trouble* contains a Derridean/feminist gloss on the use of "etc." in a somewhat different, though comparable, context:

> The theories of feminist identity that elaborate predicates of color, sexuality, ethnicity, class, and able-bodiedness invariably close with an embarrassed "etc." at the end of the list. Through this horizontal trajectory of adjectives, these positions strive to encompass a situated subject, but invariably fail to be complete. This failure, however, is instructive: what political impetus is to be derived from the exasperated "etc." that so often occurs at the end of such lines? . . . It is the *supplément*, the excess that necessarily accompanies any effort to posit identity once and for all. This illimitable *et cetera*, however, offers itself as a new departure for feminist political theorizing. (143)

20. In *Joyce and the Law of the Father*, Frances Restuccia uses the phrase to designate the way Joyce "works through Catholicism to free it" (125). In describing her collection of notes and clippings toward *Three Guineas*, Woolf remarked that she had "enough powder to blow up St. Pauls" (*D* 4:77).

21. See Gordon Ray, *H. G. Wells and Rebecca West*. Ray says that the nicknames "appear to have been the invention of Rebecca, who in her life with Wells reverted for a time to the warmth of her childhood circle before 'she had been tripped into the snare of growing up' " (36). The quotation is from West's autobiographical novel, *The Fountain Overflows*. It is interesting that Woolf also uses the metaphor of the snare in "Lappin and Lapinova."

22. Woolf's half-joking remark refers to her own inability to leave Leonard behind and run off to visit Vanessa in Cassis. "[T]he fact is," she writes, "we are so unhappy apart that I can't come" (*L* 6:294). This, too, distinguishes the Woolves from Orlando and Marmaduke. It also distinguishes 1938 from 1928, when Virginia traveled to France with Vita—but missed Leonard fearfully when she arrived at Avallon to find no letter waiting.

Chapter V
Monstrous Conjunctions

1. According to Alex Zwerdling, "Woolf's name does not appear among the sponsors of the many organizations engaged in war resistance between 1914 and 1941. . . . One does not find her mentioned in the histories of the Peace Pledge Union or the No-Conscription Fellowship or the League of Nations Society or the Women's International League for Peace and Freedom. . . . But she was intimate with many people whose primary activities were given to such work, most especially Leonard, and she was in deep sympathy with their aims" (*Virginia Woolf and the Real World* 274).

2. In fact, it was Freud who was a benefactor on this occasion. He gave Virginia a narcissus.

3. And yet she—or she and Leonard, to whom the first "we" seems to refer—had thought about it: "[W]e had often felt guilty." It is interesting, too, that between her transcription of Freud's question and that of her answer, a day intervenes: the former ends her entry for January 29, the latter begins the next entry. There is an actual gap on the page.

4. In 1936, Aldous Huxley published a pamphlet, "What Are You Going to Do about It?" which "made a case for 'constructive peace' with a plan to establish alternative societies of pacifists, affiliations of small groups, like religious orders" (Lee, *Virginia Woolf* 680).

5. According to the *Princeton Encyclopedia of Poetry and Poetics*, metonymy's "major effect is to communicate through abstract, intangible terms the concrete or tangible."

6. This is another tactic *Quack, Quack!* has in common with *Three Guineas*. In the first edition of *Three Guineas*, Virginia Woolf included photographs of judges and soldiers in full costume as aids to her satire.

7. "Groups have never thirsted after truth," Freud writes in *Group Psychology*. "They demand illusions, and cannot do without them. They constantly give what

is unreal precedence over what is real; they are almost as strongly influenced by what is untrue as by what is true. They have an evident tendency not to distinguish between the two" (16–17).

8. *Male* parthenogenesis is, of course, doubly unnatural. Behind the metaphor is an analogy to rape: the fascist produces his poem not without recourse to, but without the consent of, the feminine. In *Virginia Woolf and the Fictions of Psychoanalysis*, Elizabeth Abel writes about Woolf's descriptions in *Three Guineas* of the fascist as a male mother (92).

9. Certainly rape, actual and metaphorical, is never far from Woolf's mind when she considers forms of authoritarianism. In *Between the Acts*, a book whose backdrop, whose raison d'être, is the fascist threat across the Channel, the main female character keeps remembering a rape she reads about in the morning paper.

10. Art Berman, in *Preface to Modernism*, ascribes such stylistic and thematic changes to the larger artistic movement: "Modernism gradually relinquishes the transcendentalist tendencies that fascism increasingly appropriates for itself" (239).

11. In her biography of Roger Fry, Woolf quotes Fry's own memory of two childhood incidents in a garden. One involved his first great passion, the second his first great disillusionment. His passion was for a bush of bright red poppies. The disillusionment occurred when Fry's mother told him to pick her one of the buds of his poppy plant, then scolded him for having done so. Woolf thus conveys her own sense of prelapsarian innocence as a marvelous fiction—the parent-God has dictated the Fall already before the official "beginning" of the narrative.

12. And Virginia begins her last novel with a broken promise: "The county council had promised to bring water to the village, but they hadn't" (*BA* 3). The statement may seem trivial, but it is the book's second sentence and suggests an atmosphere defined by broken words and the failure of decency and responsibility on the part of authorities.

13. The sense of despair is heightened by the disparity between Woolf's intention and the actual implication of her words. By "nibbling" she means her daily efforts to write—but the image of a mouse nibbling at a page actually suggests the destruction of the written word.

14. It is possible to read Giles's act as a fascistic rejection of modernist art, in keeping with his rejection of the homosexual William Dodge. In *Preface to Modernism*, Art Berman writes that fascist art and architecture were a "revived neoclassicism": "For [fascists, modern art's] ironies, its tolerance of opposites in suspension so essential to the modernist aesthetic, are weaknesses, degeneracies" (245, 234). Woolf's attempt in *Between the Acts* to forge a new aesthetic, a third term beyond modernism, suggests that the suspension of opposites is no longer a viable experiment when suspension in the political realm amounts to dangerous inactivity. She differs from Giles in seeking creative means to break the deadlock.

15. In fact, Leonard and Virginia's names were on a hit list compiled by the Nazis in case they did invade England. See Hermione Lee, *Virginia Woolf* 718.

16. My own reading of La Trobe's personality and accomplishment strikes a compromise between the interpretations of two other critics, Melba Cuddy-Keane and Judith L. Johnston. In her essay, "The Remediable Flaw: Revisioning Cultural History in *Between the Acts*," Johnston says that La Trobe "sounds like an authoritarian peace-monger. . . . Even though she articulates a different message, she, like

Mussolini or Hitler, encourages hostility, panders to her audience, and seeks to manipulate their sympathies" (267). Cuddy-Keane, in "The Politics of Comic Modes in Virginia Woolf's *Between the Acts*," places the interpretation of the pageant and its success or failure with the readers. It "can be judged a success," she maintains, "if we think not of what she has taught the community but of how she has stimulated them to think. As opposed to a failed leader, La Trobe thus represents a positive alternative to leadership: a background rather than a foreground figure, a prompter and catalyst rather than a director and guide" (279).

17. The title of this section of the chapter derives from *Between the Acts*: "[La Trobe] set down her glass. She heard the first words" (212).

18. Surprising antisemitic passages occur in other works by Virginia in the thirties. "The Duchess and the Jeweller," a story published in *Harper's Bazaar* in 1938, began, in effect, as "The Duchess and the Jew." The eponymous jeweler was Jewish in the first draft; later, Woolf canceled all suggestions of ethnic identity, but the character remains slimy. Slime occurs, quite literally, in a puzzling passage in *The Years* when Sara cannot dissociate the ring around the bathtub in her boardinghouse from the Jew who apparently creates it.

Works Consulted

Works by the Woolfs

Woolf, Leonard. *After the Deluge: A Study of Communal Psychology.* Vol. 1. New York: Harcourt, Brace and Company, 1931.

———. *Barbarians at the Gate.* London: Victor Gollancz, 1939.

———. *Beginning Again: An Autobiography of the Years 1911 to 1918.* New York: Harcourt Brace Jovanovich, 1963.

———. *Diaries in Ceylon, 1908–1911* and *Stories of the East: Three Short Stories on Ceylon.* In *Ceylon Historical Journal* 9, nos. 1–4 (July 1959 to April 1960).

———. *Downhill All the Way: An Autobiography of the Years 1919 to 1939.* New York: Harcourt Brace Jovanovich, 1967.

———. *Empire and Commerce in Africa: A Study in Economic Imperialism.* New York: The Macmillan Company, 1920.

———. *Growing: An Autobiography of the Years 1904 to 1911.* New York: Harcourt Brace Jovanovich, 1961.

———. *The Hotel.* New York: The Dial Press, 1963.

———. *In Savage Times.* New York: Garland Publishing, 1973.

———. *The Journey Not the Arrival Matters: An Autobiography of the Years 1939 to 1969.* New York: Harcourt Brace Jovanovich, 1969.

———. Leonard Woolf Papers, University of Sussex (unpublished).

———. *Letters of Leonard Woolf.* Edited by Frederic Spotts. New York: Harcourt Brace Jovanovich, 1989.

———. *Quack, Quack!* New York: Harcourt, Brace and Company, 1935.

———. *Sowing: An Autobiography of the Years 1880 to 1904.* New York: Harcourt Brace Jovanovich, 1960.

———. *Stories of the East.* See *Diaries in Ceylon.*

———. *The Village in the Jungle.* Hogarth Press, 1971.

———. *The War for Peace.* London: George Routledge & Sons, 1940.

———. *The Wise Virgins: A Story of Words, Opinions and a few Emotions.* New York: Harcourt Brace Jovanovich, 1979.

———, ed. *The Intelligent Man's Way to Prevent War.* London: Victor Gollancz, 1933.

Woolf, Leonard and Virginia. *Two Stories.* London: Hogarth Press, 1917.

Woolf, Virginia. "Anon." Edited by Brenda Silver. *Twentieth Century Literature* 25, nos. 3–4 (1979): 385.

———. *Between the Acts.* New York: Harcourt Brace Jovanovich, 1941.

———. *The Captain's Death Bed and Other Essays.* New York: Harcourt Brace Jovanovich, 1950.

———. *Collected Essays,* Vol. 1. New York: Harcourt, Brace & World, 1967.

———. *The Complete Shorter Fiction.* Edited by Susan B. Dick. New York: Harcourt Brace Jovanovich, 1985.

Woolf, Virginia. "Anon." *The Death of the Moth and Other Essays*. New York: Harcourt Brace Jovanovich, 1942.

———. *The Diary of Virginia Woolf*. Edited by Anne Olivier Bell. 5 vols. New York: Harcourt Brace Jovanovich, 1977–1984.

———. *Granite and Rainbow: Essays*. New York: Harcourt Brace Jovanovich, 1958.

———. "Introductory Letter" to *Life as We Have Known It*, edited by Margaret Llewelyn Davies. London: Hogarth Press, 1931.

———. "A Letter to a Young Poet." In *The Hogarth Letters*, edited by Hermione Lee. Athens: University of Georgia Press, 1986.

———. *The Letters of Virginia Woolf*. Edited by Nigel Nicolson and Joanne Trautman. 6 vols. New York: Harcourt Brace Jovanovich, 1975–1980.

———. *The Moment and Other Essays*. New York: Harcourt Brace Jovanovich, 1948.

———. *Moments of Being: Unpublished Autobiographical Writings*. Edited by Jeanne Schulkind. New York: Harcourt Brace Jovanovich, 1976.

———. *Mrs. Dalloway*. New York: Harcourt, Brace & World, 1925.

———. *Night and Day*. New York: Harcourt Brace Jovanovich, 1920.

———. *Orlando: A Biography*. New York: Harcourt Brace Jovanovich, 1928.

———. "The Prime Minister." Unpublished MS, Berg Collection, New York Public Library.

———. *Roger Fry: A Biography*. New York: Harcourt Brace Jovanovich, 1940.

———. *A Room of One's Own*. New York: Harcourt Brace Jovanovich, 1929.

———. *Three Guineas*. New York: Harcourt Brace Jovanovich, 1938.

———. *To the Lighthouse*. New York: Random House, 1937.

———. *The Voyage Out*. New York: Harcourt Brace Jovanovich, 1920.

———. *The Years*. New York: Harcourt Brace Jovanovich, 1937.

Other Sources

Abel, Elizabeth. *Virginia Woolf and the Fictions of Psychoanalysis*. Chicago: University of Chicago Press, 1989.

Achebe, Chinua. "An Image of Africa: Racism in Conrad's *Heart of Darkness*." In Joseph Conrad, *Heart of Darkness*, edited by Robert Kimbrough. New York: W. W. Norton & Co., 1988.

Beer, Gillian. *Virginia Woolf: The Common Ground*. Ann Arbor: University of Michigan Press, 1996.

Beja, Morris, ed. *Critical Essays on Virginia Woolf*. Boston: G. K. Hall & Company, 1985.

Bell, Clive. *Old Friends*. London: Cassell Publishers, 1988.

———. *Warmongers*. London: The Peace Pledge Union, 1938.

Bell, Quentin. *Virginia Woolf: A Biography*. New York: Harcourt Brace Jovanovich, 1972.

Benjamin, Jessica. *The Bonds of Love: Psychoanalysis, Feminism, and the Problem of Domination*. New York: Pantheon Books, 1988.

Berman, Art. *Preface to Modernism*. Urbana: University of Illinois Press, 1994.

Biale, David, Michael Galchinsky, and Susannah Heschel, eds. *Insider/Outsider: American Jews and Multiculturalism*. Berkeley and Los Angeles: University of California Press, 1998.

Black, Eugene C. *The Social Politics of Anglo-Jewry, 1880–1920*. Oxford: Basil Blackwell, 1988.

Bloom, Harold, ed. *Virginia Woolf's Mrs. Dalloway*. New York: Chelsea House Publishers, 1988.

———, ed. *Virginia Woolf: Modern Critical Views*. New York: Chelsea House Publishers, 1986.

Bowlby, Rachel. *Virginia Woolf: Feminist Destinations*. Oxford: Basil Blackwell, 1988.

———, ed. *Virginia Woolf*. New York: Longman Group, 1992.

Brantlinger, Patrick. *Rule of Darkness: British Literature and Imperialism, 1830–1914*. Ithaca: Cornell University Press, 1988.

Butler, Judith. *Gender Trouble*. New York: Routledge, 1990.

Caramagno, Thomas C. *The Flight of the Mind: Virginia Woolf's Art and Manic-Depressive Illness*. Berkeley and Los Angeles: University of California Press, 1992.

Cesarani, David, ed. *The Making of Modern Anglo-Jewry*. Oxford: Basil Blackwell, 1990.

Cheyette, Bryan. *Constructions of "the Jew" in Modern English Literature and Society: Racial Representations, 1875–1945*. Cambridge: Cambridge University Press, 1993.

———, ed. *Between "Race" and Culture: Representations of "the Jew" in English and American Literature*. Stanford: Stanford University Press, 1996.

Clements, Patricia, and Isobel Grundy, eds. *Virginia Woolf: New Critical Essays*. London: Vision Press, 1983.

Conrad, Joseph. *Heart of Darkness*. Edited by Robert Kimbrough. New York: W. W. Norton & Co., 1986.

Cooper, Frederick and Laura Ann Stoler, eds. *Tensions of Empire: Colonial Cultures in a Bourgeois World*. Berkeley and Los Angeles: University of California Press, 1997.

Cooper, Howard, and Paul Morrison. *A Sense of Belonging: Dilemmas of British Jewish Identity*. London: Weidenfeld and Nicolson in Association with Channel Four Television, 1991.

Cuddy-Keane, Melba. "The Politics of Comic Modes in Virginia Woolf's *Between the Acts*." *PMLA* 105, no. 2 (March 1990).

Davies, Margaret Llewelyn, ed. *Life as We Have Known It: By Co-operative Working Women*. Introduction by Virginia Woolf. London: Hogarth Press, 1931.

Defromont, Françoise. "Mirrors and Fragments." In *Virginia Woolf*, edited by Rachel Bowlby. New York: Longman Group, 1992.

Derrida, Jacques. *The Ear of the Other: Otobiography, Transference, Translation*. Edited by Christie V. McDonald. Translated by Peggy Kamuf. New York: Schocken Books, 1985.

DeSalvo, Louise A. "Virginia, Virginius, Virginity." In *Faith of a (Woman) Writer*, edited by Alice Kessler-Harris and William McBrien. New York: Greenwood Press, 1988.

———. *Virginia Woolf: The Impact of Childhood Sexual Abuse on Her Life and Work*. Boston: Beacon Press, 1989.

———. *Virginia Woolf's First Voyage: A Novel in the Making*. London: Macmillan Press, 1980.

DeSalvo, Louise A., and Mitchell A. Leaska, eds. *The Letters of Vita Sackville-West to Virginia Woolf*. New York: William Morrow and Company, 1985.

Dettmar, Kevin J. H., ed. *Rereading the New: A Backward Glance at Modernism*. Ann Arbor: University of Michigan Press, 1992.

DiBattista, Maria. "*Between the Acts*: The Play of Will." In *Virginia Woolf: Modern Critical Views*, edited by Harold Bloom. New York: Chelsea House Publishers, 1986.

————. *Virginia Woolf's Major Novels: The Fables of Anon*. New Haven: Yale University Press, 1980.

Dirks, Nicholas B., ed. *Colonialism and Culture*. Ann Arbor: University of Michigan Press, 1992.

Dollimore, Jonathan. *Sexual Dissidence: Augustine to Wilde, Freud to Foucault*. Oxford: Clarendon Press, 1991.

Dowling, David. *"Mrs. Dalloway": Mapping Streams of Consciousness*. Boston: Twayne, 1991.

DuPlessis, Rachel Blau. *Writing beyond the Ending: Narrative Strategies of Twentieth-Century Women Writers*. Bloomington: Indiana University Press, 1985.

Fassler, Barbara. "Theories of Homosexuality as Sources of Bloomsbury's Androgyny." *Signs* 5, no. 2 (Winter 1979): 237–51.

Ferrer, Daniel. *Virginia Woolf and the Madness of Language*. London: Routledge, 1990.

Finestein, Israel. *Jewish Society in Victorian England: Collected Essays*. London: Vallentine Mitchell & Co., 1993.

Fokkema, Douwe, and Hans Bertens, eds. *Approaching Postmodernism*. Amsterdam and Philadelphia: John Benjamins Publishing Company, 1986.

Freedman, Ralph, ed. *Virginia Woolf: Revaluation and Continuity*. Berkeley and Los Angeles: University of California Press, 1980.

Freud, Sigmund. *Civilization and Its Discontents*. New York: W. W. Norton & Company, 1961.

————. *Group Psychology and the Analysis of the Ego*. New York: W. W. Norton & Company, 1959.

Gallop, Jane. *The Daughter's Seduction: Feminism and Psychoanalysis*. Ithaca: Cornell University Press, 1982.

Garnett, Angelica. *Deceived with Kindness: A Bloomsbury Childhood*. New York: Harcourt Brace Jovanovich, 1984.

Garnett, David. *Flowers of the Forest*. London: Chatto, 1953.

Gerzina, Gretchen Holbrook. *Carrington: A Life*. New York: W. W. Norton & Company, 1989.

Gilbert, Sandra M., and Susan Gubar. *No Man's Land: The Place of the Woman Writer in the Twentieth Century*. Vol. 2, *Sexchanges*. New Haven: Yale University Press, 1989.

Gilman, Sander. *Jewish Self-Hatred: Anti-Semitism and the Hidden Language of the Jews*. Baltimore: Johns Hopkins University Press, 1986.

Gordon, Lyndall. *Virginia Woolf: A Writer's Life*. New York: W. W. Norton & Co., 1984.

Gottlieb, Laura Moss. "The War between the Woolfs." In *Virginia Woolf and Bloomsbury: A Centenary Celebration*, edited by Jane Marcus. Bloomington: Indiana University Press, 1987.

Guth, Deborah. " 'What a Lark! What a Plunge!': Fiction as Self-Evasion in *Mrs. Dalloway*." *Modern Language Review* 84, no. 1 (1989): 18–25.

Heilbrun, Carolyn. *Toward a Recognition of Androgyny*. New York: Alfred A. Knopf, 1973.

————. *Writing a Woman's Life*. New York: Ballantine Books, 1988.

Higginson, C. "The Concept of Civilisation in the Work of Leonard and Virginia Woolf." Ph.D. Diss. University of Sussex, 1986.

Homans, Margaret, ed. *Virginia Woolf: A Collection of Critical Essays*. Englewood Cliffs, NJ: Prentice-Hall, 1993.

Hovey, Jaime. " 'Kissing a Negress in the Dark': Englishness as a Masquerade in Woolf's *Orlando*." *PMLA* 112, no. 3 (May 1997): 393–404.

Hussey, Mark. "Refractions of Desire: The Early Fiction of Virginia and Leonard Woolf." *Modern Fiction Studies* 38, no. 1 (Spring 1992): 127–46.

————, ed. *Virginia Woolf and War: Fiction, Reality and Myth*. Syracuse: Syracuse University Press, 1991.

Hyam, Ronald. *Empire and Sexuality: The British Experience*. Manchester: Manchester University Press, 1991.

Hynes, Samuel. *The Auden Generation: Literature and Politics in England in the 1930s*. Princeton: Princeton University Press, 1972.

JanMohamed, Abdul R. *Manichean Aesthetics: The Politics of Literature in Colonial Africa*. Amherst: University of Massachusetts Press, 1983.

Johnston, Judith L. "The Remediable Flaw: Revisioning Cultural History in *Between the Acts*." In *Virginia Woolf and Bloomsbury: A Centenary Celebration*, edited by Jane Marcus. Bloomington: Indiana University Press, 1987.

Knopp, Sherron E. " 'If I Saw You Would You Kiss Me?': Sapphism and the Subversiveness of Virginia Woolf's *Orlando*." *PMLA* 103, no. 1 (January 1988).

Lee, Hermione. *Virginia Woolf*. New York: Alfred A. Knopf, 1997.

Lehmann, John. *Thrown to the Woolfs*. London: Weidenfeld and Nicolson, 1978.

Lentricchia, Frank, and Thomas McLaughlin. *Critical Terms for Literary Study*. Chicago: University of Chicago Press, 1990.

Levy, Paul. *Moore: G. E. Moore and the Cambridge Apostles*. New York: Holt, Rinehart and Winston, 1979.

Loewenstein, Andrea Freud. *Loathsome Jews and Engulfing Women: Metaphors of Projection in the Works of Wyndham Lewis, Charles Williams, and Graham Greene*. New York: New York University Press, 1993.

Majumdar, Robin, and Allen McLaurin, eds. *Virginia Woolf: The Critical Heritage*. London: Routledge and Kegan Paul, 1975.

Marcus, Jane. *Art and Anger: Reading Like a Woman*. Columbus: Ohio State University Press, 1988.

————. *Virginia Woolf: A Feminist Slant*. Lincoln: University of Nebraska Press, 1983.

————. *Virginia Woolf and Bloomsbury: A Centenary Celebration*. Bloomington: Indiana University Press, 1987.

Marcus, Jane. *Virginia Woolf and the Languages of Patriarchy.* Bloomington: Indiana University Press, 1987.

Marder, Herbert. *Feminism and Art: A Study of Virginia Woolf.* Chicago: University of Chicago Press, 1968.

Medcalf, Stephen. "The Village in the Jungle." *Adam International Review* 37 (1972): 75–79.

Meyerowitz, Selma S. *Leonard Woolf.* Boston: Twayne Publishers, 1982.

Mezei, Kathy, ed. *Ambiguous Discourse: Feminist Narratology and British Women Writers.* Chapel Hill: University of North Carolina Press, 1996.

Moi, Toril. *Sexual/Textual Politics: Feminist Literary Theory.* New York: Methuen, 1985.

Nandy, Ashis. *The Intimate Enemy: Loss and Recovery of Self under Colonialism.* Delhi: Oxford University Press, 1983.

Nicolson, Harold. *Diaries and Letters, 1939–1945.* New York: Atheneum, 1967.

———. "Marriage: A Discussion between Vita Sackville-West and Harold Nicolson." BBC broadcast, reprinted in *Listener* 1 (June 26, 1929): 899–900.

———. *Why Britain Is at War.* Harmondsworth: Penguin, 1939.

Nicolson, Nigel. *Portrait of a Marriage: V. Sackville-West and Harold Nicolson.* New York: Atheneum, 1973.

Noble, Joan Russell, ed. *Recollections of Virginia Woolf by Her Contemporaries.* London: Sphere Books, 1989.

Norris, Margot. *Joyce's Web: The Social Unraveling of Modernism.* Austin: University of Texas Press, 1992.

Novak, Jane. *The Razor Edge of Balance: A Study of Virginia Woolf.* Coral Gables: University of Miami Press, 1975.

Ondaatje, Michael. *Running in the Family.* New York: Vintage International, 1993.

Ozick, Cynthia. "Mrs. Virginia Woolf: A Madwoman and Her Nurse." In *Art and Ardor: Essays.* New York: E. P. Dutton, 1984.

Paul, Janis M. *The Victorian Heritage of Virginia Woolf: The External World in Her Novels.* Norman, OK: Pilgrim Books, 1987.

Phillips, Kathy J. *Virginia Woolf against Empire.* Knoxville: University of Tennessee Press, 1994.

Poole, Roger. *The Unknown Virginia Woolf.* Cambridge: Cambridge University Press, 1978.

Raitt, Suzanne. *Vita and Virginia: The Work and Friendship of V. Sackville-West and Virginia Woolf.* Oxford: Oxford University Press, 1993.

Ray, Gordon N. *H. G. Wells and Rebecca West.* New Haven: Yale University Press, 1974.

Restuccia, Frances L. *Joyce and the Law of the Father.* New Haven: Yale University Press, 1989.

Rose, Phyllis. *Parallel Lives: Five Victorian Marriages.* New York: Random House, 1983.

———. *Woman of Letters: A Life of Virginia Woolf.* New York: Harcourt Brace Jovanovich, 1978.

Rosenbaum, S. P., ed. *The Bloomsbury Group.* Toronto: University of Toronto Press, 1975.

Rosenthal, Michael. *Virginia Woolf.* London: Routledge & Kegan Paul, 1979.

Russell, Bertrand. *Which Way to Peace?* London: M. Joseph, 1936.

Sackville-West, Vita. *Challenge.* New York: Avon Books, 1975.

———. *Country Notes in Wartime.* Garden City: Doubleday, Doran and Company, 1941.

Said, Edward. *Culture and Imperialism.* New York: Alfred A. Knopf, 1993.

———. *Orientalism.* New York: Random House, 1978.

Schlack, Beverly Ann. *Continuing Presences: Virginia Woolf's Use of Literary Allusion.* University Park: Pennsylvania State University Press, 1979.

Scott, Bonnie Kime. *The Gender of Modernism.* Bloomington: Indiana University Press, 1990.

———. *Refiguring Modernism.* Bloomington: Indiana University Press, 1995.

Sedgwick, Eve Kosofsky. *Between Men: English Literature and Male Homosocial Desire.* New York: Columbia University Press, 1985.

Showalter, Elaine. *A Literature of Their Own: British Women Novelists from Brontë to Lessing.* Princeton: Princeton University Press, 1977.

Silver, Brenda R. "Periphrasis, Power, and Rape in *A Passage to India.*" *Novel,* Fall 1988, 86–105.

Spater, George, and Ian Parsons. *A Marriage of True Minds: An Intimate Portrait of Leonard and Virginia Woolf.* New York: Harcourt Brace Jovanovich, 1977.

Spilka, Mark. *Virginia Woolf's Quarrel with Grieving.* Lincoln: University of Nebraska Press, 1980.

Spivak, Gayatri C. "Unmaking and Making in *To the Lighthouse.*" In *Women and Language in Literature and Society,* edited by Ruth Borker, Nelly Furman, and Sally McConnell-Ginet. New York: Praeger, 1980.

Stevenson, Randall. *Modernist Fiction: An Introduction.* Lexington: University Press of Kentucky, 1992.

Strachey, Lytton. *Elizabeth and Essex.* New York: Harcourt, Brace and Company, 1928.

———. *Eminent Victorians.* New York: Harcourt Brace Jovanovich, n.d.

Tratner, Michael. *Modernism and Mass Politics: Joyce, Woolf, Eliot, Yeats.* Stanford: Stanford University Press, 1995.

Suleiman, Susan. "Naming and Difference: Reflections on 'Modernism *versus* Postmodernism' in Literature." In *Approaching Postmodernism,* edited by Douwe Fokkema and Hans Bertens. Amsterdam and Philadelphia: John Benjamins Publishing Company, 1986.

Valente, Joseph. *James Joyce and the Problem of Justice.* Cambridge: Cambridge University Press, 1995.

Waugh, Patricia. *Feminine Fictions: Revisiting the Postmodern.* London: Routledge, 1989.

White, Luise. *The Comforts of Home: Prostitution in Colonial Nairobi.* Chicago: University of Chicago Press, 1990.

Willis, J. H., Jr. *Leonard and Virginia Woolf as Publishers: The Hogarth Press, 1917–41.* Charlottesville: University Press of Virginia, 1992.

Wilson, Duncan. *Leonard Woolf: A Political Biography.* New York: St. Martin's Press, 1978.

Wurgaft, Lewis D. *The Imperial Imagination: Magic and Myth in Kipling's India*. Middletown, CT: Wesleyan University Press, 1983.

Young, Robert J. C. *Colonial Desire: Hybridity in Theory, Culture and Race*. London: Routledge, 1995.

Zwerdling, Alex. *Virginia Woolf and the Real World*. Berkeley and Los Angeles: University of California Press, 1986.

Index